Michael Morrison
Web development expert, game designer, entrepreneur

Faster Smarter

HTML & XML

Take charge of your Web code—
faster, smarter, *better*!

PUBLISHED BY
Microsoft Press
A Division of Microsoft Corporation
One Microsoft Way
Redmond, Washington 98052-6399

Library of Congress Cataloging-in-Publication Data
Morrison, Michael, 1970-
    Faster Smarter HTML & XML / Michael Morrison.
       p. cm.
    Includes index.
    ISBN 0-7356-1861-5
    1. HTML (Document markup language)   2. XML (Document markup language)   I.
Title.

   QA76.76.H94 M67   2002
   005.7'2--dc21   2002029541

Printed and bound in the United States of America.

1 2 3 4 5 6 7 8 9   QWE   8 7 6 5 4 3

Distributed in Canada by H.B. Fenn and Company Ltd.

A CIP catalogue record for this book is available from the British Library.

Microsoft Press books are available through booksellers and distributors worldwide. For further informa-
tion about international editions, contact your local Microsoft Corporation office or contact Microsoft
Press International directly at fax (425) 936-7329. Visit our Web site at www.microsoft.com/mspress.
Send comments to *mspinput@microsoft.com*.

ClearType, FrontPage, Microsoft, Microsoft Press, MSDN, MSN, PhotoDraw, Visual Basic, Windows,
and Windows Media are either registered trademarks or trademarks of Microsoft Corporation in the
United States and/or other countries. Other product and company names mentioned herein may be the
trademarks of their respective owners.

The example companies, organizations, products, domain names, e-mail addresses, logos, people, places,
and events depicted herein are fictitious. No association with any real company, organization, product,
domain name, e-mail address, logo, person, place, or event is intended or should be inferred.

Acquisitions Editor: Alex Blanton
Project Editor: Kristen Weatherby
Series Editor: Kristen Weatherby

Body Part No. X08-95129

Table of Contents

Part I: Getting Started with HTML

This part gets you started by introducing you to the HTML language and why it is such an important part of Web page creation. The chapters in this part provide a base of HTML knowledge to build on throughout the book.

Part II: Beyond the Basics

This part digs deeper into HTML by guiding you through topics such as the use of image maps to provide visual navigation to your Web pages, the use of tables, and the importance of graphical design tools. It also shows you how to publish Web pages online and how to interact with the user with forms. The chapters in this part provide you with the knowledge to take your Web pages to a whole new level.

Part III: Adding Style to Your Pages

This part is all about style as you learn how to use style sheets to improve the appearance of Web pages. You find out how to create style sheets that format text and position content on a Web page with precision, as well as how to integrate multimedia into your pages.

Part IV: Beyond HTML with XML

This part tackles XML, an important technology that is closely linked to HTML. You learn how to use XML to organize data, as well as how to use style sheets to process and transform XML content. You also explore XHTML, which represents the merger of XML and HTML. The chapters in this part help you to boldly face the future of HTML and the Web.

To my wife, Masheed, who constantly
amazes me with her capacity to love.

Acknowledgments

Thanks to Alex Blanton and Kristen Weatherby at Microsoft Press, as well as the rest of the Microsoft Press gang, and to Tempe Goodhue, Chris Russo, and Stephanie English at nSight. All these people have held me to a high standard to ensure that this become a top-notch book. A big thanks goes to my literary agent, Chris Van Buren, who keeps me in business. And finally, a tremendous thanks to my wife, Masheed, and my parents, who have always pledged their undying support to every facet of my life.

Introduction

It has been said that the Web has brought the power of the printing press to the individual, power that comes from the simple fact that ideas change the world. People have traditionally used the printed word to share their ideas, but today they are making a rapid move toward electronic media such as Web pages—although I doubt that printed paper is going away just yet. By learning to create your own Web pages, you can take part in this free exchange of knowledge and have the chance to change the world in your own unique way.

Regardless of how lofty or simple your motivations for creating Web pages may be, you have to start with the language that serves as the foundation of the Web: HTML. HTML is a language used to describe what you see on a Web page, including the text, images, and how they are arranged next to each other. HTML isn't a programming language, as some people think, but is instead a language used to describe information so that it can be displayed in a Web browser.

Although HTML has done a wonderful job of making the Web a reality, it isn't perfect. For this reason, it can be helpful to use additional Web technologies to make HTML more effective. These technologies include Dynamic HTML (DHTML), Extensible Markup Language (XML), and style sheets, all of which are explained clearly throughout the book using practical examples.

My goal with this book isn't to make you an HTML guru, or to teach you everything that is possible using HTML. Instead, I want to provide you with the practical knowledge you need to hit the ground running as you create Web pages of your own. There are plenty of books and online resources you can use to get detailed information about advanced features and tricks to using HTML. However, you must first have a solid foundation and comfort level with Web page creation. I hope you'll find that this book strikes a delicate balance between building your Web development knowledge base and challenging you with real-world examples.

This Book Could Be for You

This book is geared toward anyone who wants to create a Web page or a complete Web site but has no experience with HTML or Web publishing. You are expected to have basic computing skills, such as opening and saving files, installing and running programs, and so on. It also helps if you already have a Web page or Web site in mind that you'd like to begin building. It's often difficult to learn a new skill without having a good reason to apply it, which is why I encourage you to have a "pet project" in mind while you're working through the book. You can then gradually build the project as you work through the examples in each chapter and learn new skills.

If the whole process of taking an idea from paper and making it an online reality appears daunting at this moment, please don't stress out. You'll find that the transition from the printed page to the screen is really not so difficult to follow. You may also be surprised to find out how simple it is to get started creating simple Web pages and trying them out in a Web browser, even without using an Internet connection. When you are ready to publish a page on the Web, you'll be glad to know that there are plenty of options available to you, some of them free. The point I'm trying to make is that this book quickly addresses many of the most common questions associated with Web publishing and has you creating real Web pages from the start.

The book is organized into four parts, with each part building on the previous one by introducing you to new facets of Web page design and development.

- **Part I: Getting Started with HTML** Get your feet wet with HTML through a gentle introduction to the language and what it has to offer you in terms of constructing Web pages. You find out the relationship between HTML and other Web technologies such as DHTML and XML. You also build your very first Web page in HTML, not to mention learn how to arrange text, format images, and connect Web pages with hyperlinks. This part of the book provides you with plenty of practical HTML knowledge, as well as priming you for what's to come.

- **Part II: Beyond the Basics** Push beyond the basics of HTML by exploring interesting topics, such as how to provide visual navigation to your Web pages with image maps. You learn how to arrange rows and columns of information in tables, which can be very useful in certain situations. You also learn how to use graphical design tools to help streamline Web page design, as well as how to publish pages on the Web. Toward the end of this part you find out how to gather information using forms, as well as how to dynamically interact with a Web page using Dynamic HTML.

- **Part III: Adding Style to Your Pages** Learn about style and how to use style sheets to dramatically improve the appearance of Web pages. You begin by learning the fundamentals of style sheets and how they work. You then move on to learn how to format text and position content on a Web page using styles. As if using styles isn't enough to make your pages more exciting, this part concludes by showing you how to incorporate multimedia, including sound and video clips, into your Web pages.

■ **Part IV: Beyond HTML with XML**   Take a few steps beyond HTML and find out about XML, which is one of the key technologies shaping the future of the Web. You learn how to organize data using XML, as well as how to use a special type of style sheet to process and transform XML documents for display within a Web browser. This part concludes by examining the merger of HTML and XML, which is the new extensible hypertext markup language known as XHTML.

You'll find the book to be written in a very accessible, easy-to-understand style that is perhaps unlike other technical books you might have read. This isn't a graduate thesis on Web design, but a practical guide written from the perspective of someone who has faced a new technology and appreciates learning with a hands-on approach. There are several elements sprinkled liberally throughout the chapters that you'll find useful as you navigate your way through HTML and XML. Every chapter includes tips, notes, sidebars, and lingo elements that help to provide additional information related to the topic at hand. Also, each chapter concludes with a "Key Points" section that summarizes the most important topics in the chapter in a bulleted list. Finally, there are three appendixes that include highly useful information such as an HTML quick reference, HTML resources on the Web, and a guide to using custom colors in Web pages.

All of the examples shown throughout the book are available for download from my Web site at *http://www.michaelmorrison.com/cbook_fshtml.html*. The examples provide a great place to start in creating Web pages, especially if you're the kind of person who likes to learn by tweaking something that already exists, as opposed to starting from scratch.

System Requirements

The Web itself is *cross-platform*, which means that it doesn't favor or otherwise require you to use any particular computer operating system. The only thing that matters is that you have a Web browser on your computer that is reasonably up to date. By "reasonably" I mean that the Web browser isn't more than a couple of years old. This is because the Web has come a long way in a fairly short period of time, so it's important to have a Web browser that supports all of the latest Web technologies. The good news is that most Web browsers are free, so you can easily upgrade your Web browser if you do happen to have an old version.

Beyond a Web browser, a few other software applications are mentioned throughout the book, although they are not required. Microsoft FrontPage is a visual Web development environment that is used as an example of how you can edit HTML code and test it in a visual environment. Although FrontPage is designed for the Windows operating system, there are similar equivalents on other operating systems, some of which I mention in the book. So, regardless of whether you are a Windows, Macintosh, Linux, or some other operating system user, you'll be able to work through the book and tinker with all of the example code. The Web truly has no favorite when it comes to operating systems, which is actually quite remarkable. More importantly, it gives everyone an equal footing when it comes to creating Web pages and tapping into the power of the "online printing press."

Support

Every effort has been made to ensure the accuracy of this book. Microsoft Press provides corrections for books at the following address:

http://mspress.microsoft.com/support/

The code for most of the examples that appear in the book is available for download from my Web site:

http://www.michaelmorrison.com/cbook_fshtml.html.

If you have comments, questions, or ideas regarding this book, please send them to Microsoft Press via e-mail to:

mspinput@microsoft.com

or via postal mail to:

Microsoft Press
Attn: *Faster Smarter* Editor
One Microsoft Way
Redmond, WA 98052-6399

Please note that product support is not offered through the above addresses.

Part I

Getting Started with HTML

Part I gets your feet wet with Hypertext Markup Language (HTML) by gently introducing you to the language and what it has to offer in terms of constructing Web pages. You find out the relationship between HTML and other Web technologies, such as Dynamic HTML (DHTML) and Extensible Markup Language (XML). You also build your very first Web page in HTML, not to mention learn how to arrange text, format images, and connect Web pages with hyperlinks. This part of the book provides you with plenty of practical HTML knowledge and also primes you for what's to come.

Chapter 1

An Introduction to HTML, DHTML, and XML

As you may already know, HTML is one of a long string of acronyms that litter the landscape of the Web. If there's one thing techies love, it's a good acronym—and the more letters, the better. This chapter cuts right to the chase with acronyms by exploring three of the most common ones related to Web pages: HTML (Hypertext Markup Language), DHTML (Dynamic HTML), and XML (Extensible Markup Language).

While the remainder of the book explores the inner workings of these three technologies, this chapter paints the big picture of what they have to offer and how they relate to one another. By gaining an understanding of the practical usefulness of these technologies and how they complement each other, you'll be much better equipped to push forward and learn how to do interesting things with them. Besides, you'll also be picking up three new acronyms to unleash on unsuspecting friends at your next nerd cocktail party.

What Is HTML?

They key to understanding *HTML* is in the relationship between HTML and the Web. The Web is a vast sea of documents—Web pages—that are interconnected so that you can jump from one page to the next. This means that Web pages are written in HTML, just as a letter you write to a friend in Rome is written in Italian. The obvious difference is that HTML is a computer language understood by Web browsers, and Italian is a human language understood by people in Italy. HTML is required on the Web to format text and images, as well as to add character and personality. It gives you options that help you communicate the precise message you want to send.

Lingo   *HTML* is the official language of Web pages and stands for Hypertext Markup Language.

HTML also provides the critical linking mechanism that allows pages to link to one another. Without HTML, the Web would be nothing more than a bunch of dull text documents with no interconnectivity—no formatting, no style, no images, and really no fun! The most significant feature of HTML is called *hyper-linking*, which is the ability to link pages together. Hyperlinking allows you to jump from one page to another by simply clicking a link. Hyperlinks are commonly used in navigation bars for Web sites. For example, when you see a button or image on a Web page that says Products, there's a good chance that a hyperlink will link you to the Products page of the Web site when you click the button or image.

Lingo   A *hyperlink* is a reference from one Web page to another Web page.

If you think of the Web as a big book, then hyperlinks are the dog-eared pages that make it easier to find what you're looking for in the book. The Web is not a book, however. It contains tons of incredibly disorganized pages, making hyperlinks a necessity when it comes to navigating through pages in any meaningful way. You will learn much more about hyperlinks and how to code them in HTML in Chapter 5, "Connecting Pages with Hyperlinks." For now, I just want to make the point that the hyperlink is the one feature of HTML that is responsible for making the Web possible.

Your Pen Pal the Web Browser

If HTML is so important in making Web pages pretty and connecting them, why don't you see it when you're on the Web busily shopping for lava lamps or researching Bigfoot sightings? The answer is that no one but Web page designers and Web browsers speak the language of HTML. When you design a Web page in HTML, you are in effect writing a personal letter to a Web browser about what you'd like a page to look like. It might go something like this:

Dear Browser,

Please place the picture of my pet salamander, Ernest, in the upper-left corner of the screen and write his name in bold just below the picture. To the right of Ernest, please list his vital statistics including height, weight, color, and sliminess. Below all of that, please include a link so that my friends can e-mail their best wishes for Ernest's improved health. One more thing—please make the background of the page pink, Ernest's favorite color.

Yours Truly,
Michael

Although this narrative description of the conversation between Web designer and Web browser is obviously not valid HTML code, it does convey the information that is typically described using HTML. The problem is that computers aren't very smart. You must give them detailed instructions to get exactly what you want on a Web page. HTML is the language used to communicate the detailed instructions.

Putting on Your HTML X-Ray Glasses

You might be struggling to believe that all of the Web pages you've ever seen are constructed using HTML. To put your mind at ease, I want to teach you a little trick that allows you to view the actual HTML code for any Web page. Along with showing you that all pages have HTML under the hood, this trick will prove valuable later on in your HTML career because it allows you to explore pages to see how other designers pulled off certain looks. To view the HTML code for a Web page, follow these steps in Microsoft Internet Explorer:

1   Visit one of your favorite Web sites.

2   Choose Source from the View menu.

A new window will immediately open, showing letters and symbols like you've never seen them before. That is the HTML code for the page. You can use this trick to view the HTML code for any Web page, although I have to warn you that many pages out there are extremely complicated and difficult to understand.

Try This!   Try the View Source trick on one of your favorite Web pages and try to make sense of the HTML code in the page. Don't worry if it looks like a mess; many commercial Web pages rely on complex HTML code.

> **Tip**   If you aren't using Internet Explorer as your Web browser, you can still view the HTML code for a Web page. In Netscape Navigator, the menu command is named Page Source. You'll find that other browsers also support this feature, although the specific menu commands vary to some degree.

As you progress through this book, you will come to view HTML code as meaningful information and realize that it can be your friend. By the way, the HTML code you create for Web pages in this book won't look nearly as messy as the code that you typically see on the Web. The HTML code for complex Web sites has a tendency to evolve into something far removed from a fast read. You will learn to create HTML code that is much cleaner and easier to understand.

> **Note**   HTML isn't the only language being used on the Web to create Web pages. Web page designers are beginning to adopt a new standard for Web pages known as XHTML. I told you techies love acronyms! XHTML is a more structured form of HTML that is based upon XML, which you will learn about a little later in this chapter. Many people expect the language XHTML to some-day alleviate many of the inconsistencies associated with how browsers display HTML. You will learn a great deal more about XHTML in Chapter 18, "XHTML: XML Meets HTML."

The Significance of HTML

As an engineering student years ago, I constantly found myself asking the question "Why do I need to know this?" The piles of information I had to learn were seemingly unrelated to anything I wanted to do in the real world. Although no one ever answered that question for me, I can help you out in regard to HTML. Why do you need to know HTML? The surprising answer is that you don't need to know HTML. With so many excellent Web development tools around, you can create some pretty interesting Web pages without having a clue about HTML. So what's the deal? Have you bought this book, only to learn in the first chapter that you don't need it? Of course not.

Although you may not need to know HTML to create Web pages, it's an immeasurable asset to know HTML when something doesn't work as you expected it to in a Web page, or when you're pushing the limit to do something unique. Keep in mind that whatever tool you use to create Web pages, the end result is always HTML. When you don't know HTML, you are at the mercy of the tool. Anyway, you may be the kind of person who likes complete control over a situation. Knowing HTML guarantees that you will have complete control over your Web pages. Creating Web pages using a Web tool without knowing HTML is kind of like being dependent on a calculator to calculate 2 + 2.

Note   There are some Web design tools that don't generate HTML code. For example, Macromedia Flash is one such tool. It generates special animation files that must be embedded in HTML so that they will work properly. Since Flash doesn't generate HTML code, you must know HTML in order to place Flash animations in your Web pages unless you use an additional Web page design tool such as Macromedia Dreamweaver.

There is another reason you should know HTML. The Web is a community that is based largely on sharing. It is common for a technique used to get a desired effect on a Web page to appear later on someone else's page. I'll let you decide if "imitation is the highest form of flattery." But the reality is that you can learn to do incredible things by studying the HTML code of Web pages that you like. Understand that I'm not endorsing or recommending that you make a habit of borrowing ideas and HTML from others, and I'd certainly advise against lifting *content* from other Web sites. In some cases it may be illegal, and in others just not cool. What I am saying is that if you see a page you like, take a look at the code and figure out how to make your own HTML magic.

Lingo   *Content* is a general term used to describe the information presented on a Web site. Content typically includes text, images, and any multimedia presentations, such as music and videos.

Web Pages as Intellectual Property   Similar to books and music, Web pages are considered intellectual property and therefore have rights associated with them. What this means is that an author of a Web page automatically has rights over the original material in the Web page, which prevents others from using the material without permission. This presents a double-edged sword for new Web authors such as yourself; on the one hand, it's great to have legal protection over your Web page creations but, on the other hand, it puts you at risk if you borrow too much from other Web pages. The way to safely avoid risk is to only borrow *techniques*, not content. In other words, use other Web pages as a means of learning how to do interesting things with HTML and then apply those techniques to your own content.

What Is DHTML?

In order to gain an appreciation of *DHTML*, you must first learn exactly what constitutes a dynamic, or interactive, Web page. Interactivity implies that you can do something to a page and have it respond to your actions. For example, you might click a button to change the appearance of an image on the page, or maybe drag the mouse over a piece of text to change the color of the letters. Interactive Web pages can also carry out more advanced tasks, such as retrieving and displaying information from a database.

Lingo   *DHTML* is a grouping of technologies used to create interactive Web pages, which are also sometimes referred to as *dynamic Web pages*. That's where the D in the acronym comes from: Dynamic.

DHTML is not a special version of HTML, or even a version of HTML at all, which is unfortunately quite confusing considering how it is named. Instead, DHTML consists of a combination of the following three Web technologies:

- HTML
- *Cascading style sheets* (CSS)
- Web scripting

Lingo   *Cascading style sheets*, or *CSS*, is not an attraction at a water park, as its name sounds. It is actually a technology used to add a fine degree of control over how text and images on a Web page are laid out and formatted.

The practical implication of this combination is that it allows you to change the HTML code for a Web page after the page has been loaded and displayed in a Web browser. In other words, the HTML code for a Web page is no longer etched in stone when you create the page. Using DHTML, you can interact with the user and alter the content of a page at any time. Specifically, you can use *Web script* code to alter the styles of Web content based upon user interactions such as clicking or dragging the mouse. You can also directly change the content of Web pages by using script code.

Lingo   *Web scripting* represents a type of programming that uses small chunks of programming code (script code) to control Web pages and how they are displayed. A *script* is a small program written in a scripting language such as JavaScript or VBScript that is capable of being run on a Web page. Scripts can be written to perform a variety of different tasks, and therefore play an important role in DHTML.

One of the main requirements for using DHTML is having access to the pieces and parts of a Web page at the programming level. In other words, a script must be able to access HTML code in a Web page so that it can process it and make changes, which is how interactivity is achieved. In order to make this possible, Web browsers are required to provide a feature known as the *Document Object Model*, or DOM for short. The DOM essentially creates a programmatic interface around all of the content in a Web page, making it possible for any part to be accessed and modified with script code.

Lingo   Although it may sound like a mob kingpin, the *DOM* is actually a layer of software in a Web browser that exposes pieces of a Web page as objects that can be referenced in script code. Or put another way, the DOM allows you to write scripts that access and modify parts of a Web page.

Although it sounds somewhat technical, the DOM really isn't all that difficult to use, especially when you think about what it does. The DOM simply provides you with a means of accessing and tinkering with specific parts of a Web page, such as the size of a font or the name of an image. Without the DOM, it would be virtually impossible to alter a Web page using script code. This means a lot of the Web sites that you know and love wouldn't work too well because Web scripting is used a great deal in interactive commercial Web sites. Even if you aren't planning to create the next Amazon.com, you'll likely find scripting with the DOM to be extremely handy in certain situations.

See Also   You will learn a great deal more about the DOM and how it is used to create interactive DHTML Web pages in Chapter 11, "Dynamic HTML."

What Is XML?

Moving right along in our triple crown of Web acronyms, we arrive at *XML*, which is perhaps the most misunderstood technology of the three. In addition to being another lovable acronym, XML is a groundbreaking technology that aims to completely change the way information is structured on the Web. XML is known as a *meta-language*, which means that it is used to create other markup languages. This may sound a bit confusing, but what I mean is that XML provides the necessary structure and rules for describing any kind of information in a meaningful way. Using XML, you could create a unique markup language to model just about any kind of information. In fact, you could use XML to create your very own version of HTML. Or perhaps on a more personal level, I could create a markup language called Michael's Markup Language, or MML, that I use to code information specific only to me. The bottom line is that XML is a flexible way to organize information, any information, in a consistent manner.

Lingo   *XML* stands for *Extensible Markup Language*, and its purpose is to provide a means of describing any kind of information.

Okay, it's great that XML is open-ended enough to be useful for representing any kind of information, but that doesn't necessarily explain why it's being covered in a book about creating Web pages. Fair enough. While it is true that XML must be viewed in a context much broader than the Web, there are some very important Web-centric uses for XML. One of the first applications of XML is to restore some order to the Web through yet another markup language (and acronym!) called XHTML. XHTML, which stands for Extensible Hypertext Markup Language, represents a merger of sorts between XML and HTML, and is covered in Chapter 18, "XHTML: XML Meets HTML."

Another way that XML fits into the Web equation is through custom markup tags that make it possible to add meaning to the content in Web pages. Although I'm jumping ahead a little, let me point out that a markup tag is a little piece of code in a Web page that somehow describes a piece of information. For example, to make a word appear bold you use the <b> tag, like this:

```
<b>I'm feeling mighty bold!</b>
```

HTML defines a rich set of tags that are primarily designed around how content on a Web page is to appear. While that's certainly useful, it doesn't factor in the meaning of the content. XML makes it possible to add additional markup tags for giving meaning to information on a page. For example, you might use

XML to code a joke on a Web page using a special <joke> tag, which clearly states that the content it highlights is a joke:

```
<joke>Knock knock.</joke>
```

I still haven't answered the question: Why does it matter whether or not you know the meaning of the content? So, let's consider a practical benefit of knowing the meaning of content on the Web.

You've no doubt used a search engine to look for information on the Web. Imagine that you are compiling a list of jokes for your next family gathering or Oscar ceremony, and you want to search the Web for some real knee-slappers. The obvious approach would be to use a search engine and perform a search on the word "joke," which would find some joke sites. Yet this method would probably never find the jokes that individuals have placed on their Web pages—there is nothing for the search engines to find. This is because search engines look for important words, also known as *keywords*, so Web developers must be diligent about embedding the right words in their pages. If you've simply put a few jokes on your personal Web page, it's doubtful you'll take the time to add the word *joke* as one of your keywords.

On the other hand, what if every joke on the Web was coded with our new <joke> tag? Instead of searching for inconsistent and often misused keywords, search engines would search for the <joke> tag. Presto! A list of all the jokes on the Web. Step aside, Jerry Seinfeld. This works because the jokes are now tagged based upon their meaning, making it possible to perform more intelligent searches. Here you have the main premise of XML—adding context to content.

The advantages of XML extend far beyond search engines, but they do come to mind as the most obvious and immediate beneficiaries of a Web with XML-based pages. XML is also in vogue now as a means of shuttling information back and forth between Web-based applications such as online stores. XML has already proven to be a highly efficient and simple means of storing and transferring information between different kinds of computing systems, both on and off the Web.

Comparing XML and HTML

Now that you have a basic understanding of what XML is and what it can do, you're probably wondering how XML relates to HTML. Is XML a newer, more advanced version of HTML? The answer is a resounding no! XML is not a version of HTML at all. If anything, HTML is a version of XML. To understand this, you have to grasp how XML works. XML defines markup languages by describing the structure of documents of a given type. You use HTML to develop a Web page, which can be considered a type of XML document. It would be reasonably accurate to say that HTML is an application of XML. More specifically, HTML is considered an *XML vocabulary*.

> **Lingo**   An *XML vocabulary* is a language that describes a document of a certain type. For example, HTML is an XML vocabulary used to describe Web pages. Many XML vocabularies are in use today. In addition to HTML, a few examples include SVG (Structured Vector Graphics) for two-dimensional graphics and MathML (Mathematical Markup Language) for mathematical equations.

So, HTML is a specific markup language used to create Web pages, while XML is a general markup language used to create many languages. The critical point is that XML can be used to create markup languages for any kind of information, not just Web pages. This is why you often see the word *document* used instead of *page* when referring to XML content. As applied to HTML, the term *Web page* conjures up an image of a page displayed in a browser, but the term *HTML document* simply refers to content marked up with HTML. Although a Web page is in fact an HTML document, a distinction between the two emerges as you explore other XML markup languages and their documents. Although it may be simple in theory, the big picture of XML is an elusive concept. The biggest challenge for most people is figuring out how they can use it. XML is usually described in such general terms that it's hard to pinpoint its practical implications. Sure, I mentioned the search engine example, but you may have guessed that my dream XML search engine doesn't exist yet.

> **Note**   I hate to muddy things, but I must point out that, technically speaking, HTML isn't a true XML markup language. XML imposes strict structural requirements on Web pages and other documents. HTML currently doesn't meet these requirements, so there's a special version of HTML known as XHTML that serves as a true XML markup language. You will learn about XHTML in Chapter 18, "XHTML: XML Meets HTML."

Another irony of XML is that you can't do much with it by itself. Unlike HTML, which solves a specific problem, XML is not a solution by itself. Instead, it lays the ground rules for solving problems. To understand this, consider the fact that there is no such thing as a generic XML Web browser. A Web browser is inherently an HTML-based program, and it can't process the content of XML documents for display, other than just showing the raw XML code. More important, XML doesn't even specify what content should look like when displayed, which is also why a generic XML browser isn't possible.

Note   Although it isn't possible to browse generic XML beyond viewing the raw code, it is possible to apply styles to XML code so that content can be viewed in a Web browser. You will learn how to do this in Chapter 17, "Styling XML with XSL."

Please forgive me if this discussion of XML and HTML seems rather abstract. Believe me, I don't stay up late at night pondering the meaning of life in terms of XML. The fact of the matter is that XML involves a significant shift in how you perceive the Web, which is why it's necessary to clarify exactly how XML and HTML relate to one another.

See Also   *You revisit XML and learn how to do some practical things with it in Part IV, "Beyond HTML with XML."*

Key Points

- HTML stands for Hypertext Markup Language, which is the standard language used to create Web pages.

- An author of a Web page automatically has rights over the page just as if it were a traditional written document.

- DHTML is not a specific technology, but a merger of three technologies (HTML, CSS, and Web scripting) that makes it possible to create interactive Web pages.

- XML stands for Extensible Markup Language, which is a general markup language used to create other markup languages for specific types of information.

- Although it has many applications outside of the Web, XML has a lot to offer the Web in terms of adding meaning to Web content and cleaning up the overall structure of Web pages.

- XML is not a newer version of HTML, or even a competitor of HTML. In the long run, XML will likely help HTML to become more structured and reliable.

Chapter 2

Your First HTML Web Page

The previous chapter explained that HTML is a computer language used to describe how information is presented on a Web page. You can think of HTML as the bare-knuckle approach to creating Web pages; it requires you to use special words and symbols to create effects such as bold text and bulleted lists. Knowing this, you might wonder why you shouldn't just buy Microsoft FrontPage or some other Web design tool that allows you to blissfully create Web pages without learning HTML. The answer is that you certainly can buy such a tool and create Web pages without ever learning any HTML. There's even a good chance that you'll use one of these tools after you learn HTML. But creating Web pages without knowing HTML is like using autopilot and not knowing how to fly—it just isn't safe. Okay, I'm exaggerating a little, but you get the idea: it's important to understand HTML to be truly creative with Web pages.

The goal of this chapter is to begin to take the mystery out of HTML by showing you how simple it is to create your first Web page. The idea is to start doing real things with HTML—whether that's building the next eBay or simply a Web site to immortalize your pet salamander.

Inside a Web Page

The medical profession is generally quite good at diagnosing ailments and quickly recommending a course of action for nursing us back to health. But when doctors reach a consensus that they have no clue as to what is wrong, the scariest of all medical procedures, exploratory surgery, may be necessary. This is when a surgeon opens you up just to have a look around. Although exploratory surgery can be something to dread, it also can be a lifesaver. Likewise, making an incision right down the middle of a sample Web page can give new life to your own project.

If you recall from the previous chapter, I wrote a hypothetical letter to a Web browser explaining how to lay out a Web page for a pet salamander named Ernest. If you take a look at Figure 2-1, you'll see a real Ernest the Salamander Web page that was created based upon that letter.

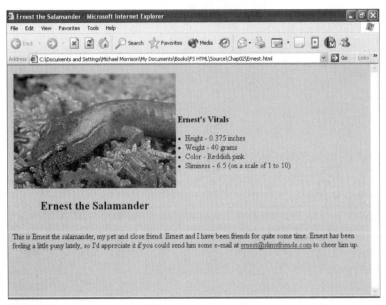

Figure 2-1   The Ernest the Salamander Web page is a good example of how to structure a simple page using HTML code.

Along with giving our friend Ernest a place on the Web, this page serves as a good example of how to write clean, concise HTML code. Although I don't expect you to understand the code yet, you should at least be able to pick out some of the elements on the page, such as the text. Following is the code for the Ernest the Salamander Web page:

```
<html>
<head>
  <title>Ernest the Salamander</title>
</head>

<body bgcolor="pink">
  <table>
    <tr>
      <td align="center">
      <p>
      <img src="Ernest.jpg">
      <br>
      <h2>Ernest the Salamander</h2>
      </p>
      </td>

      <td>
      <p>
      <h3>Ernest's Vitals</h3>
      <ul>
      <li>Height - 0.375 inches</li>
      <li>Weight - 40 grams</li>
      <li>Color - Reddish pink</li>
      <li>Sliminess - 6.5 (on a scale of 1 to 10)</li>
      </ul>
      </p>
      </td>
    </tr>
  </table>
  <p>
  This is Ernest the salamander, my pet and close friend. Ernest and I
  have been friends for quite some time. Ernest has been feeling a little
  puny lately, so I'd appreciate it if you could send him some e-mail at
  <a href=mailto:ernest@slimyfriends.com>ernest@slimyfriends.com</a> to
  cheer him up.
  </p>
</body>
</html>
```

That may seem like a lot of code for such a simple Web page, but the amount has to do with how the code is organized. The first thing you'll probably notice about this HTML code is all the angle brackets (<>). In HTML, angle brackets enclose special codes, called *tags*, which indicate the structure and format of the *content* on the page. HTML consists of many tags that do a variety of different formatting and organizational tasks. The most important tag in a Web page is the `<html>` tag, which identifies the page as an HTML document. Notice that this tag actually consists of two tags:

1   A *start tag* (`<html>`), which is located at the beginning of the page

2   An *end tag* (`</html>`), which, not surprisingly, is at the end of the page

---

Lingo   A *tag* is a special HTML code enclosed in angle brackets (`<>`) that is used to indicate the structure and format of content on a Web page. Many tags in HTML come in pairs that consist of a *start tag* and an *end tag*, such as `<b>` and `</b>` for bold formatting; the start tag is placed before the content being tagged, and the end tag is placed after the content.

All the content in an HTML document must appear within the two `<html>` tags.

Lingo   Although I clarified the meaning of the word "content" in the previous chapter, it's worth quickly revisiting it. *Content* is simply the text and images that are displayed on a Web page. You use HTML to mark up content so that it is displayed in a certain way. For example, the phrase "Ernest the Salamander" is content, and the HTML tags `<h2>` and `</h2>` are used to format this phrase in a certain font size.

The other two tags most relevant to the overall structure of the Web page are the `<head>` and `<body>` tags. These tags are important because they describe the two major sections of all Web pages, the head and the body. The *head* of a Web page is placed near the beginning of the page, and describes general properties of the page such as the title. The *body* appears below the head and contains the content of the Web page. Like the `<html>` tag, the `<head>` and `<body>` tags consist of both start and end tags that enclose the content appearing in each section. An end tag is simply the start tag plus a forward slash that immediately follows the opening angle bracket (`</`). Following are a few examples of end tags: `</html>`, `</head>`, and `</body>`.

Lingo   The *head* of a Web page appears near the beginning of the page, and serves as a place to store general properties about the page, such as the page title. The *body* appears below the head and is used to store the actual content of the page.

The Brains of a Web Page

In general, the head of a Web page contains information about the page that isn't displayed by a browser, and the body contains everything that you see when you view the page. In other words, the head of a Web page contains information about the page such as the page's title and keywords that are used to help search engines find the page, but none of the page's content. The most important piece of information stored in the head of a Web page is the *title*, which is identified by the `<title>` tag. In the salamander example page, the third line of HTML code contains the title:

```
<title>Ernest the Salamander</title>
```

Lingo   The *title* of a Web page serves as a unique means of identifying a page. The title of a page is important because Web browsers use it to identify the page; when you add a Web page to your Favorites in Internet Explorer, the title is what is used to determine the name of the page.

Although the title of a Web page isn't considered part of the page's content, it is important because it serves to identify the page. When you bookmark a page or add it to your Favorites list, the browser uses the title of the page to identify it. If you were to bookmark the Ernest the Salamander page, you would see the page referred to as "Ernest the Salamander" in your Favorites list.

Placing Content in a Web Page

The body of an HTML document contains the content that is displayed by a Web browser. When you create a Web page later in this chapter, you will spend the majority of your time in the body of the page because that's where all the content is located.

Note   You might have noticed that I use the terms *Web page* and *HTML document* interchangeably. You may not think of a Web page as a document, but strictly speaking it is, just as your resume is probably a Word document. I've tried hard to interchange the words only when it makes sense to do so, but don't forget that *Web page* and *HTML document* mean the same thing. In many ways *HTML document* is a more formal description of a Web page because a Web page is simply a document coded in HTML.

Common HTML Tags and Attributes

Now you know a little about HTML tags and how they're used to describe the different parts of an HTML document. It's time to take a closer look at tags and how they are used to describe content within a Web page. Although you've learned about a few tags already, let me warn you that HTML is loaded with tags that do all kinds of different things. Table 2-1 lists some of the most common HTML tags, which you will put to use in your first Web page in the next section of this chapter. Keep in mind that you'll continue to learn about additional tags as you progress through the book. Although this is only a sampling of the tags used in HTML, you'll find yourself using these routinely in your Web pages.

Table 2-1 Commonly Used HTML Tags

Tag(s)	Usage
<html></html>	Identifies the document as an HTML document
<head></head>	Identifies the head of the HTML document
<body></body>	Identifies the body of the HTML document
<title></title>	Specifies the title of the HTML document
<h1></h1>...<h6></h6>	Sets the size of text to one of six preset sizes
<p></p>	Denotes a paragraph in the page
<b></b>	Bolds text
<i></i>	Italicizes text
<u></u>	Underlines text
<img>	Places an image on the page
<a>	Establishes a hyperlink (anchor)
 	Creates a line break, moving the insertion point to the next line
<ul></ul>	Denotes an unordered list of bulleted items
<ol></ol>	Denotes an ordered list of numbered items
<li></li>	Identifies an item within an ordered or unordered list

Before you can begin putting the tags in the table to use, it's important to learn about *attributes*, which play an important role when working with tags. Simply put, attributes are used to describe the properties of a tag. Take a look at this example:

```
<p align="left">
Let's sing a lament,
The world isn't round
it's twisted and bent.
</p>
```

Lingo   An *attribute* is a customizable option for a tag that allows you to provide details about how the tag is to impact content.

This is a paragraph of text, which consists of the `<p>` tag followed by text, followed by a `</p>` tag. Can you guess what the attribute is and what it is used for? The `align` attribute is part of the `<p>` tag, and it allows you to specify how text in a paragraph is arranged on the page: left-aligned, right-aligned, or centered. In this example, the `align` attribute is set to `left`, which results in the paragraph of text being left-aligned.

Note   HTML is not a case-sensitive language, which means that you can enter tags and attributes in either uppercase or lowercase, or a mixture of the two. However, it is a good practice to use lowercase for tags and attributes, because it is a strict requirement of XHTML, which you will learn about in Chapter 18, "XHTML: XML Meets HTML." XHTML is a somewhat more finicky version of HTML. Because it represents the future of the Web, you might as well start thinking in terms of coding documents that meet its stricter guidelines. One of these guidelines is using lowercase for tags and attributes.

Attributes are used heavily in HTML to describe the specific properties of a tag. Not all tags support attributes, but it's important to familiarize yourself with the attributes for those tags that do. Attributes are always specified as part of a start tag and always consist of the attribute name followed by an equal sign followed by the attribute value. This is another example of a tag with an attribute:

```
<body bgcolor="pink">
...
</body>
```

In this example, the `bgcolor` attribute is used to set the background color of the Web page to pink. If you are an astute kind of reader, you might recognize this code from the Ernest the Salamander Web page earlier in the chapter. The `bgcolor` attribute is part of the `<body>` tag, and is capable of being set with various color values. Notice that the attribute is specified as part of the start tag, which is a strict requirement of HTML.

Note   A requirement that isn't so strict is enclosing attribute values in quotation marks. The only time you absolutely must enclose an attribute in quotation marks is when it contains spaces. Otherwise, you are free to specify it without quotes. On the other hand, as you learn later in the book, XHTML isn't quite so liberal, so you might want to get into the habit of using quotation marks.

Some HTML tags have *required attributes*, which are attributes for which you must supply values any time you use the tag. The idea is that required attributes contain information that is essential to the usage of the tag. A good example of a required attribute is the src attribute that is part of the image tag (<img>). The image tag is used to place images on a Web page. A critical part of image placement is identifying the image file to be displayed, which is specified in the src attribute. That's why the src attribute is a required attribute. Following is an example of the src attribute at work:

```
<img src="Ernest.jpg">
```

Caution   You should be careful to make sure and set values for any required attributes that a tag may have.

This example demonstrates how to display the image in the file Ernest.jpg using the <img> tag and the src attribute. The image tag (<img>) indicates that an image is to be displayed, and the src attribute within the tag identifies the image file associated with the image, which in this case is Ernest the Salamander.

Many tags support multiple attributes, and the attributes are listed one after the next in the start tag, separated by a space. You will learn a great deal more about attributes as you dig deeper into HTML tags.

Writing Your First Web Page in HTML

I'm generally the kind of person who likes to learn how to do something new by jumping in with both feet. Although I have plenty of scars to justify why this might not always be the best approach to learning all new activities—off-road skateboarding, for example—the learn-by-doing approach has served me well, technically speaking. For this reason, I want you to cut your teeth on HTML by creating a Web page for yourself. Relax, though, I'm going to give you most of the code, and I'm going to give you all of the details to be sure that you understand what's going on.

Tip   The code for all of the examples throughout the book is available for download from my Web site at the following URL: *http://www.michaelmorrison.com/cbook_fshtml.html*.

Honor Thyself

Few of us can resist sharing with others our noblest interests and proudest moments. What better way to honor yourself and share a little with the world than by creating your own personal Web page? I encourage you to start out with a personal Web page as your first HTML project, because it deals with a subject you know better than any other—yourself! If you're worried about having to do research for this one, you may need to take time to reflect before continuing this chapter.

Note   For the purposes of demonstrating how to put together a personal Web page, this section leads you through the development of a personal page for a fictitious character called Sparky the Clown. Feel free to insert your own personal information in place of Sparky's.

To get started on your personal page, create a text document using your text editor of choice. If you're using Microsoft Windows, Notepad will suffice. Whatever editor you use, be sure to save your file as a text-format file, and use .*html* as the extension.

If you're on a different type of computer with a different operating system, then find a suitable program that will let you edit straight text files. The first code you need to enter is the skeletal template that describes the overall structure of the page:

```
<html>
<head>
</head>

<body>
</body>
</html>
```

This code establishes that you are indeed creating a Web page (HTML document) and that it has a head and a body, two important requirements of all Web pages. Now, name the page using the `<title>` tag:

```
<title>Sparky's Personal Page</title>
```

Do you remember where this line of code goes? A big celebratory ding if you said the head of the page! That's right, the title of a page is not considered part of the page's content, and must be placed between the `<head>` and `</head>` tags.

Caution   If you don't provide a title for your Web page and someone attempts to bookmark it in his or her Web browser, the browser won't know what to name the bookmark. So, be sure to provide a title for all of your Web pages.

Adding a Splash of Color

Next on the agenda is to spice up the page with background and text colors. You use the `bgcolor` attribute of the `<body>` tag to specify the background color, and the `text` attribute to specify the text color. The `bgcolor` and `text` attributes are optional. By default, all Web pages use whatever colors are set up as default colors in your Web browser, usually white with black text.

The following are the predefined colors you can use as values for the `bgcolor` and `text` attributes: `white`, `black`, `silver`, `gray`, `maroon`, `red`, `green`, `lime`, `navy`, `blue`, `purple`, `fuchsia`, `olive`, `yellow`, `teal`, and `aqua`. Keep in mind that the text on your page must contrast with the background color in order to be seen, so selecting black text on a black background is definitely a bad idea. After selecting background and text colors for your personal page, the `<body>` tag should look something like this:

```
<body bgcolor="silver" text="navy">
```

Caution   If the text color of a Web page doesn't contrast with the background color, it will be very hard for people to read the text on the page. So, make sure that you choose colors carefully so that there is plenty of contrast. Black text on a white page provides the utmost contrast, which is why you see so many pages that are black on white. Even so, you can certainly find other color combinations that still provide reasonable contrast.

Tell Me Something About Yourself

Now that you're within the body of the Web page, you can start entering content, such as headings. *Headings* provide a good way to break up content into clearly labeled sections. In the case of your personal Web page, adding a heading immediately lets everyone know who you are. The `<h1>`, `<h2>`, `<h3>`, `<h4>`, `<h5>`, and `<h6>` tags allow you to format text at predefined sizes for headings. The `<h1>` tag creates the largest heading and should work great for displaying your name on the page:

```
<h1>Sparky the Clown</h1>
```

You're now ready to begin describing yourself, and what better way to do that than to display an image of yourself. The `<img>` tag embeds images in Web pages, as you saw earlier in the chapter. If you don't have an image of yourself, feel free to find an interesting clip art image to use for the time being. A clip art image is an image that is made available as part of a collection of images, and once you've purchased the collection you can usually use the images as much as you want in your own Web pages. Microsoft offers a sizable collection of clip art on the Web that is completely free. Check out Microsoft's Design Gallery Live at *http://dgl.microsoft.com/* to access their clip art collection.

Anyway, getting back to the `<img>` tag, the `src` attribute of the `<img>` tag is used to identify the file containing the image that you want to display. You can also control the alignment of the image with respect to nearby text by using the `align` attribute. The following is an example of how you might embed an image of yourself in your personal page:

```
<img src="Sparky.jpg" align="top">
```

> **Tip** Any images or other files referenced from within a Web page should be placed in a folder easily accessible from the Web page. In the case of the Sparky example page, the Sparky.jpg image file should be placed in the same folder as the Sparky.html file.

Keep in mind that most Web pages are organized into paragraphs. It's a good idea to start your personal page with an opening paragraph that includes the image you just coded as well as some introductory text. Paragraphs are enclosed within `<p>` and `</p>` tags. You might use these tags to structure the opening paragraph this way:

```
<p>
<img src="Sparky.jpg" align="top">
This is the personal Web page of Sparky the Clown. Click
<a href="mailto:sparky@sillyclowns.com">here</a> to e-mail Sparky.
</p>
```

Notice that the `<img>` tag is placed within the paragraph just before the text. It is important to note that the setting of the `align` attribute forces the image to be aligned with the top of the text in this paragraph. Another interesting thing about this code is the usage of the `<a>` tag to provide an e-mail hyperlink. You use the `href` attribute of the `<a>` tag to set the target for the link, which in this case is the e-mail address for Sparky the Clown. Substitute your own e-mail address after the colon following `mailto`, and you're good to go.

> **Note** Just in case you're worried that I'm glossing over some details, you will be learning a great deal more about images in Chapter 4, "Decorating Pages with Images." For now, I just wanted to tell you enough about images so that you could make your first Web page a little more exciting.

Listing Your Activities

To wrap up your personal page, you might want to include a list of your favorite activities. These can be hobbies, sports, or anything else you enjoy. Because your activities list is logically separate from the introductory paragraph, you might include it in its own paragraph using the <p> tag. Taking things a step further, this is a great time to use the unordered list tag, <ul>, in conjunction with the list item tag, <li>. The idea behind these two tags is that you set up a bulleted list with the <ul> tag, and then identify each item within the list using <li> tags. This is an example of how your activities list might be structured:

```
<p>
These are some of Sparky's primary interests:
<ul>
<li>Jumping off balconies</li>
<li>Doing silly little backflips</li>
<li>Floating children with helium balloons</li>
</ul>
</p>
```

It's important for you to remember to close tags that come in pairs. For example, end the <ul> tag with </ul> and the <li> tag with </li>. Otherwise, a Web browser could get confused and do ugly things to the content of your page.

Try This!   Modify the list of activities to suit your own personal activities. Feel free to add more activities by using the <li> and </li> tags if you're the adventurous type, or remove activities if you tend to have a one-track mind.

Taking a Peek at the Finished Page

While you've been busy doing a personal inventory of activities and carefully committing them to HTML code, you may not have realized that you've already written your first Web page in HTML! The following code contains the complete Sparky.html Web page, which should mirror your own personal page in structure and form.

```
<html>
<head>
  <title>Sparky's Personal Page</title>
</head>

<body bgcolor="silver" text="navy">
```

```
<h1>Sparky the Clown</h1>
<p>
<img src="Sparky.jpg" align="top">
This is the personal Web page of Sparky the Clown. Click
<a href="mailto:sparky@sillyclowns.com">here</a> to e-mail Sparky.
</p>
<p>
These are some of Sparky's primary interests:
<ul>
<li>Jumping off balconies</li>
<li>Doing silly little backflips</li>
<li>Floating children with helium balloons</li>
</ul>
</p>
</body>
</html>
```

Before you began reading this chapter, you might have looked at this code and thought it was incomprehensible. Now, only a few pages later, you are speaking simple HTML. Figure 2-2 shows the finished Sparky the Clown Web page as viewed in Internet Explorer.

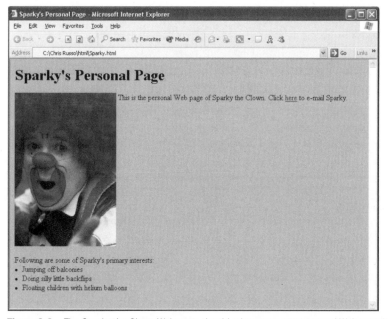

Figure 2-2   The Sparky the Clown Web page should mirror your own personal Web page in structure and form even if you don't look like a clown.

In case you're wondering how to view your new masterpiece, just fire up your Web browser. (You probably have an icon handy on your desktop). Once the browser window opens, perform these steps to open your page:

1   Choose Open from the File menu.

2   Browse and select the HTML file on your hard drive.

3   Click OK to open your page in the browser.

You may not have realized it until now, but you can view Web pages stored on your local hard drive as if they were located out on the Web. In fact, this is how you test all of your Web pages as you assemble them on your computer. If you have something against menus and you're using Windows, another quick way to open a local Web page is to drag the Web page file onto the Web browser window. When you let go of the file after dragging it onto Internet Explorer, for example, Internet Explorer will open the file and display it just as if it was located on the Web.

Publishing Your First Web Page

Although it's certainly a thrill to view your first Web page in a browser and instantly see the results of your foray into HTML, the real reason you want to create Web pages is so you can share them with the world. To share Web pages with the world, you must publish them, which simply means that you will copy them to a special computer on the Internet. This computer, connected to the Web, is set up specifically to store Web pages. Before I get into any more specifics about how a page is published, it's worth taking a moment to explain how the Web works in terms of accessing Web pages.

If you have any geeky friends, you may have heard your Web browser referred to as a "Web client." These are probably the same friends who insist on describing every piece of electronic equipment they own as either analog or digital. Not to worry, the term Web client is quite straightforward and helps to explain how the Web works. When you view a Web page in a Web browser, the page is actually being delivered to the browser by a special program known as a *Web server*. Its only job is to receive requests for Web pages and serve them up for viewing. The Web browser, the client, asks a Web server to deliver a certain page, and the server obliges. This relationship between the Web browser and server is known as a *client-server* relationship, which is why browsers are referred to as *Web clients*.

Lingo   The Web is organized as a *client/server* environment where Web pages are delivered from Web servers to Web clients. A *Web server* is a computer permanently connected to the Internet that stores Web pages, while a *Web client* is a computer that connects across the Internet to a Web server in order to retrieve Web pages.

As a Web surfer, all you've had to concern yourself with was the client side of the equation because you interacted only with the browser. When you begin publishing Web pages, you will have to pay some attention to the server side of the equation. You must either install Web server software on a computer that's always connected to the Internet, or use a Web hosting service. Either way, the Web pages you create will be stored on the computer with the Web server, as opposed to your personal computer. You will still create the pages locally on your own computer and test them there. Once they are ready to go live, you must copy your pages to a Web server. Copying a Web page to a Web server is similar to copying a file on your hard drive. The difference is that you are copying the Web page file across the Internet. It sounds tricky, but special programs designed for this task make it almost as simple as copying files between folders on your own hard drive.

Note   Most visual Web development tools, such as Microsoft FrontPage, include a feature that automatically copies, or publishes, pages to a Web server via File Transfer Protocol (FTP), which alleviates the need to use a special FTP program. A *visual Web development tool* is a tool that uses a graphical user interface to allow you to practically point and click your way through the creation of Web pages.

I want to reiterate that you don't need access to a Web server of any kind to learn HTML and develop your own Web pages. Web servers come into play only when you want to publish pages for the whole world to view. So, if you want to create a family Web site that is only going to be viewed on your local computer and doesn't need to be on the Web, you can simply develop the pages on your computer and view them in a Web browser straight from the hard drive. Of course, you probably have plans of making your Web pages much more publicly accessible, in which case you must publish them to a Web server. When you are ready to publish pages, you might find that your existing Internet service includes Web hosting space as part of your deal. If this is the case, you can contact your *Internet Service Provider* (*ISP*). They'll tell you how to copy the pages to the appropriate Web server and publish them. You can also pay a monthly fee for a Web hosting service through an ISP.

Lingo   An *Internet Service Provider*, or *ISP*, is a company that provides an Internet connection. Popular ISPs include the Microsoft Network (MSN), AOL, Earthlink, and a variety of telephone and cable companies who offer their own Internet services.

Getting Your Own Dot-Com

If you're interested in having your own dot-com name, then you'll need to register the name and set up a Web hosting service. Services offered by Network Solutions (*http://www.networksolutions.com/*) and EasyDNS (*http://www.easydns.com/*) and allow you to see if your name is available. These are companies that oversee domain name registrations, and that also offer hosting services for Web sites at relatively little cost. Also, if you are a member of the Microsoft Network (MSN) or America Online (AOL), there is Web space included with your service that you can use to host your pages.

If working through all this Web hosting information felt like being in the middle of a whirlwind, that's because it was. My intention in this section isn't to teach you everything there is to know about publishing Web pages. You learn all the ins and outs of Web page publication in Chapter 9, "Publishing Pages on the Web." For now, your first page is up and running. Bask in the limelight!

Note   In addition to .com names, you can also register names with .net, .org, .biz, and several other domain extensions.

Try This!   If you have a domain name in mind for a Web site you'd like to create, stop reading right now and see if it's available. It's never too early to register a domain name if you know you will use it at some point in the future.

Publishing Web Pages in Windows XP

If you're using Microsoft Windows XP, you have a built-in tool that allows you to quickly publish pages on the Web. I'm talking about the Microsoft Web Publishing Wizard, which you can run by following these steps:

1   Open My Computer and navigate to the folder containing your page.

2   Click the folder to highlight it in File Explorer.

3   Click Publish The Selected Items To The Web in the left-hand pane of File Explorer.

Note   If you're using a version of Windows that's prior to Windows XP, you can still access the Web Publishing Wizard by clicking the Start menu and then choosing Programs, Accessories, Internet Tools, and Web Publishing Wizard. However, the steps required to publish a page using the old version of the Web Publishing Wizard differ somewhat from the steps discussed here, which apply to Windows XP.

Figure 2-3 shows the opening screen of the Web Publishing Wizard. To get started publishing your personal page, click Next. You will then be prompted to check and uncheck the files associated with the pages you wish to publish (Figure 2-4). If you're using the Web Publishing Wizard in an older version of Windows, then you may have to browse and select the files.

Figure 2-3   The Web Publishing Wizard is a program that simplifies the process of publishing Web pages.

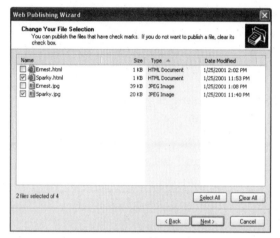

Figure 2-4   The first step in the Web Publishing Wizard is to select the files for the Web page to be published.

After selecting the files that go with your Web page, click Next to continue. You are then prompted to select the Internet service to which you are copying the page. The services available to you are dependent upon what Internet service your computer is already configured to use. For example, my computer offered Xdrive Plus and MSN Communities, but yours might also offer Yahoo! Briefcase if you're a Yahoo! user.

After selecting an Internet service, click Next to continue. You are then prompted to use an existing location on the Internet service, or to create a new one. This is the location on the Internet where your Web page is to be copied. Since this is the first time you're publishing a Web page, you should indicate that you want to create a new location.

Clicking Next continues along with the Web Publishing Wizard. However, the remaining steps are entirely dependent on the specific Internet service that you're using to store your Web page. For example, if you're creating your own MSN Community storage location, you must specify whether it is public or shared. You then enter your MSN or Microsoft Passport user ID to create the community. On the other hand, the specific procedure for creating a Yahoo! Briefcase will vary to some degree, even though the end result is the creation of a storage location for your Web page.

Regardless of which Internet service you use to store your Web page, the Web Publishing Wizard eventually gets around to copying the files for your Web page to a server at the Internet service. Figure 2-5 shows the Sparky Web page files being copied to an MSN Community storage location that I created.

Figure 2-5   One of the final steps in the Web Publishing Wizard is to watch while the files are copied to a Web server.

It takes a few moments for the page to copy across the Internet, but once it's finished you can view your page online by entering its *address* in a Web browser. Fortunately, the Web Publishing Wizard concludes by confirming the address of your page so that there aren't any mysteries as to where it's located (Figure 2-6). Assuming that you specified for your Web page to be public, anyone with Web access anywhere around the world can now enter your Web page address (URL) to view the newly published page!

Lingo   An Internet *address* is like an online version of a mailing address. The technical term for an Internet address is *URL*, which stands for *Uniform Resource Locator*. All you need to know at this point is that an Internet address, or URL, uniquely identifies a Web page in the same way that your mailing address uniquely identifies your house.

Figure 2-6   The final step in the Web Publishing Wizard confirms that the page has been successfully copied and provides you with the address of the page on the Web.

Key Points

- Although you could probably get through life without knowing HTML, it will give you much more freedom and flexibility in creating your own Web pages.

- A tag is a special HTML code enclosed in angle brackets (<>) that is used to indicate the structure and format of content on a Web page.

- Every Web page consists of two parts, the head and body, which serve as places to store general properties about the page and the content of the page, respectively.

- The title of a Web page isn't considered part of the page's content, but it's important because Web browsers use it to identify the page.

- An attribute is a customizable option for a tag that allows you to provide details about how the tag is to impact content.

- HTML is not a case-sensitive language, which means that you can enter tags and attributes in uppercase, lowercase, or a mixture of the two.

- If the text color of a Web page doesn't contrast with the background color, it will be very hard for people to read the text on the page, so it's important to carefully choose colors so that there is plenty of contrast.

- The Web is organized as a client/server environment where Web pages are delivered from Web servers to Web clients.

- Windows XP includes a utility called the Web Publishing Wizard that makes it easy to publish your Web pages on the Internet.

Chapter 3

Dressing Up Text

As you learn how to use various HTML tags to format text in Web pages, you'll find that HTML provides you with a surprising amount of control over how text appears on a page. Yet, text formatting in HTML is not the same as text formatting within a word processor or desktop publishing program. A word processor or desktop publishing program gives you exacting control over the size and placement of text on a printed page, but HTML merely provides an approximation of how text will be displayed on a Web page. This may seem like a small distinction, but it does matter—especially if you have desktop publishing experience. If you don't, lucky you. Your blissful ignorance will allow you to embrace HTML text formatting easily.

Organizing Text

A picture may be worth a thousand words, but I doubt you would go along with a federal initiative to do away with all text in American newspapers and replace it with pictures. Fortunately, Congress has not pushed for such an initiative...yet. The point is that although Web pages are a visual medium with a multitude of graphics, text still reigns as the preferred means of presenting information.

Because of the importance of text to a Web page, organizing and formatting text so that it's easy to read is a critical part of constructing any Web page. Text formatting is therefore an important part of HTML.

Text and the Head of a Page

You learned in the previous chapter that a Web page is organized into two main sections: the head and the body. Although each of these sections may contain text, only the body houses text content that shows up in the Web browser window. Before going into how text is organized in the body of a Web page, let's recap why you'll find text in the head section.

The `<title>` tag, nestled cozily between the start and end `<head>` tags, allows you to specify the title of a Web page. This title isn't displayed in the contents of a browser window, but it does appear in the title bar of the Web browser. For example, the following HTML code specifies the title of a Web page:

```
<head>
  <title>Ralph's Rock Collection</title>
</head>
```

> **Note**   In addition to holding the title of a Web page, the head section can store scripting code. *Scripting code*, which is code written in a programming language that appears within the body of the page, executes tasks such as calculating a mortgage payment or accessing information in a database. You will learn about scripting in Chapter 8, "Dynamic HTML."

When viewed in a browser, the page shows up with the title in the bar at the top. This title is also the basis for naming *favorites*, also called *bookmarks*, in a browser. For this reason, be sure to use `<title>` tags in the head section of all of your Web pages. And, choose descriptive names that give your pages names with meaning beyond the context of the individual page. For example, a page named "Table of Contents" could be from one of a jillion Web sites. On the other hand, you're sure to recognize a favorite named "Ralph's Rock Collection: Table of Contents." Although certain other tags can be used within the `<head>` tag, the `<title>` tag is the only one that should be placed on every Web page.

A Body Full of Text

The drama starts to unfold in the body section of a Web page. Recall that the body of a page is where you put the travelogue you wrote during your trip to Easter Island or the pictures of the antique fishing lures you want to sell. In other words, the material that appears on the page in the Web browser is located in the body. The `<body>` tag takes on the responsibility of housing the content in the body of a page. You have two options when it comes to placing content in the body of a page. You can insert it directly into the body or within paragraphs in the body. It is usually better to break text into paragraphs because this organizes the content more efficiently than simply dropping text into the body.

Two particularly useful tags for organizing text within the body are the `<p>` and `<div>` tags. These tags define paragraphs and sectional divisions, respectively. The paragraph tag (`<p>`) is quite popular and separates paragraphs from one another. Unlike the old-fashioned typewriter, modern HTML doesn't normally observe carriage returns; it requires HTML code for *newlines*, and a new line is started for each paragraph tag.

Lingo A *newline* is a special text character used to indicate that a new line is to start in a sequence of text. In a simple text processor, a newline is inserted in a text document whenever you press Enter. You press Enter to make the cursor go to a *new line*, hence the name "newline." When an HTML document is rendered in a Web browser as a Web page, newlines are ignored as white space. In other words, you have to explicitly state in the document that you want to start a newline via a tag such as the paragraph tag.

Although a new line will appear in your HTML code every time you hit Enter in Notepad, it will disappear when you test the page on your browser. In fact, all white space created by using keystrokes (more than one space, tab, and returns) is removed when it is displayed on the browser. In practical terms, this means your beautifully spaced paragraphs in HTML code probably will not be positioned on the page the way you intend. You must apply tags. On the other hand, those new lines in Notepad are invaluable for helping you to organize and easily view the code you've written.

If you don't want to go to the trouble of identifying paragraphs with the `<p>` tag, you can also use the `<br>` tag, which represents a line break. When a Web browser encounters a `<br>` tag, it interprets it as a request for a new line and moves down a line and back to the left margin before displaying the next text in the document. Here is an example of how to separate two sentences using the `<br>` tag:

```
<body>
This sentence wants to be alone.
<br>
This sentence also wants a little space.
</body>
```

This approach works fairly well, but in some ways is considered poor usage of HTML. It doesn't provide enough logical organization for text content. The <br> tag tells the browser to move down and start a new line, while the <p> tag is more informative in that it tells the browser that this is a paragraph. The <p> tag not only has an impact on the appearance of the text, but also adds meaning by declaring that this text is a complete paragraph. In other words, context is added when you specify paragraphs of text with the <p> tag, as opposed to specifying newlines with the <br> tag. Here is the same example, marked up using the <p> tag to identify the two separate paragraphs:

```
<body>
<p>
This sentence wants to be alone.
</p>
<p>
This sentence also wants a little space.
</p>
</body>
```

Unlike the <br> tag, the <p> tag includes start and end tags that must be placed around the paragraph, but you wouldn't know that by looking at the majority of Web pages. Web developers typically use the <p> tag in the same manner as the <br> tag, to establish a new line for text. This means that the <p> is often mistaken as a way to separate paragraphs, as opposed to its correct usage: enclosing paragraphs. Fortunately, Web browsers aren't too discerning when it comes to how the <p> tag is used, which explains why the incorrect technique works in all of the popular browsers.

As a conscientious Web developer, you should stick with the appropriate use of the <p> tag, which is using both the start and end tag to *enclose* paragraphs, not *separate* them. Come to think of it, I encourage you to use all HTML tags as they were intended, regardless of what you might be able to get away with. Demonstrate your rebellion against the establishment by getting a tattoo or a nose ring, but not by bending the rules with HTML.

Note   For the record, <br> tags are not evil. As in life, there is a time and place for everything in HTML. You legitimately need a simple newline in some situations, and the <br> tag is perfectly suited for the task. However, given the choice between using a tag that simply changes the way text looks versus using a tag that adds meaning to the text as well, always use the more meaningful tag. It's kind of like the difference between a Mother's Day card with meaning versus one that just looks pretty.

Several of the <p> tag's attributes allow you to fine-tune paragraph formatting. The most common is undoubtedly the `align` attribute, which can be set to any one of the following values:

- `left`—aligns the paragraph text to the left.
- `right`—aligns the paragraph text to the right.
- `center`—centers the paragraph text.

Note   The latest version of HTML, HTML 4.0, phases out the `align` attribute of the <p> tag and encourages you to use style sheets, which are covered in Chapter 12, Chapter 13, and Chapter 14. Style sheets offer a more advanced method of formatting Web content at the cost of being more difficult to use than most of the tags and attributes they are intended to replace. And the easier-to-use tags won't go away anytime soon. So, it's important to learn how to format text using the tags and attributes that are still prevalent in most Web pages, even if the powers-that-be are urging us to move toward style sheets.

Here is an example of how to center a line of text using the `align` attribute with the <p> tag:

```
<p align="center">
This text is centered on the page.
</p>
```

The `align` attribute brings up an interesting question about attribute values: What happens if you don't specify an attribute? Attributes that aren't required have default values. In the case of the `align` attribute, the default value is `left`, which is why paragraph text is left-aligned if you don't specify an alignment.

The <div> tag serves a function similar to the <p> tag, although it's somewhat more general. The <div> tag is used to divide an HTML document into sections and plays more of an organizational role than the <p> tag. The <p> tag identifies a section of a document as specifically being a paragraph, while the <div> tag separates the section from the rest of the document and doesn't distinguish the section as being a paragraph of text. The <div> tag is often used to identify a section of a document for scripting purposes. You will learn about scripting in Chapter 11, "Dynamic HTML."

Basic Text Formatting: The Look or the Meaning?

After you've organized text into paragraphs or sections, you can begin formatting it using various HTML formatting tags. HTML provides two different types of formatting tags: content-based tags and physical tags. *Content-based tags* are used to add meaning, or context, to a piece of text, which affects how the text is displayed. *Physical tags*, on the other hand, provide no meaning and deal directly with how text is displayed.

Lingo   Although the terms sound somewhat technical, *content-based tags* and *physical tags* are just different ways of describing content in a Web page. Content-based tags pertain primarily to what content means, while physical tags dictate how content looks. In reality, content-based tags typically affect the appearance of content, too, it's just that the emphasis is on giving the content meaning.

To better understand the difference between the two approaches to describing Web page content, consider the names of the infamous 1930s gangsters "Baby Face" Nelson and Frank "The Enforcer" Nitti. Although Baby Face describes the juvenile appearance of this Prohibition-era bank robber, it tells you nothing about him or what he did. Without knowing anything about the many people he killed, you might think he was just an average guy with a youthful appearance. The Enforcer, on the other hand, indicates all you need to know about Al Capone's favorite henchman. The name is both colorful and descriptive, leaving no doubt that he was a dangerous man. To draw an analogy between these names and HTML formatting tags, Baby Face provides a physical description, and The Enforcer provides a content-based description.

Note   There are two different types of tags because in some instances you care more about how a Web page looks than assigning meaning to its content, and vice versa. Of course, this creates a constant struggle in HTML coding between a desire to make a page look good and a desire to give its content more meaning. These two desires run contrary to each other because adding meaning to HTML content doesn't always result in a visually appealing Web page. Fortunately, there's no true right or wrong when it comes to this struggle. Throughout this book, I attempt to describe the ideal situation: Adding meaning to the content while taking practical aesthetics into account. I can't help it—I'm an idealist!

The next couple of sections describe the content-based tags and physical tags used to format text in HTML. In addition to these tags, there are a few others that don't clearly fall into either category. These are *heading tags*, which identify sectional headings in an HTML document. These six heading tags describe headings of various sizes, in order of decreasing significance: <h1>, <h2>, <h3>, <h4>, <h5>, and <h6>. By decreasing significance, I mean that <h1> might be used to describe the title of a book, <h2> could be used for the chapter titles, and <h3> could be the chapter subsections. The heading tags affect the display of heading text because the size and weight of the text increases with the significance of the tag. Figure 3-1 shows text formatted with the six different heading tags, as viewed in Internet Explorer.

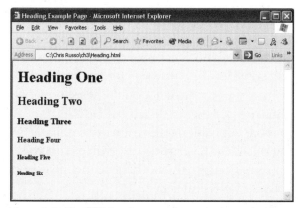

Figure 3-1 The HTML heading tags allow you to format heading text, which is displayed in a font size related to the specific heading tag used.

The body content for the Web page shown in Figure 3-1 looks like this:

```
<body>
<h1>Heading One</h1>
<h2>Heading Two</h2>
<h3>Heading Three</h3>
<h4>Heading Four</h4>
<h5>Heading Five</h5>
<h6>Heading Six</h6>
</body>
```

Tip The code for this example, as well as all of the examples throughout the book, is available for download from my Web site at the following URL: *http://www.michaelmorrison.com/cbook_fshtml.html.*

Notice that each of the heading tags requires both a start and an end tag. The heading tags serve as a great way to identify headings in a Web page without getting into the display specifics of font sizes. Keep in mind, however, that the browser ultimately determines how the specific heading sizes are displayed. This is a perfect example of how HTML fails to give you complete control over text formatting. Instead of specifying an exact font size, a heading tag lets the browser determine the best way to display the text on the page. It is possible to get more specific about the formatting of text in HTML documents, but it requires the help of style sheets, which are covered in Chapter 12, "Style Sheet Basics."

Content-Based Text Formatting

Content-based text formatting involves using HTML tags to mark up text according to the meaning of the text as opposed to how it is displayed. The motivation for using content-based formatting is that text content may be viewed in a variety of different ways. For example, consider Web browsers for the visually impaired that read content aloud instead of displaying it on the screen. In this scenario, an emphasis (<em>) tag makes more sense than a bold (<b>) tag because the text can be read with more expression to give it more emphasis. In other words, bold has no meaning outside of displaying text, while emphasis applies to text both written and spoken. Consequently, whenever possible, you should use content-based tags instead of physical tags.

These are the HTML content-based formatting tags, along with brief descriptions of their use:

- <cite>—identifies a bibliographic citation, such as a book or magazine article title.
- <code>—identifies monospaced code, such as programming code.
- <dfn>—indicates definitions, such as might appear in an online dictionary.
- <em>—adds emphasis to text.
- <kbd>—identifies text that is typed on a keyboard.
- <samp>—identifies a sequence of literal characters.
- <strong>—adds strong emphasis to text.
- <var>—identifies variables in code, such as programming code.

All of these tags require both start and end tags enclosing text content. Here is an example using the `<em>` and `<strong>` tags to mark up a sentence of text:

```
<p>
The collapse of the market came as an <em>enormous</em>
surprise to many, and delivered a <strong>crushing</strong>
blow to many individual portfolios.
</p>
```

Figure 3-2 shows the results of this code, illustrating how Internet Explorer displays `<em>` text in italics and `<strong>` text in bold.

Figure 3-2   The HTML content-based formatting tags allow you to format text based on its meaning, which indirectly impacts how it is displayed.

Tip   Although I've referred to the content-based formatting tags as being useful for formatting text, you can use them to format images as well. Because the emphasis is on the meaning of content, you can mark up an image with the `<strong>` tag to indicate that the image has a strong meaning with respect to other content on a page. You will learn how to use images in Chapter 4, "Decorating Pages with Images."

Physical Text Formatting

Content-based formatting tags allow you to format text according to its meaning, and physical formatting tags define how to format text based on how you want it to appear in a Web browser. Physical formatting tags have served as the primary means of formatting text on the Web since its inception, which is why it isn't realistic to assume that content-based tags are going to take over any time soon. The convenience of physical tags is significant when it comes to specifying clearly how text is to be displayed.

In some cases, you'll find that browsers render a content-based tag the same as a physical tag. For example, text formatted with the <em> content-based tag appears as italicized text in most browsers, but the same result is achieved with the <i> physical tag. The difference is that you aren't guaranteed italics with the <em> tag because it doesn't directly address how text is displayed, whereas the <i> tag does. The moral of the story is that if you want to achieve a specific appearance with text, use a physical tag, but if you want to assign meaning to the text, use a content-based tag. There is a chance that both tags may end up yielding the same result in a browser, but by using one or the other you are indicating a preference for text appearance versus text meaning.

Here are the physical formatting tags, along with brief descriptions of their use:

- <b>—indicates bold text.
- <big>—increases the font size of default text.
- <blink>—indicates blinking text.
- <i>—indicates italicized text.
- <s>—indicates strikethrough text.
- <small>—decreases the font size of default text.
- <sub>—indicates subscript text.
- <sup>—indicates superscript text.
- <tt>—indicates a monospaced font (all characters are the same width) for text.
- <u>—indicates underlined text.

Similar to the content-based tags, these physical text-formatting tags are used to enclose text content and must have both start and end tags. Here is an example using several of the mark-up tags:

```
<p>
When I was <small><small>smaller</small></small> than I am now,
I dreamed of being much <big><big>bigger</big></big>. As
<b>excited</b> as I was about the prospect, the amount of time
it would take to get there made me <i>sad</i>.
</p>
```

Try This! Take some time to experiment with physical formatting tags. Just start out with a paragraph of text and try applying each tag to a different word to see how it affects the text when viewed in a Web browser.

Figure 3-3 shows the formatted paragraph in Internet Explorer.

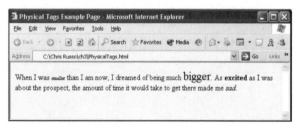

Figure 3-3   The HTML physical formatting tags allow you to format text for specific display.

You may wonder why the `<small>` and `<big>` tags are used repeatedly. It's simple. Each occurrence of the `<small>` and `<big>` tags decreases or increases the size of text by a certain amount. The basic idea behind this approach is that the physical formatting tags acknowledge six font sizes. When you use one of the `<small>` or `<big>` tags, the enclosed text is decreased or increased one size. To further decrease or increase the font size, you must use the tags repeatedly, as in the example.

Note   Technically speaking, the `<blink>` tag was never part of the HTML standard. Instead, it is a Netscape extension that is still supported to this day. Many Web designers view the `<blink>` tag as the worst example of inconsistency among Web browsers because Internet Explorer doesn't support its use. Your best bet is to avoid using it. In addition, the `<u>` and `<s>` tags are both phased out of HTML 4.0, but they are still commonly used in many Web pages.

Working with Lists

If you're the kind of person that likes to keep up with personal top ten lists, then you're really going to love HTML. Maybe you keep an ongoing list of your top ten favorite movies, or possibly even your top ten favorite Madonna hairstyles. Either way, you'll be glad to know that you can use a handy feature of HTML to put your lists on the Web. I'm referring to HTML lists, which are used to break a sequence of text into an ordered or unordered list. *Ordered lists*, also known as *numbered lists*, typically outline the steps required to perform a process. An *unordered list* might be used to specify the ingredients for a recipe, for example. There are actually three types of lists supported in HTML:

- Unordered lists contain bulleted items.
- Ordered lists contain numbered items.
- Definition lists contain terms with corresponding definitions.

Different tags specify each type, and they are covered in the next few sections.

Tip   Although it isn't imperative to place each item on a line of its own in HTML code, it makes the code easier to read and understand.

Unordered Lists

Unordered lists consist of items displayed with a bullet next to each one. The `<ul>` tag encloses an unordered list. Within the list, individual items are coded with the `<li>` tag. The following code demonstrates how to use these tags to create an unordered list:

```
<p>
Following are the sports in which I regularly participate:
<ul>
<li>Hockey</li>
<li>Cycling</li>
<li>Skateboarding</li>
<li>Wiffle Ball!</li>
</ul>
</p>
```

Note   Because the items in an *unordered list* are identified by bullets, as opposed to numbers or letters, they are considered unordered. You learn about ordered lists in the next section.

Figure 3-4 shows the formatted paragraph viewed in Internet Explorer.

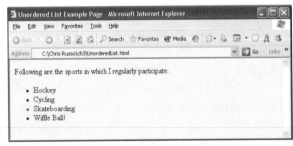

Figure 3-4   The `<ul>` tag allows you to create unordered lists of items.

Notice that the `<ul>` tag consists of both start and end tags that enclose the entire list. The `<li>` tag identifies each item within the list and also requires both a start and an end tag.

The `<ul>` tag supports a `type` attribute that allows you to change the type of bullet shown next to each item in the list. The following values are acceptable for use with the `type` attribute. Note that `disc` is the default bullet:

■ The `disc` value indicates a solid circle.

■ The `circle` value indicates a hollow circle.

■ The `square` value indicates a solid square.

Note   The `type` attribute of `<ul>` isn't used too often, even in older Web pages, because most pages rely on the default `disc` bullet style.

Numbered Lists

Ordered lists are similar to unordered lists, with the exception that they are identified by numbers when displayed, instead of bullets. The numbering starts with 1 by default and increases by one for each value in the list. The `<ol>` tag is used to create ordered lists. Here is an example of a simple ordered list similar to the unordered list you previously examined:

```
<p>
Following are the sports I regularly participate in,
ranked in order from most favorite to just fun-to-do:
<ol>
<li>Skateboarding</li>
<li>Hockey</li>
<li>Cycling</li>
<li>Wiffle Ball!</li>
</ol>
</p>
```

Figure 3-5 shows the formatted paragraph viewed in Internet Explorer.

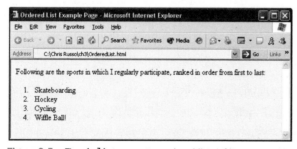

Figure 3-5   The `<ol>` tag creates ordered lists of items.

Figure 3-5 illustrates how numbers are assigned to items in an ordered list, even though no numbering appears in the HTML code. You might be concerned about the potential limitations on ordered lists, such as always beginning with an Arabic 1 and proceeding from there. Fortunately, HTML permits you to change both the starting number and the type of numbering system used in ordered lists. The `start` attribute allows you to specify the starting number for a list, and the `type` attribute specifies the type of numbering system. Here are the allowed values for the `type` attribute, along with an example of the associated numbering system:

- 1—1, 2, 3, 4... (default)
- A—A, B, C, D...
- a—a, b, c, d...
- I—I, II, III, IV...
- i—i, ii, iii, iv...

To change the numbering system for an ordered list, simply assign one of these values to the `type` attribute. Next is an example of using both the `start` and `type` attributes to alter the numbering of an ordered list:

```
<p>
Following are some of my favorite letters:
<ol type="A" start="5">
<li>The letter E!</li>
<li>The letter F!</li>
<li>The letter G!</li>
<li>The letter H!</li>
</ol>
</p>
```

In this example, the type of list is set to "A" to display capital letters next to the items. The starting number of the list is set to "5", which results in identifying the first item with the letter E, which is the fifth letter of the alphabet.

Definition Lists

If Noah Webster had had access to HTML in 1806, he would have appreciated definition lists for marking up terms and their associated definitions. Webster published the first American dictionary, which evolved over the last two centuries into today's popular Merriam-Webster dictionary. Although you probably aren't putting together your own dictionary, you may still find definition lists useful.

Definition lists consist of terms and their definitions. A definition list is enclosed within <dl> start and end tags, and each term in the list is identified by the <dt> tag. Another tag, the <dd> tag, must follow the <dt> tag in a definition list to provide the definition of the preceding term. I realize that this sounds confusing, but I promise it's really pretty simple. This example shows how these tags fit together to create a list of definitions:

```
<p>
Following are a few technologies related to Web page
development, along with a brief description of each:
<dl>
<dt>Java</dt>
<dd>A programming language designed to add interactivity to Web
pages through special programs called applets that run within
the context of a page.</dd>
<dt>JavaScript</dt>
<dd>A scripting language designed to add interactivity to Web
pages by embedding script code directly in HTML code.</dd>
<dt>VBScript</dt>
<dd>A scripting language that serves a similar role as
JavaScript, but that is loosely based upon Microsoft's popular
Visual Basic programming language.</dd>
</dl>
</p>
```

Figure 3-6 shows the formatted text viewed in Internet Explorer.

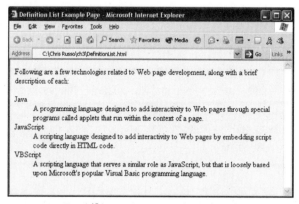

Figure 3-6   The <dl> tag allows you to create definition lists containing terms and their definitions.

As you can see in the example, creating definition lists is straightforward; you enclose the entire list with the start and end <dl> tags, and then mark up the terms and definitions with the <dt> and <dd> tags, respectively.

Note   Regarding lists in general, the list tags are all designed to support nesting—which means that you can nest lists within other lists. Because of this, it's important to make sure that you match every start and end tag properly.

One Last Comment

We all have one of those friends who has a comment about everything. As much as you may love to hear their musings on current events, too many comments annoy. Not so in HTML. HTML *comments* describe the code. More specifically, comments in HTML code identify information that isn't part of the document's content and isn't processed or displayed. Comments are marked up with the special comment delimiters: <!-- and -->.

Lingo   A *comment* in HTML code is used to store information that isn't part of the document's content and therefore isn't displayed in a Web browser. This kind of information could include something as important as a copyright notice or simply a note to yourself reminding you to update part of the page at a later date.

Here is an example of a simple comment placed in HTML code:

```
<!-- Finish the following paragraph -->
<p>
It all began innocently enough in the fall of 1987...
</p>
```

In this example, the comment is used to describe work that needs to be done to the document.

Try This!   Add some comments to the personal Web page that you created in the previous chapter. If you're struggling to think about what needs to be commented on, consider adding comments regarding information you'd like to add the page. In other words, try using comments as sort of built-in "To Do" list within your Web page.

Comments can also be used to temporarily ignore lines of HTML code during testing. The most popular and important use of comments is placing scripting code, such as code written in JavaScript or VBScript. Web browsers capable of interpreting such code will routinely scan comments in a document to see if there is any scripting code. In this way, comments can certainly do more than just contain information that won't be displayed. However, from the perspective of pure HTML code, browsers simply ignore comments.

Caution   Comments cannot be nested within each other. When a Web browser encounters the `<!--` that signals the start of a comment, it continues ignoring everything until it finds the `-->` end delimiter, which signals the end of the comment. If you nest a comment about an image within another comment about a paragraph of text, the browser will end the comment at the first `-->` end delimiter for the image comment and not know what to do with the paragraph comment. The moral of the story is that each comment must learn to fly on its own two tags—or fall from the nest.

Key Points

- The `<p>` and `<div>` tags are used to define paragraphs and sectional divisions, respectively, and come in handy when it comes to organizing text on a Web page.

- The `<br>` tag offers a quick and dirty approach to inserting a new line in a Web page.

- Many attributes have a default value that is assumed if you don't explicitly specify a value for the attribute.

- Physical and content-based HTML tags provide a means of distinguishing between marking up content for display and associating meaning with the content.

- List tags allow you to create bulleted or numbered lists of items, or even lists containing definitions of terms.

- In both unordered and ordered lists, the `<li>` tag is used to specify each individual item in a list.

- Comments allow you to add information to a Web page that isn't displayed by a Web browser.

Chapter 4

Decorating Pages with Images

It's difficult to go anywhere on the Web without encountering images of some sort. They convey meaning, share information, and serve as window dressing for the majority of Web pages in existence. Although it is certainly possible to misuse images from a graphic design perspective, almost anyone would argue that Web pages benefit from them. Images helped spur the Web's rapid acceptance and will continue to draw attention to the Web as it evolves. This chapter will show you how to display images using HTML. More specifically, you will learn about the single tag that embeds images in Web pages. You'll also get friendly with the basic types of images, along with the details about when to use them.

The Whole Picture on Images

I mentioned previously that nerds like me love to throw around acronyms when discussing technology. If you've ever heard talk about images or scanned pictures, you've likely heard the terms JPEG and GIF. These two acronyms, which you will learn more about shortly, refer to the two most commonly used types of images on the Web. Before I get into the specifics of how the two image types differ—and why they are necessary—let me get to the heart of exactly what an image is.

If your monitor's resolution is set to 800×600, the picture on your screen has 800 pixels across and 600 pixels down—that's almost half a million pixels! Although all images are ultimately displayed as a rectangular group of pixels, they are stored in a variety of different ways. The manner in which an image is stored is determined by an image format—a number of different image formats have been developed, each offering some unique combination of image file size and display quality. Two major formats, appropriate for different types of images, are commonly used on the Web and are supported by most Web browsers.

■   The *JPEG image format*, named after the Joint Photographic Experts Group and pronounced "jay peg," helps photographs travel lightly, with a format especially designed for storing them efficiently. These image files typically have a .jpg or .jpeg file extension.

■   The *GIF image format*, named for the Graphics Interchange Format and most often pronounced "jif," more efficiently stores images that are not photographs, such as illustrations and diagrams. These image files typically have a .gif file extension.

Try This!   Check your screen's resolution in Windows by following these steps:

1   Double-click Display in the Control Panel.

2   Selecting the Settings tab in the Display Properties window.

3   The screen resolution displayed represents the width and height of your screen in pixels.

Note   A third image format showing up on the Web is called *PNG*, which stands for Portable Network Graphic and is pronounced "ping." The PNG image format is intended to eventually replace GIF. It compresses image files even more than GIF and avoids licensing problems associated with the technology underlying GIF. Although PNG images are likely to grow in popularity during the next few years, they're not likely to seriously challenge GIF's popularity for a while.

So, how do the two most popular image formats differ? Basically, both are designed to store certain types of images. By choosing the appropriate format for an image, you keep the size of the image file at a minimum while maintaining its quality. To summarize what this means to you: Store photographic images in the JPEG format. GIF works best for other images, such as illustrations.

You probably know from experience that images often take a noticeable amount of time to download over most Internet connections. Keeping image sizes to a minimum is the most efficient way to speed things up, so making the right format choice is critical in Web pages. Despite the growing number of users with high-speed Internet access, you can't count on the average Web surfer to have such a connection, at least not yet. And even with high-speed Internet access, network congestion increases download time.

Lingo High-speed Internet connections are often referred to as *broadband* connections. Examples of broadband Internet connections include cable and DSL modems, as well as direct corporate connections such as T1 and T3 lines. If you are using a traditional modem to dial an Internet service, you do not have a broadband connection.

The JPEG format is designed for photorealistic images with many shades of color, and it significantly reduces the size of the image file. Photorealistic images are primarily photographic images that were either scanned from a photograph or taken as pictures using a digital camera. On the other hand, the JPEG format doesn't fare so well with illustrations, and it is not the ideal image format for them.

For illustrations and virtually any image that isn't photorealistic, GIF is your best choice. Non-photorealistic images include most hand-drawn artwork, as well as the majority of clip art that comes with popular desktop publishing tools such as Microsoft Publisher. In addition, the GIF image format provides flexibility that isn't available with a JPEG image: transparency and animation. These are popular features for Web page development.

Lingo *GIF transparency* lets you "see through" a region of a GIF image, allowing the background color of a Web page to show through. Think about the weather report on your local news broadcast; the reporter appears in front of the computer-generated weather map. The real background that the reporter is standing in front of is a solid color that is interpreted as being transparent, which allows the weather map to be displayed in its place as a backdrop.

Lingo *GIF animation* is a GIF feature that allows images to change appearance over time. More specifically, an *animated GIF* includes multiple image frames, which are displayed in succession to yield the effect of motion. Although animated GIF images can be annoying if overdone, they can be quite compelling when used properly. You will learn more about animated GIF images later in this chapter, in the section titled "Using Animated Images."

Working with Images

Would it come as a big surprise if I told you that there are 12 different HTML tags involved in formatting and displaying images? Images are certainly powerful, and they offer a lot of bang for the buck in terms of Web page design. So it wouldn't be surprising if a large number of complex tags were involved. Interestingly though, only two HTML tags are necessary to put an image on a Web page: <img> and <a>. The difference between these tags has to do with how you tell the Web browser to display an image.

This brings up an important distinction between images and text. They are not stored in the same place. Text belongs with the HTML code, but an image is stored in an external file. An image file has to be referenced, or called, from HTML code to have the image displayed on the Web page. The actual image is always located in a separate file.

What's the big deal? This changes the perspective. From an HTML perspective, you are dealing with a file other than the Web page. You must reference an image file in one of two ways:

■ A reference to the file in which an *inline image* is stored displays the image directly on the Web page with the surrounding text and other images. The more common of the two approaches, an inline image basically parallels the way traditional desktop publishing handles images.

■ A reference to an *external image* is a link to the image file, which is displayed only when someone clicks the link. These external images work differently in that they are not displayed directly on the Web page with the link.

The next section describes how to use inline images, while you tackle external images a little later in the chapter in the section titled "Linking to External Images."

Displaying Inline Images

A simple HTML <img> tag places an inline image—a photo of a scenic waterfall, for example—on the Web page. This tag has one required attribute, src, used to identify the address of the image to be displayed. Briefly mentioned in Chapter 1,"An Introduction to HTML, DHTML, and XML," such an address is also known as a *URL*, or Uniform Resource Locator. You will learn a great deal about URLs in the next chapter, but for now just keep in mind that they identify the location of files on the Internet. The URL of the image specified in the src attribute includes the image file name, along with any other path information. If you specify just the image file name, the Web browser assumes that the image is located in the same directory as the Web page's file. I realize this may seem confusing at this stage, but it's fairly simple when you see how it works. Look at this example of an <img> tag that displays an inline image:

```
<img src="Jump.jpg">
```

I told you it was simple! This example uses a *relative path* to identify the image file, looking for it where the Web page file itself is located. Here is a similar example that instead uses an *absolute path* to reference the image file:

```
<img src="http://www.thetribe.com/images/Jump.jpg">
```

This second example is a little more complicated, but it's not so confusing when you understand what's going on. In this example, the absolute path of the image file is specified, which means that the complete address of the image file is used. This is similar to using those four extra digits in your ZIP code. You must use an absolute path if you are displaying an image that isn't stored in the same directory as your Web page file.

> **Note** A good way to think of the difference between relative and absolute paths is to consider how you give your phone number to people. If it's someone who lives in your city, you probably just give him or her the local seven-digit number. On the other hand, you tell someone out of state the entire 10-digit number, including the area code. In the local example, the seven-digit number is relative because the area code is assumed. In the national example, the 10-digit number is absolute, because it represents your complete phone number. If you happen to live in a highly populated area where you have to use 10 digits to call your next-door neighbor even though you have the same area code, please accept my condolences. Oh for the good old days of 7-digit numbers.

Another good example of heavily used absolute paths is eBay listings. If you list an item on eBay, you can't place the image of the item directly on eBay's Web servers. Instead, you must use an image hosting service or place the image on your own server. When you create the eBay listing, you enter the absolute path to the image so that it can be displayed with the listing.

Formatting Images

Like text, images are considered Web page content, so the `<img>` tag can be used anywhere text can appear. You can place images in the middle of paragraphs or even in headings. Images are also susceptible to many of the same formatting issues as text, such as using the `<br>` tag to move to the next line of a page, which spaces images out vertically. You can also place images in paragraph tags by themselves to separate them from surrounding text. You will see some examples of how this is done in the next few pages.

In addition to the required `src` attribute, the `<img>` tag has another important attribute: `alt`. The `alt` attribute is used to assign text to an image—a succinct text label that describes the image, for example. This text is displayed in lieu of an image when the display of images has been disabled in a browser or when a Web browser doesn't support images. Alternate text is important because if an image cannot be displayed, people who use those Web browsers will at least see text explaining the image instead of simply a blank rectangle where the image should be. Because most Web browsers can display images without a hitch these days, the text in the `alt` tag now serves an additional purpose: as the little text box that appears if you pause the mouse pointer over an image. The words in the box are specified by the `alt` attribute. Here is an example of using the `alt` attribute to provide information about an image:

```
<img src="Jump.jpg" alt= "Here I am catching a little air.">
```

To get a feel for how this image might fit into the context of a real Web page, take a look at the following code:

```
<html>
<head>
  <title>Mountain Biking at Tsali</title>
</head>

<body>
<h2>My Tsali Mountain Bike Trip</h2>
<p>
Tsali is a system of mountain bike trails in western North
Carolina on the edge of the Smoky Mountains. I recently took a
trip there with a couple of friends. Following is a picture
from the trip:
</p>
<img src="Jump.jpg" alt="Here I am catching a little air.">
</body>
</html>
```

Pause with the mouse pointer over the image and Internet Explorer displays a small text window containing the alternative text, as shown in Figure 4-1.

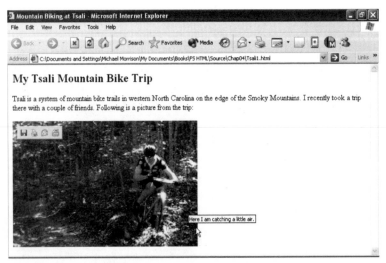

Figure 4-1   The `<img>` tag allows you to place inline images adjacent to a paragraph of text and can provide optional descriptive text for the image.

Tweaking the Size of Images

The `<img>` tag includes a couple of attributes that allow you to set the width and height of an image: `width` and `height`. Wait a minute, aren't the width and height of the image determined when you create it? Yes, but the `width` and `height` attributes of the `<img>` tag aren't used only to change the size of an image. Knowledgeable Web page designers often use `width` and `height` attributes to improve the efficiency of images on Web pages.

It works like this: When a Web page is first loaded, the browser assesses each image to determine its width and height. During this process, the browser resizes and relocates parts of the page to accommodate the images. If you specify the width and height of each image with the `width` and `height` attributes, the browser knows the measurements of the image. Consequently, it doesn't waste time figuring them out, and presto—happy Web surfers see the page displayed more quickly. For this reason, it's a good idea to specify the width and height for your Web page images—just make sure that they match up with the actual width and height (in pixels) of each image so that the image doesn't get stretched or shrunken unintentionally.

Of course, if you want to change the size of an image on a Web page then you might consider altering its `width` and `height` attributes. Specify a width and height that differs from the actual size of an image, and the browser will stretch or shrink the image to fit. Although this can be a problem if it is unintended, it is a benefit if you want to resize an image within a page. Using thumbnails of images is an example of where this is useful. Consider the scenario of displaying several images in the previous mountain bike Web page. If you displayed them all as large as the jump image, they would take up a lot of space on the page. A solution is to provide a series of thumbnail images that link to the external full-size images. Instead of creating smaller thumbnail images, you might want to use the `width` and `height` attributes of the `<img>` tag to decrease the size. On the other hand, there is a problem with this solution. Any idea what it is?

Note   Thumbnail images allow you to present a greater number of small images within a page; the viewer clicks on a thumbnail image to see the full-size image. You will learn how to use thumbnail images later in the chapter in the section entitled "Linking to External Images."

The problem with resizing images using the `<img>` tag, as opposed to resizing the image file and creating a new thumbnail image, is that the full-size image must still be downloaded to the Web browser. It takes longer to download the image than to display one you resized using an image editing tool. Don't forget that the main reason for using thumbnail images is that they take up less space and are faster to transfer. So, I don't recommend using the width and height attributes to decrease the size of an image; it is useful only if you want to increase the size of an image. In this case you have to pay careful attention to image distortion in the larger image.

Caution   It's generally not a good idea to use the width and height attributes of the <img> tag to make an image smaller because the full-size image will still have to be downloaded, which is much less efficient than resizing the image manually using an image editing tool.

Giving Images Room to Breathe

Because images often appear alongside text and other content, you might wonder about the spacing of images with respect to other content. Fortunately, the <img> tag allows you to precisely control the space around an image with the hspace and vspace attributes. For example, if you want two pixels of space on the top and bottom of an image, just set the vspace attribute to "2". Likewise, the hspace attribute specifies the number of pixels on the left and right sides of an image. These attributes primarily come into play when you have text flowing around images or images placed next to each other. In these situations, you want to provide some visual distance between each element.

Building Walls around Images

If you've tried adding space around an image and you still doubt that it's safe, you can go a step further and create a border for the image. A border is simply a colored line drawn around an image. Borders are made possible by the border attribute of the <img> tag, set to the width of the border, in pixels. To create a border that is 5 pixels wide around an image, use code similar to this:

```
<img src="Jump.jpg" border="5">
```

Figure 4-2 shows the image from Figure 4-1 surrounded by a 5-pixel border.

Figure 4-2 The `border` attribute of the `<img>` tag allows you to place a border around an inline image.

If you choose to use both borders and spacing, the border is applied to each edge of the image, then the space is applied to the border.

Borders may occur with your images whether you want them to or not. When you use an image as a hyperlink—more on this in the next chapter—most Web browsers automatically display a border that is 2 pixels wide around the image. If you don't want a border around a linked image, use the `border` attribute and set it to zero.

Aligning Images

In the previous chapter you learned to control the alignment of text within a paragraph, but you didn't find out how to control the alignment of text near images. Keep in mind that images can be placed directly in a paragraph of text, which can present some tricky problems in terms of aligning the image with surrounding text. Fortunately, the `<img>` tag provides the `align` attribute, which controls the positioning of an image and the flow of text around it. Here are the possible values for the `align` attribute and their functions:

- `left`—aligns the image along the left margin, flowing text around it to the right.

- `right`—aligns the image along the right margin, flowing text around it to the left.

- `top`—aligns the top of the image along the top edge of the current line of text, or the tallest image in the current line.

- `texttop`—aligns the top of the image along the top edge of the current line of text.

- `middle`—aligns the center of the image along the bottom of the current line of text, commonly referred to as the baseline of the text.

- `absmiddle`—aligns the center of the image along the middle of the current line of text, or the tallest image in the current line.

- `center`—aligns the center of the image along the middle of the current line of text, or the tallest image in the current line, which duplicates the effect of `absmiddle`.

- `bottom`—aligns the bottom of the image along the bottom of the current line of text, which is usually the baseline of the text.

- `baseline`—aligns the bottom of the image along the bottom of the current line of text, which is usually the baseline of the text. This duplicates the effect of `bottom`.

- `absbottom`—aligns the bottom of the image along the bottom of the current line of text, or the bottom of the tallest image in the line.

Note   The `border` and `align` attributes are more examples of those pesky deprecated parts of HTML, meaning that they will eventually be phased out and replaced with style sheets. But like most deprecated tags and attributes, the `border` and `align` attributes are still in use throughout the Web—and, realistically, will be around for some time. It's worth pointing out that the `texttop`, `absmiddle`, `absbottom`, `baseline`, and `center` values for the `align` attribute were never a part of standard HTML. Nonetheless, they are supported by most browsers and have enjoyed wide usage.

Rather than go through exhaustive examples of how each of these alignment values affects the positioning of an image, let's look at a simple example. This HTML code illustrates how you can control the flow of text around an image using the `align` attribute:

```
<html>
<head>
  <title>Mountain Biking at Tsali</title>
</head>
```

```
<body>
<h2>My Tsali Mountain Bike Trip</h2>
<p>
Tsali is a system of mountain bike trails in western North
Carolina on the edge of the Smoky Mountains. I recently took a
trip there with a couple of friends. Following is a picture
from the trip:
</p>
<p>
<img src="Jump.jpg" alt="Here I am catching a little air."
hspace="10" align="left">
In this photo, I'm catching a little air off of a jump located
on the Right Loop of the Tsali trail. This jump was the last
in a series that provided a refreshing change of
pace from the fast descents and smooth climbing the trail had
to offer.
</p>
</body>
</html>
```

This is the mountain bike Web page mentioned earlier in the chapter, with some text added. Notice that the `hspace` attribute is set to 10, which provides 10 pixels of space on the left and right sides of the image. The `align` attribute is set to `left`, which aligns the image along the left margin of the page, forcing the text to flow around the picture on the right. Figure 4-3 shows this page viewed in Internet Explorer.

Figure 4-3   The `hspace` and `align` attributes of the `<img>` tag were used to fine-tune the placement of the image.

Linking to External Images

Earlier in the chapter, I mentioned that external images are images that don't appear inline with other content on a Web page. Instead, they are referenced externally and viewed separately from the page where they are referenced. Sound confusing? All will soon be clear.

The main difference between an external image and an inline image is that an external image isn't displayed automatically. You must click a link to view it. External images are coded using the <a> tag, which establishes a hyperlink to the image. You will learn more about hyperlinks in Chapter 5, "Connecting Pages with Hyperlinks." For now I'll cover enough to get you going with external images. The idea behind the <a> tag is to enclose content that will serve as a hyperlink to some other Web page or resource, or in this case, an image. To reference an external image, you simply sandwich HTML content between <a> start and end tags, and reference the image using the href attribute. Here is an example:

```
<p>
Here is a <a href="Jump.jpg">picture</a> of me jumping.
</p>
```

In this example code, the word "picture" refers to the external image, Jump.jpg, which is displayed in most Web browsers when the user clicks the word. Notice that the href attribute is used to specify the URL of the external image, in this case the image file name, a relative path. Recall that thumbnail images are often used as a means of referencing external images. Here is an example of how you might use a small thumbnail image, SmJump.jpg, to reference a larger external image:

```
<a href="Jump.jpg"><img src="SmJump.jpg"></a>
```

This code looks a little more complex, so let's dissect it to see what's happening. The thumbnail image, SmJump.jpg, serves as the source of the hyperlink. It is displayed on the Web page with a border around it. When you click the thumbnail image, the larger external image, Jump.jpg, is displayed in the browser window. Here is additional code that uses this technique to add thumbnail images to the mountain bike Web page:

```
<p>
<a href="Jump.jpg"><img src="SmJump.jpg" alt="Here I am
catching a little air." hspace="10" align="left"></a>
<a href="Cruise.jpg"><img src="SmCruise.jpg" alt="Here I am
cruising by Fontana Lake." hspace="10" align="left"></a>
In these photos, I'm catching a little air off of a jump
located on the Right Loop of the Tsali trail, as well as
```

```
cruising by Fontana Lake on the Left Loop. The jump picture
shows the last in a series that provided a change
of pace from the fast descents and smooth climbs. The cruise
picture shows how the water in the lake was lowered due to dam
maintenance.
</p>
```

Figure 4-4 shows the results of adding this code and a bit more text to the mountain bike Web page. Notice in the figure that, by using thumbnails, you fit more content on the page, even allowing the page to be smaller. You can have more information on the page, and the page loads faster. You click on thumbnails you're interested in to see the full-size image. It's a win-win situation!

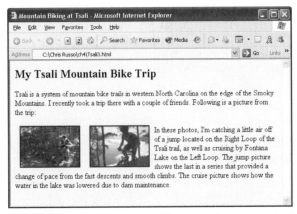

Figure 4-4   Thumbnail images provide a convenient means of optimizing a Web page for arrangement and size by using the `<a>` tag in conjunction with the `<img>` tag.

Using Background Images

You've no doubt seen Web pages with interesting backgrounds that often have a textured appearance. Admit it, you've lost sleep wondering how it's possible to display an image behind a Web page. This is known as a *background image*. And despite how restless you are over them, I'm here to tell you that they are simple to use and can either dramatically improve a Web page or make it almost impossible to read. That's right, background images are both incredibly cool and highly dangerous at the same time. The positive side of background images is obvious, but the negative side is that a bold image lacking good contrast with the text on the page can render the text illegible. Be careful when you choose background images for your Web pages.

Caution   It is extremely important not to get carried away with background images and select images that are too bold or don't contrast well with text on the page. As a rule, background images should have solid, muted colors so that text "pops out" over them.

Background images are used differently than the images you've encountered so far in this chapter. A background image isn't displayed by using the familiar `<img>` tag. The `<body>` tag has an attribute named `background` that specifies the background image. The following line of code demonstrates how to use this attribute:

```
<body background="DirtBack.gif">
```

Try This! See if you can find a better background image (tire treads maybe) for the mountain biking Web page and then change the page so that it uses the new image.

Figure 4-5 shows how this code affects the mountain bike page you saw in Figure 4-3. Although it is somewhat difficult to see in a grayscale figure, the background image used in the example contains muted colors, which makes the black text clearly visible when it appears on top of the background. It is important to provide contrast between the color of the text on the page and the colors used in the background image.

It is also important to ensure that the background image is designed so that it tiles appropriately. The edges of the image must line up with one another so that no seams are visible. The edges of the background image are a concern because most background images are fairly small. The complete background is created by repeating the image multiple times across and down the page like a tiled floor in a house. This is why background images are sometimes referred to as *tiled images*. Unless you are adept at using image editing tools to carefully manipulate images, you are better off not trying to create tiled images. Try looking for Web sites that offer free background images that tile seamlessly.

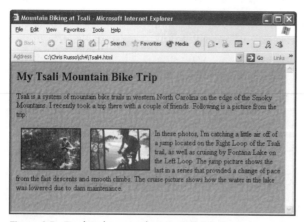

Figure 4-5 The `background` attribute of the `<body>` tag allows you to specify a background image for the Web page.

Another topic related to the background of Web pages is the `bgcolor` attribute, which allows you to set the background color of a Web page instead of using a background image. You normally use either the `bgcolor` or `back ground` attribute, not both, because a background color will be hidden by a background image unless the image contains transparent areas. You specify colors in the `bgcolor` attribute by using the name of a predefined color or a special number that identifies a custom color. To learn how to specify custom colors in HTML, take a look at Appendix C, "Using Custom Colors." If you want to go with a predefined color, you can choose from the following list:

aqua	black	blue	fuchsia
gray	green	lime	maroon
navy	olive	purple	red
silver	teal	yellow	white

For example, setting the background of a Web page to the predefined color `olive` would look like this:

```
<body bgcolor="olive">
```

One other attribute of the `<body>` tag is the `text` attribute used to set the text color for the page. Although both the `background` and `text` attributes are now deprecated, they are prevalent in the HTML of existing Web pages. The `text` attribute finds more usage in pages where the background has been set to an image or a color other than white, the default color. When using the `text` attribute, the color value is specified as either one of the predefined colors listed or as a special custom color number.

Using Animated Images

I mentioned earlier that the GIF image format supports animation, which makes it possible to display cartoons and animated effects. The interesting thing about animated GIFs is that all of the parameters of the animation are specified when creating the image. The image looks like any other from the perspective of HTML code. In other words, you don't have to do anything special when displaying animated images with the `<img>` tag.

To create animated GIFs, you must use a special graphics tool. At one point Microsoft shipped a tool called GIF Animator with its FrontPage Web development environment, but unfortunately, this tool is no longer available. So you'll have to find a graphics tool that supports the creation of animated GIFs. One such tool that I can recommend is GIF Movie Gear by Gamani Productions, which is available online at *http://www.gamani.com*. This is by no means the only useful graphics tool capable of creating animated GIFs, so feel free to look around and decide for yourself which tool suits your needs and budget best.

Note   Internet Explorer supports another type of animation known as marquee text animation. This animated text makes use of the `<marquee>` tag, an Internet Explorer extension to HTML that is not a part of standard HTML.

The main point is that there is nothing special required of animated GIFs from the perspective of HTML. You place an animated image on a Web page using the `<img>` tag, and the Web browser takes care of the rest. All of the real work with animated images takes place when the image is created.

Key Points

- An image is an arrangement of little colored squares known as pixels.

- The JPEG image format is perfect for storing photographic images because it is especially designed for storing them efficiently.

- The GIF image format is ideal for storing Web page images that are not photographs, such as illustrations and diagrams.

- The `<img>` tag allows you to place inline images, which are helpful whenever you need to display an image directly on a Web page alongside text.

- The `<a>` tag allows you to place external images, which are displayed only when you click a link to navigate to them.

- The `align` attribute of the `<img>` tag allows you to control the alignment of inline images relative to text and other images around them.

- You can place an image as the background of a Web page by using the `background` attribute of the `<body>` tag.

Chapter 5

Connecting Pages with Hyperlinks

Like people, Web pages benefit from good relationships. Of course, Web page interactions boil down to one page having a link to another page. This connectivity between Web pages is the true killer feature of the Web and the primary reason for its rapid integration into modern culture. The ability to link Web pages, with no regard for their physical location, makes for an unbelievably powerful system of sharing information. The impact of this system is so significant that it's redefining entire industries. The Web has changed and is continuing to change the way we live—how we shop, how we learn, and how we communicate.

This chapter tackles the subject of linking Web documents using hyperlinks. You can effectively weave a web of your own documents within your Web site. Perhaps even more interesting, you can create links to other documents and resources on the Web. In effect, you can incorporate the Internet at large into your own valuable resources.

What Is a Hyperlink?

As a Web user, you've no doubt heard the term *hyperlink* used in conjunction with Web pages. Hyperlinks are an important part of virtually all Web pages, and they have nothing to do with hyperactivity. Hyperlinks are used to connect a Web page with another resource on the Web. That resource might be another Web page, an external image, or an e-mail address. Hyperlink text is usually displayed in a different font color to distinguish it from other text, and it is typically underlined as well. When you hover the mouse pointer over hyperlink text, the pointer changes—usually to a hand symbol—to indicate that clicking the text will take you to linked material. Hyperlink images are also displayed a little differently than other images. They are sometimes shown with a default 2-pixel-wide border around them. Figure 5-1 shows how hyperlink text stands out in a paragraph.

Lingo   A *hyperlink* is a connection between an HTML element such as text, an image, or anything else on the page and another resource.

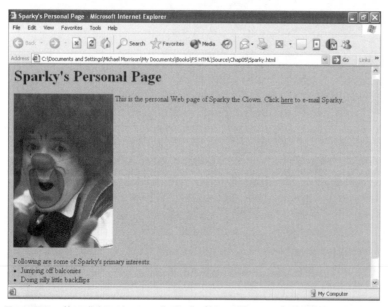

Figure 5-1   Hyperlink text is generally displayed in a different color and with an underline to help distinguish it from other text.

Tip   Chapter 4, "Decorating Pages with Images," shows how to remove the border that is automatically drawn around hyperlink images.

This figure should look somewhat familiar because it's based on the same file that was used in Chapter 2, "Your First HTML Web Page." I'm using it again because it contains a good example of a simple text hyperlink. The word "here" in the second sentence is a text hyperlink and provides an e-mail link so that you can e-mail your good friend Sparky the Clown. When you click the link, the Web browser will automatically launch the program that handles e-mail. It addresses a message to the recipient, who in this case is Sparky. Let's take a look at how an image can be used as a hyperlink. Figure 5-2 shows a Web page with a couple of familiar image hyperlinks.

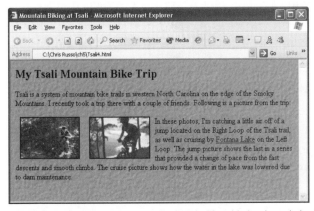

Figure 5-2   Hyperlink images are displayed with a thin border to help distinguish them from other images.

Notice the 2-pixel-wide border around the thumbnail mountain bike images—both are hyperlinks. You'll learn how to analyze the code for both text and image hyperlinks shortly. First, though, take a moment to learn or review the basics of Uniform Resource Locators, which we know by the name *URLs*.

Understanding URLs

As you may already know, URLs identify Web pages and other resources, such as images. You can type a URL in the address box near the top of your Web browser to open the Web page with that address. Similarly, hyperlinks rely on URLs to nail down the exact location of the linked resource on the Web. Given the importance of URLs to hyperlinks, it's worth spending a little time to understand them better.

Note   Minor debate continues over the correct pronunciation of "URL." I prefer saying the letters as if you were spelling a word: U-R-L, or "you are el." However, you'll also hear it pronounced "earl," so that it rhymes with "girl."

IP Addresses and URLs

Web resources ultimately reside on computers connected to the Internet, and each of those computers must be identifiable to get to the resources. To find an image that is located on the Web, you must first find out which computer (Web server) the image is stored on. Servers on the Internet are uniquely identified by *host names*. Every server connected to the Internet has its own unique host name that is used as a means of identification. Host names for servers connected to the Internet are similar to social security numbers for people, in that they provide a means of uniquely identifying every online server. Most URLs contain a host name that helps identify the location of a Web page or other resource.

Note   A *host name* uniquely identifies a server connected to the Internet that serves up Web pages.

If the term "host name" sounds somewhat technical, allow me to calm your nerves by revealing that you're already quite comfortable with host names. I'd be willing to bet that you've memorized several host names and could list them right now. You see, the name of every Web site is a host name. So *www.amazon.com*, *www.ebay.com*, *www.yahoo.com*, and *www.msn.com* are all host names.

Dissecting a URL

Host names may be clever or informative or both. But what do they have to do with URLs and hyperlinks? Keep in mind that Web browsers use URLs to navigate to specific pages on the Web. Here's an example of a complete URL:

```
http://www.tailspintoys.com/toys.htm
```

A URL consists of a protocol, a host name, and a resource. The three components of the URL *http://www.tailspintoys.com/toys.htm* are

- **http**   The protocol for the resource
- **www.tailspintoys.com**   The host name of the computer where the resource is stored
- **toys.htm**   The resource (in this case a Web page)

Lingo   The `http` portion of a URL specifies the protocol of the URL. A *protocol* defines how the exchange of information takes place over the Internet. Different types of information require different protocols. For example, the protocol used to send Web pages over the Internet (*HTTP*, or Hypertext Transfer Protocol) differs from the protocol used to send e-mail messages over the Internet (*SMTP*, or Simple Mail Transfer Protocol).

These three components are required to fully specify an absolute URL. HTML tags that expect URL values allow you to use relative URLs, which are less specific. A relative URL might simply contain the resource portion of the URL, in which case the host name is assumed to be the same as that of the Web page. For example, this is a legitimate relative URL for an image:

```
Logo.gif
```

Because Web pages and other resources also exist in folders within a Web site, you may need to precede the name of the document with the name of its folder to specify a resource within a relative URL:

```
images/Logo.gif
```

In this example, the file Logo.gif is located in a folder named "images" on the Web server. If this relative URL is used in a Web page that is stored on the server with the host name *www.tailspintoys.com*, the URL is then equivalent to the following absolute URL:

```
http://www.tailspintoys.com/images/Logo.gif
```

If you're worried that I'm straying too far from HTML with this URL information, let me point out that URLs are very important in HTML coding. They are used any time a resource is referenced externally. You've already been using URLs when specifying inline images files with the `<img>` tag. URLs are also used with hyperlinks and external images in conjunction with the `<a>` tag, which you'll learn about next.

Try This!   Quick, go to any of your favorite Web sites and follow these steps:

1   Wait for the page to load.

2   Look at the Address bar in your Web browser and identify the URL of the page.

3   See if you can pick apart the different pieces of the URL.

URLs and Web Resources

Throughout this chapter I've used the word *resource* a great deal, probably to the point that you're tired of it. The reason for my apparent obsession is that resources are incredibly important from the perspective of URLs and hyperlinks. Why? Well, a hyperlink is just a reference to a resource, which in turn is identified by a URL. To get the most out of hyperlinks, you must understand what

kinds of resources are available as well as how to identify them with URLs. Here
are the major types of URLs, along with a brief description of each:

- **Web page**   Used to identify an HTML document available for down-
  loading and viewing with HTTP

- **FTP**   Used to identify a file available for download with *FTP* (File
  Transfer Protocol)

- **E-mail**   Used to identify an e-mail address to which you can send an
  e-mail message

- **Newsgroup**   Used to identify a newsgroup or a message within a
  newsgroup

- **File**   Used to identify a file on the local file system

Now that you know more about the main types of resources, URLs will
probably start to make more sense. Revisiting the URL you saw earlier, *http://
www.tailspintoys.com/toys.htm*, you see that the protocol for the Web page
resource is specified as http. This is the protocol Web servers use to deliver
pages to Web browsers, often called clients. The protocol changes when you
use a different type of URL, such as an FTP or e-mail URL. The protocol name
for FTP is ftp, the name for e-mail is mailto, the name for newsgroups is news,
and the name for files is file. Here are sample URLs for each of these types:

```
ftp://michael:zed@ftp.tailspintoys.com/docs/products.txt
mailto:sales@tailspintoys.com
news:alt.skateboarding
file:///C:/Books/FSHTML/Source/Chap05/Tsali4.html
```

These examples demonstrate the different formats that URLs can take; the
format used depends on the type of the URL. In the case of the FTP URL, a user
name (michael) and password (zed) are provided first, followed by the host
name of the site containing the file (ftp.tailspintoys.com), followed by the
path (docs/) and then the file itself (products.txt).

The e-mail URL consists of the word mailto followed by the recipient's e-mail
address. It's up to the Web browser to invoke an e-mail program to handle the
details of composing and sending the message. Internet Explorer will typically use
either Outlook or Outlook Express to send e-mail through an e-mail URL.

The news URL consists of the word news followed by the name of a *newsgroup*. If you know the ID of a specific message within a newsgroup, you can
specify it in lieu of the newsgroup name. In the example, the newsgroup
alt.skateboarding is specified.

Lingo   For the uninitiated, *newsgroups* are special messaging systems on the Internet where you can hold open discussions with other people. Newsgroups were widespread prior to Web browsers and are still popular. Most Web browsers allow access to newsgroups. For example, to access newsgroups in Internet Explorer, select Mail and News from the Tools menu, followed by Read News.

The final URL type is the file type, which consists of the word `file` followed by a path on the local hard drive. The path appears much as you might enter it in the Run window, which is accessible by clicking Run on the Start menu in Windows. The exception that sometimes catches us all is that the slashes are entered as forward slashes instead of the familiar backslashes that are used in Windows paths. For example, a Windows path is specified using backslashes, like this: *Windows**Favorites*. However, a URL path is specified using forward slashes, like this: */Windows/Favorites*. Keep in mind that file URLs apply only to the local file system, which means you can't refer to remote files on the Internet. File URLs are what you use to open Web pages stored on your local hard drive, such as those you create as you work through this book.

Try This!   Open a Web page directly from your hard drive (just double-click it in Windows Explorer) and take note of the URL for the page that appears in the Address bar of your Web browser. See if the file URL type is being used to reference the page.

Working with the `<a>` Tag

The magical HTML tag used to create hyperlinks is the `<a>` tag, which stands for "anchor." One of the uses of the `<a>` tag is *anchoring*, which I'll tell you about later in the chapter. However, the most common use of this tag is creating hyperlinks to text and images. You've already seen a few examples of this tag in action in previous chapters, and it's time to take a closer look at how it works.

Linking to Web Pages

A hyperlink created with the `<a>` tag consists of two items: the name of the hyperlinked HTML content and a target resource. The *hyperlinked HTML content* is text or an image and is enclosed within the `<a>` and `</a>` tags. The *target resource* for the hyperlink is specified in the `href` attribute of the `<a>` tag and consists of a URL that identifies the resource. Any of the URL types you learned earlier are OK to use with the href attribute, but the HTTP URL type is used to link to Web pages. Here is an example of such a hyperlink:

```
<p>
We offer many interesting products that you can
<a href="Order.html">order</a> from our online store.
</p>
```

Lingo   When text or an image is used as the source for a hyperlink, it is referred to as *hyperlinked content*, while the resource to which it points is known as the *target resource* of the hyperlink.

In this example, the word "order" is the hyperlinked text that links to the Order.html Web page. This is a good example of a relative URL because no host name or path is specified for the target Web page. For the hyperlink to work properly, the Order.html file must be located in the same folder as the referring page. The same code could have used an absolute URL, which would look something like this:

```
<p>
We offer many interesting products that you can
<a href="http://www.tailspintoys.com/Order.html">order</a> from our
online store.
</p>
```

Notice how the full URL is specified in this example, including the protocol type, the host name, and the resource file name.

Caution   If you choose to use absolute paths in the URLs for hyperlinks, it's important to remember that the links will be broken if you rename folders or move files around. Relative paths are often a better idea because they are tougher to break if you need to reorganize your Web site.

Linking to Other Resources

Creating hyperlinks based on the other URL types is similar to creating links to Web pages. Here is the same example code expanded to include an e-mail URL:

```
<p>
We offer many interesting toys and games that you can
<a href="http://www.tailspintoys.com/Order.html">order</a> from our
online store. For additional information, please feel free to
send us <a href="mailto:sales@tailspintoys.com">e-mail</a>.
</p>
```

This code demonstrates how to link to an e-mail URL using the mailto protocol type. As you can see, the mailto protocol type is followed by an e-mail address. When the user clicks the word "e-mail," his Web browser will launch his e-mail program and start a new message with sales@tailspintoys.com as the recipient.

Practical Linking with the <a> Tag

To see how the <a> tag works in the context of a real Web page, look over the following code. It shows a modified version of the mountain bike Web page you saw in the previous chapter and includes several hyperlinks to text and images:

```
<html>
<head>
  <title>Mountain Biking at Tsali</title>
</head>

<body background="DirtBack.gif">
<h2>My Tsali Mountain Bike Trip</h2>
<p>
Tsali is a system of mountain bike trails in western North
Carolina on the edge of the Smoky Mountains. I recently took a
trip there with a couple of friends. Following are pictures
from the trip:
</p>
<p>
<a href="Jump.jpg"><img src="SmJump.jpg" alt="Here I am
catching a little air." hspace="10" align="left"></a>
<a href="Cruise.jpg"><img src="SmCruise.jpg" alt="Here I am
cruising by Fontana Lake." hspace="10" align="left"></a>
In these photos, I'm catching a little air off of a jump
located on the Right Loop of the Tsali trail, as well as
cruising by <a href="http://www.greatsmokies.com/community
/fontana.htm">Fontana Lake</a> on the Left Loop. The jump picture shows the
last in a series that provided a change of pace from the fast descents and
smooth climbs. The cruise picture shows how the water in the lake was lowered
due to dam maintenance.
</p>
<p>
<br clear="left">
For more information on the Tsali trails, contact my friend
<a href="mailto:christheyeti@thetribe.com">Chris the Yeti</a>
: <a href="mailto:christheyeti@thetribe.com">
<img src="ChrisYeti.jpg" align="middle"></a>
</p>
</body>
</html>
```

In this code, you can see the external image hyperlinks that were already in the code from Chapter 4, "Decorating Pages with Images." The new hyperlinks include a link to a remote Web page containing information about Fontana Lake in North Carolina and a couple of e-mail links. One of the e-mail links is associated with the text "Chris the Yeti," and the other with the image file ChrisYeti.jpg. You can click either the text or the image to follow the e-mail hyperlink. Figure 5-3 shows this page as viewed in Internet Explorer.

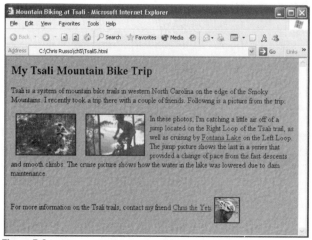

Figure 5-3   The mountain bike Web page shows several examples of using hyperlinks to link text and images with external images, Web pages, and e-mail addresses.

Anchor Hyperlinks

Although the <a> tag is commonly used to describe hyperlinks to other Web pages, it can also be used to identify *anchors* within a Web page. An anchor is a reference to a specific location within a Web page. Anchors are invisible to the user and are used purely for linking purposes within a Web site.

Lingo   An *anchor* is a named point in a Web page that serves as a bookmark for the page.

You create anchors using the <a> tag and the name attribute by specifying the name of the anchor in the name attribute, like this:

```
<a name="bbear">All About Black Bears</a>
```

In this code, the phrase "All About Black Bears" is identified as an anchor with the name bbear. Understand that this anchor is not a hyperlink; it serves as a target for a hyperlink. Once you've named an anchor, you can link to it with a hyperlink by using the href attribute of the <a> tag. The trick to referencing an anchor in a hyperlink is that you must precede the anchor name with the # symbol. Here is an example of using the href attribute to link to an anchor:

```
<p>
The mountains of Tennessee and North Carolina are home to
<a href="http://www.tailspintoys.com/animals.html#bbear">black
bears</a>.
</p>
```

Tip   Anchor links can be relative, in which case you simply provide the # symbol and anchor name, or they can be absolute, in which case you specify a full URL with the # symbol and anchor name appended to the end.

In this code, the phrase "black bears" is linked to the anchor named bbear within the Web page:

```
http://www.tailspintoys.com/animals.html
```

If this was a real Web page posted online, upon following this link the Web browser would open the *animals.html* Web page and scroll to the anchor identified by the name bbear. Here is code for a more complete example that demonstrates how to use relative anchor hyperlinks:

```
<html>
<head>
  <title>Mountain Bike Parts</title>
</head>

<body background="DirtBack.gif">
<h2>Inventory of Mountain Bike Parts</h2>
<p>
[ <a href="#brakes">Brakes</a> ]
[ <a href="#brakelevers">Brake Levers</a> ]
[ <a href="#brakepads">Brake Pads</a> ]
</p>
<h4><a name="brakes">Brakes</a></h4>
<ul>
<li>Avid Single Digit magnesium</li>
<li>Avid Arch Rival 50 Brakes</li>
<li>Hayes Disc MC74 Hydraulic</li>
<li>Magura Clara Hydraulic Disc Brakes</li>
<li>Shimano XT V-Brake</li>
</ul>
<h4><a name="brakelevers">Brake Levers</a></h4>
<ul>
<li>Avid 2.0L Mag Levers</li>
<li>Avid Ultimate L</li>
<li>Cane Creek Direct Curve V</li>
</ul>
<h4><a name="brakepads">Brake Pads</a></h4>
<ul>
<li>Avid rim wrangler</li>
<li>Magura Pads</li>
<li>Ritchey Blk/Red</li>
<li>Shim. XTR-V</li>
</ul>
</body>
</html>
```

> **Note**   The code for this example, as well as all of the examples throughout the book, is available for download from my Web site at the following URL: *http://www.michaelmorrison.com/cbook_fshtml.html*.

This example contains code that might be suitable for an online bike shop. The code contains a list of mountain bike parts, broken down into categories. Below the title heading is a paragraph that contains a simple navigation bar for jumping to parts of the inventory list. The navigation bar is created by using the <a> tag to establish links to relative anchors. The anchors themselves are created farther into the document at each major heading. If this page sounds slightly complicated, just spend a moment studying the code and then look at Figure 5-4, which shows the page as viewed in Internet Explorer.

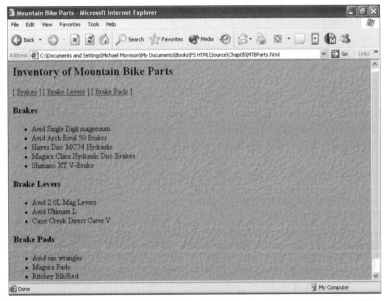

Figure 5-4   Anchors provide a means of navigating to a specific location within a Web page.

> **Note**   Anchors should refer to HTML content only. In the bike shop example, the <a> tag directly surrounds the text, as opposed to surrounding the text and the heading tags. The idea is that anchors identify a location within a document without regard for formatting. It's important to apply anchors directly to text or images; as far as anchors are concerned, formatting is secondary.

Key Points

■ Hyperlinks are the glue that binds together the massive collection of global Web pages that we call the World Wide Web.

■ You could take all the Web pages in existence and remove the links between them, and they would have virtually no value to anyone; it's the hyperlinks that make it possible to share our knowledge.

■ Hyperlinks rely on URLs to nail down the exact location of the linked resource on the Web.

■ A hyperlink is created with the <a> tag, and consists of two items: the name of the hyperlinked HTML content and a target resource.

■ An anchor is a reference to a specific location within a Web page and is created using the <a> tag.

Part II

Beyond the Basics

Part II pushes beyond the basics of HTML by exploring topics that will enable you to make your Web pages more interesting and useful. For example, it covers the use of image maps to provide visual navigation to your Web pages. You can learn how to arrange rows and columns of information in tables. You also learn how to use graphical design tools to help streamline Web page design, as well as how to publish pages on the Web. Toward the end of Part II, you find out how to gather information using forms, as well as how to dynamically interact with a Web page using Dynamic HTML.

Chapter 6

Visual Navigation with Image Maps

In the previous chapter, you learned how to use an image as the source of a hyperlink. Although images work great as the sources for individual hyperlinks, they work even better when you associate multiple links with a single image. This technique works well when you're dealing with images that can be divided into different regions that are associated with different links. This kind of image is known as an *image map*, and it is quite useful because you can click different parts of it to follow different links. Image maps present a powerful option for navigating sites.

Lingo An *image map* is an image that is divided into logical regions, each of which serves as a hyperlink to a Web resource.

In this chapter, you'll learn about the significance of image maps and the types of Web pages they are commonly used in. You'll also find out about the different approaches to creating image maps, including one that is ideally suited to today's Web browsers.

Image Map Basics

Several years ago, the hit Christmas toy was the *Tickle Me Elmo* doll, made by Fisher-Price. The selling point of the *Tickle Me Elmo* doll is that he giggles when you poke his belly, which is apparently quite a hoot if you're under the age of ten. If you tickle Elmo anywhere else, he just sits there and does nothing. Thinking about Elmo's giggle zone might help you zero in on how an image map works.

Note   If you've never heard of *Tickle Me Elmo*, I encourage you to check out your local toy store. Make sure no one is looking and then give Elmo a good poke to the belly.

Another way to visualize an image map is to think of a color-by-numbers painting, where each region in the painting is associated with a URL. Instead of painting a region a given color, you click it. Image maps can be used in a variety of different ways, the most common being for navigation bars and geometric maps. A good example of a geometric map with an image map is on the Arizona Vacation Guide Web site (*http://www.arizonavacationguide.net/Map/*). The state image map is shown in Figure 6-1, which allows you to click and learn about different attractions around the state.

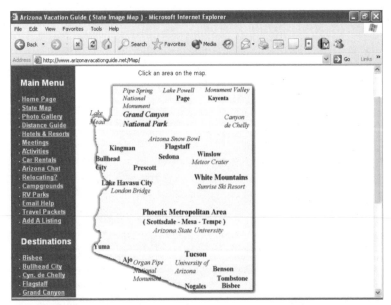

Figure 6-1   The Arizona Vacation Guide Web site includes an image map that can be used to learn more about the attractions located in the state of Arizona.

When you click one of the cities or attractions on the map, a page is opened with more detailed information. This is a powerful and intuitive image map that helps provide context to information by showing where Arizona attractions are geographically located within the state. By breaking an image down into several regions, it is possible to specify hyperlinks for each region and give an image a navigational context.

Client-Side vs. Server-Side Image Maps

Although you can create image maps several different ways using Web technology, two primary approaches have a dramatic impact on the way image maps work. Understand that when the user clicks an image map, the technology first determines the location of the mouse pointer on the computer screen, using the coordinates of the mouse click. Once the region is determined, the associated URL is used to open the Web page related to that region. The two image map approaches differ in the processing of the mouse-click coordinates. One approach handles the processing on the client, which is the Web browser on your computer. The other takes place on the Web server. Let's take a look at why there are two different approaches to image maps.

Lingo   When I refer to *coordinates*, I'm simply talking about an X,Y position on the screen. Coordinates identify the location of the mouse pointer relative to the browser window or to a point inside of an image. Coordinates are always measured in pixels, with the point (0,0) located in the upper-left corner of the browser window or image. This means that coordinate values increase to the right and down. So, if you started in the upper-left corner of an image (0,0) and counted over 10 pixels and down 5 pixels, you would arrive at the point (10,5).

Let the Server Do the Work

In the early days of the Web, browsers weren't crammed full of features. Much of the processing associated with interactive Web pages took place on Web servers. This server-based approach worked fine, but several weaknesses surfaced as the number of Web users grew rapidly. The number one problem with server processing is that it eats up valuable server resources. When you consider that a Web server may be called upon to serve thousands of users at any given time, the idea of doing additional processing beyond serving pages becomes overwhelming.

Lingo   Image maps processed on a Web server are known as *server-side image maps*. Server-side image maps place more processing duties on a Web server, which is generally not a good idea since Web servers should be primarily devoted to serving Web pages.

Giving the Client Some Responsibility

If a Web server is required to process a server-side image map, then we can reasonably expect that a Web browser is required to process a *client-side image map*. In fact, client-side image maps are processed entirely by a Web browser and basically result in a simple request for the target Web page from the server. In other words, a Web server has nothing to do with the processing of a client-side image map, which allows a browser to quickly process the information and improve the overall performance of the image map; the map-image processing—the time-intensive activity—is moved from the server to the client.

Lingo   Image maps processed within a Web browser are known as *client-side image maps*. Client-side image maps are considered more ideal than server-side image maps because the processing of the image map takes place in the client, which frees the server up to simply serve pages.

Another interesting distinction between client-side and server-side image maps is how the map information is specified. This information, as I mentioned earlier, consists of the geometric coordinates for the regions within the map, along with the URLs of the Web pages that are linked to each region. For server-side image maps, the map information is described in a special map file. The map file is placed on the Web server and referenced from an <a> tag that contains a reference to the image. Client-side map information is typically embedded directly in the Web page where the image map is located. Special HTML tags, which you'll learn about a little later in the chapter, describe the specifics of the map.

Note   Because client-side image maps don't require any processing on the server, Web pages that use client-side image maps don't have to run in an online environment with a real Web server. This is a significant benefit of client-side image maps because it allows you to deploy Web pages in offline scenarios, such as on interactive CD-ROMs.

I can tell you in no uncertain terms that client-side image maps are a significant improvement over server-side image maps. Therefore, the remainder of this chapter focuses on the creation of client-side image maps.

Tip   Client-side map information can be placed in a different Web page for sharing purposes, but the code is still basically the same. For example, if you create an image map that is used in several Web pages, it is much better organizationally to store the map information in a file by itself so that all of the pages can reference the information in one place. Otherwise you would have to duplicate the map information in every Web page.

Using Image Map Development Tools

You'll be glad to know that creating client-side image maps isn't difficult. In fact, it is incredibly easy to create them with special graphical tools—no complicated programming or technical savvy needed. Several shareware image map editing tools are available, or you can use full-featured Web development tools, such as Microsoft FrontPage. Figure 6-2 shows a bicycle image ready to be converted to an image map by simply identifying hyperlink regions on the image.

Figure 6-2   Microsoft FrontPage can be used to draw geometric regions for an image map.

In FrontPage, the tools shown along the bottom of the screen in Figure 6-2 allow you to draw geometric shapes to specify hyperlinked regions within the image. After drawing each shape, enter the hyperlink associated with the region in the Insert Hyperlink dialog box that appears. Figure 6-3 shows the creation of a hyperlink to a Web page named wheels.html that is associated with circular regions drawn around the bicycle wheels.

Figure 6-3   The Insert Hyperlink dialog box allows you to enter a URL that specifies the Web page associated with an image map hyperlink.

Try This!   If you have Microsoft FrontPage or some other visual Web development tool, try to create a simple image map by placing an image on a Web page and then identifying linked regions on the image. You'll find that visual tools really make the creation of image maps a breeze.

You might be asking, if this book is about HTML, how can you endorse the use of a visual tool to create image maps? Because the end result of the visual graphical editing is HTML code that describes the image map. Additionally, the task of specifying the regions in an image map is a visual task, which is much easier to perform with a graphical tool. Following is a portion of the image map HTML code that is generated by FrontPage:

```
<p>
<map name="FPMap0">
<area href="wheels.html" shape="circle" coords="519, 278, 118">
<area href="wheels.html" shape="circle" coords="114, 291, 104">
<area href="seat.html" shape="rect" coords="365, 7, 489, 32">
<area href="barends.html" shape="rect" coords="36, 48, 80, 76">
<area href="grips.html" shape="rect" coords="78, 57, 115, 75">
</map>
<img border="0" src="Bicycle.jpg" usemap="#FPMap0"
width="650" height="400">
</p>
```

Although this code might not entirely make sense to you at this point, a quick look reveals some clues about how image maps are described. Each area, or region, in the image map is specified as a shape followed by coordinates and values related to the position and size of the shape. Each area is associated with a single hyperlink to a location you go to when you click the area in the image.

Although it can be difficult to see by simply looking at the image map code, several of the areas in the map overlap each other. When you click in an overlapping region, the first area appearing in the code has precedence. You must take into consideration the order of the code when you create an image map with overlapping areas. I'll tackle this issue again in the next section when you construct image maps by hand in HTML code.

Coding Image Maps by Hand

You've seen HTML code for a client-side image map generated by FrontPage, but I haven't explained the specific HTML tags used to create image maps. This section describes the HTML tags and attributes that make image maps work.

Creating the Map

The primary tag used to create image maps is `<map>`, enclosing all the information associated with an image map. The `name` attribute of the `<map>` tag is used to identify the areas and hyperlinks for the map and to associate the map information with the map image itself. For example, the following code creates an image map named `bicyclemap`:

```
<map name="bicyclemap">
</map>
```

This code describes an empty map with no map information, not terribly useful. It's kind of like a city map with no streets or points of interest. Map information within the `<map>` tag is coded using the `<area>` tag, which includes several attributes for describing regions within an image map. These are the main attributes of the `<area>` tag that are used to describe areas within an image map:

- `href`—URL of the resource, usually a Web page, linked to the area

- `nohref`—specifies that the area has no hyperlinked resource

- `shape`—geometric shape of the area

- `coords`—coordinates that describe the size and position of the shape of the area

- `alt`—text description of the area

The href attribute identifies the URL of the resource linked to the area, and it can contain either a relative or an absolute URL. The nohref attribute is used to specify that the area has no resource linked to it, which means that clicking the area does nothing. The nohref attribute is useful in situations when you don't want an area of an image map to serve as a hyperlink. Because there is no real value to assign to the nohref attribute, you code it in HTML using the following format:

```
nohref="nohref"
```

Tip   The nohref attribute comes in handy in situations where you want to remove a region from a hyperlink. For example, if you were creating an image map that included a giant donut, you might use a circular shape for the donut as a whole, and then provide a smaller circle with the nohref attribute set to eliminate the donut hole from the link. Pretty slick, right?

Once you've defined the hyperlink associated with an area, using the href or nohref attributes, you're ready to describe the shape of the area. The shape attribute is used to accomplish this task, and it can have one of the following values:

- rect—rectangle described by coordinates for the upper-left and lower-right corners
- circ—circle described by coordinates for its center, along with a radius
- poly—polygon described by a series of coordinates for connected points

---

Note   You might have noticed a discrepancy between these attribute values and those generated by FrontPage in the code shown earlier in the chapter. For example, FrontPage generates image map code using the shape value circle instead of circ. Both values work in most browsers, but it is generally accepted that the abbreviated forms of the shapes are safer to use. Most browsers also support the full names of the rect and poly shape values—rectangle and polygon. However, I encourage you to use the shortened versions.

These are the only shapes supported by the shape attribute, and they are the only shapes you can use in describing areas within an image map. While these shapes may seem limiting, you'll find that the poly shape type is extremely flexible and allows you to create complex shapes if necessary. Besides, you can always create multiple links to the same resource using different shapes if you're having a hard time capturing the region with a single shape. The points used to describe each of the shapes are specified by the coords attribute, which contains a list of numbers separated by commas. The meaning of the numbers in the

coords list varies according to the type of the shape. Next are the coordinate formats for each shape:

```
shape="rect" coords="x1, y1, x2, y2"
shape="circ" coords="x, y, radius"
shape="poly" coords="x1, y1, x2, y2, x3, y3, ..."
```

All of the numbers in the coords attribute used to describe the various
shapes are specified in pixels relative to the upper-left corner of the image. The
coordinates for the rect shape consist of two points—the upper-left corner of
the rectangle and lower-right corner. The circ coordinates consist of the center
of the circle and its radius. And finally, the poly coordinates consist of a list of
points that are connected with lines to form a closed shape. Following are a few
examples of how to describe shapes using the <area> tag in conjunction with
the shape and coords attributes:

```
<area href="page1.html" shape="circ" coords="10, 10, 5">
<area href="page2.html" shape="rect" coords="5, 15, 40, 20">
<area href="page3.html" shape="polygon" coords="50, 5, 95, 45, 5, 45">
```

The first line of code creates a circular area at the point (10,10) with a radius
of 5. The second line creates a rectangular area with its upper-left corner at the
point (5,15) and its lower-right corner at (40,20). The last line of code creates a
triangular polygon by connecting the points (50,5), (95,45), and (5,45) together.

One final useful attribute of the <area> tag is alt, which allows you to provide a text description of an area. When a user pauses the mouse pointer over
an area with alt text, the text is displayed in a small window over the area. The
alt attribute therefore provides a useful way of adding context to image maps.
For example, to make them easily recognizable, you could use the alt attribute
to associate the name of each state to the regions of an image map of the United
States. This is an example of how you might use the alt attribute to describe a
triangular area:

```
<area href="page4.html" shape="polygon" coords="50, 5, 95, 45, 5, 45"
alt="This is a triangular area.">
```

Associating the Map with an Image

You've learned how to describe the areas and URLs associated with an image
map, but you haven't yet learned how to put this information together with an
image to form a complete image map. Map information described in the <map>
tag is associated with an image by using the usemap attribute of the <img> tag.
The value of the usemap attribute contains a URL that identifies the map information for the image. You create the map information using the <map> tag, and then

associate it with an image using the usemap attribute of the <img> tag. Therefore, the creation of an image map is a two-step process:

1 Within the <map> tag, create the map areas with associated hyperlinks to URLs.

2 Associate the map information with an image by using the usemap attribute of the <img> tag.

Caution   The details contained within an image map are highly dependent upon the size of an image. So, if you decide to resize an image being used as an image map, be sure to adjust the map information appropriately.

Recall that every map has a name that is identified by the name attribute of the <map> tag. This name is what you use in the usemap attribute to associate a map with an image. If the <map> tag containing the map information is located within the same Web page as the image—typically the case—you specify the name of the map preceded by a # symbol, like this:

```
<img src="Jungle.gif" usemap="#junglemap">
```

In this code, the map named junglemap must be located in the same Web page as the <img> tag. You could also reference a map that is located in a separate document by including a URL to the map. The map name effectively works like an anchor, except that the image map is specified by the name attribute of the <map> tag, as opposed to using the <a> tag. The <a> tag doesn't enter the equation at all when using client-side image maps!

Constructing a Practical Image Map

To put together all of what you've learned about client-side image maps, it's worth studying a complete example. Following is code for a skateboard Web page that uses an image map to explain each part of a skateboard:

```
<html>
<head>
  <title>Anatomy of a Skateboard</title>
</head>

<body>
<h2>The Anatomy of a Skateboard</h2>
<p>
Click on the skateboard to learn more about each major part of
it.
</p>
```

```
<p>
<map name="skatemap">
<area href="wheels.html" shape="rect" coords="89, 155, 144,
195" alt="Wheel">
<area href="wheels.html" shape="rect" coords="455, 155, 510,
193" alt="Wheel">
<area href="Wheels.html" shape="rect" coords="461, 8, 517, 47"
alt="Wheel">
<area href="Wheels.html" shape="rect" coords="87, 5, 143, 44"
alt="Wheel">
<area href="Trucks.html" shape="rect" coords="437, 79, 501,
124" alt="Truck">
<area href="Trucks.html" shape="rect" coords="477, 47, 497,
155" alt="Truck">
<area href="Trucks.html" shape="rect" coords="102, 79, 170,
122" alt="Truck">
<area href="Trucks.html" shape="rect" coords="105, 47, 128,
156" alt="Truck">
<area href="Sticker.html" shape="rect" coords="503, 109, 552,
166" alt="Sticker">
<area href="Deck.html" shape="circ" coords="77, 100, 77"
alt="Deck">
<area href="Deck.html" shape="circ" coords="521, 101, 78"
alt="Deck">
<area href="Deck.html" shape="rect" coords="81, 21, 521, 181"
alt="Deck">
</map>
<img src="Skateboard.jpg" usemap="#skatemap" border="0">
</p>
</body>
</html>
```

To better understand how the areas of the image are organized, take a look at the skateboard Web page as viewed in Internet Explorer (Figure 6-4). Especially note the small window appearing over the lower-right wheel; this is the text description provided by the alt attribute for that rectangular area.

You learned earlier in the chapter that areas are capable of overlapping in an image map and that, based on the order they were defined, areas take precedence over other overlapping areas. This is important in the skateboard image map because several of the areas overlap each other. For example, a large rectangle identifies the deck of the skateboard, which is the main body of the board. However, other components of the board appear above the deck rectangle, which means that their areas overlap the deck rectangle. To keep the deck rectangle from overriding the other areas, the smaller areas must be defined first, as evident in the HTML code for the page.

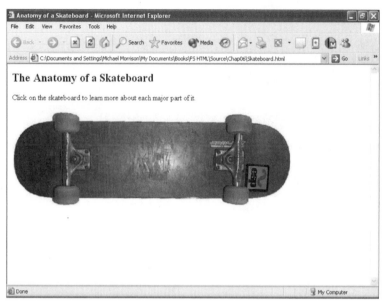

Figure 6-4   The skateboard Web page is a good example of how an image map can be used to describe different parts of a photograph.

Another interesting facet of the skateboard Web page is how the deck area is described using both circles and rectangles. The ends of the skateboard are described using circles since the board has rounded ends. The middle part of the deck is then described using a large rectangle that overlaps half of each circle. This is significant because it shows how to model a complex shape using multiple simple shapes. There is nothing magical going on here, it's just a clever use of overlapping areas.

Each of the hyperlinks associated with the skateboard image map is linked to a Web page with a simple description of each part of the skateboard. Following is code for the Trucks page, which describes the role of skateboard trucks:

```
<html>
<head>
  <title>Anatomy of a Skateboard</title>
</head>

<body>
<h2>The Anatomy of a Skateboard : Trucks</h2>
<p>
Trucks are attached to the <a href="Deck.html">deck</a> of a skateboard, and
are used for steering.
<a href="Wheels.html">Wheels</a> are attached to the ends of the trucks.
Click <a href="Skateboard.html">here</a> to return to the Anatomy of a Skateboard.
</p>
</body>
</html>
```

The Trucks Web page doesn't use image maps, but it does link back to other pages, including the main skateboard page (Figure 6-5). I wanted to show you this page because it helps demonstrate how image maps are used in the context of a complete Web site. I'll leave it up to you to think of something interesting to visually describe using image maps.

Figure 6-5 The Trucks Web page is linked to the skateboard image map and serves as a good example of how to describe an object in a single image using an image map.

Key Points

- An image map allows you to define regions in an image and link them to different Web resources.

- The two major types of image maps are client-side image maps and server-side image maps, with client-side image maps being the more desirable type because they don't place an additional workload on Web servers.

- Although it's important to understand how image maps work at the code level, Web development tools such as FrontPage can be useful because of their visual approach to specifying image map regions.

- The <map> tag is used to create map information for an image map, including the regions within the map and their related hyperlinks.

- The usemap attribute of the <img> tag is used to connect image map information described in the <map> tag with an image.

Chapter 7

Organizing Pages with Tables

Tables are grid-like structures used to divide a Web page into rectangular regions. They were originally designed to organize tabular data of the kind you might find in a spreadsheet. As HTML evolved and more features were added, however, Web developers realized that tables could also solve page layout problems. This chapter explains how to use tables both as a page layout tool and as a means of organizing tabular data. By the end of this chapter, you will have all the knowledge necessary to display in tabular form the results of a neighborhood poll about the next Presidential election. Maybe you'll be able to use your newfound table skills to come up with a better voting system than electing leaders with paper punches!

Table Basics

The most obvious way to get acquainted with tables and their role in HTML is to think of them as spreadsheets. If you've ever used Microsoft Excel, then you know that a *spreadsheet* consists of a grid of cells arranged in rows and columns of data of some sort. *Tables* are similar to spreadsheets in that they consist of cells that are arranged in rows and columns.

Lingo   A *spreadsheet* is a document used to organize data into a grid of cells arranged in rows and columns. *Tables* in HTML are similar to spreadsheets in that they consist of cells arranged in rows and columns.

Try This!   You can easily convert an Excel spreadsheet into a table in a Web page by following these steps:

1   Open the .xls spreadsheet file in Excel.

2   Select Save as Web Page from the File menu.

3   Open the resulting .htm file in a Web browser.

Although the OpenSecrets.org Web page shows the most logical use of Web page tables, they are used more often in a way that you may not know about: to control the layout of Web pages. Tables are extremely flexible and provide considerable control over the position of information. Unlike a spreadsheet, a table can be nested within another table, giving you more flexibility in organizing data. As an example, check out the Web page shown in Figure 7-1, which is from the Web site for my board game.

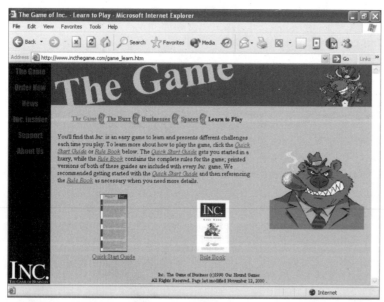

Figure 7-1   The board game Web site uses tables to control the positioning of content on a page.

Looking at this Web page, you would probably never guess that a table defines its layout. In fact, two tables are used within the page to carefully position the text and images. The tables make it possible to specify the relative position of Web content. For example, by carefully designing the size and arrangement of cells within a table, you can create effects such as vertical navigation bars and text in two columns.

The *Inc. The Game of Business* Web page shown in the figure takes advantage of a table nested within another table, which is a quite common technique when it comes to laying out Web pages.

Getting to Know the Table Tags

Can you imagine life without tables? I'm referring to the real world now, not the virtual one. We'd be relegated to eating off the floor and holding business meetings in beanbag chairs. It's not a pretty thought. Just as we have furniture manufacturers to thank for making tables available in the physical world, we have HTML to thank for tables in Web pages. The basic HTML for tables comes in the form of a few tags:

■   `<table>`—creates a table.

■   `<tr>`—identifies the beginning of a row within a table.

■   `<td>`—identifies a cell within a row.

To create a table, start with the `<table>` tag. With the table initially created, you add rows to it by including as many `<tr>` tags as necessary. Then within each `<tr>` tag, you add `<td>` tags to identify each cell. Here is an example of how to use these tags to create a simple table:

```
<table>
<tr>
  <td>January</td>
  <td>February</td>
  <td>March</td>
</tr>
<tr>
  <td>April</td>
  <td>May</td>
  <td>June</td>
</tr>
<tr>
  <td>July</td>
  <td>August</td>
  <td>September</td>
</tr>
<tr>
```

```
<td>October</td>
<td>November</td>
<td>December</td>
</tr>
</table>
```

This code creates a one-year calendar that contains months organized three across and four down. Figure 7-2 shows the resulting page.

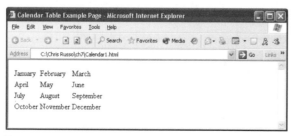

Figure 7-2   The table tags make it easy to organize information into rows and columns.

Drawing Borders around Tables

Although the calendar table in the example is functional, it could look better. One useful addition would be a *border* to visually divide the cells in the table. Conveniently, the `<table>` tag includes an attribute named `border`, which is designed specifically to accomplish this task. Set the `border` attribute to a number that determines the thickness of the table border in pixels. To change the calendar Web page so it has a border two pixels wide, you must change its `<table>` tag to

```
<table border="2">
```

The resulting table is shown in Figure 7-3.

Lingo   A *border* is a thin box drawn around a section of content on a Web page.

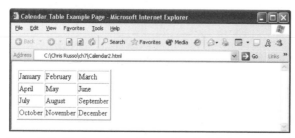

Figure 7-3   The `border` attribute of the `<table>` tag enables you to create a border around a table and between its cells.

The default value of the `border` attribute is zero, which means no border appears if you don't use the attribute. In addition to improving the look of some tables, the `border` attribute can play an important role during the early design stages. Even if you don't want borders on your finished table, it is often helpful to use them temporarily so you can see the layout of the table. Tables can get tricky, especially when you start nesting them, and borders provide an easy way to see exactly what is going on.

Heading Up Your Tables

In addition to the basic `<table>`, `<tr>`, and `<td>` tags, there is also a `<th>` tag, which is used to create *header cells*. The content in header cells is centered and in a boldface font. Header cells are used to create headings within tables, and are cells with the contents centered and bolded. Header cells don't play a signif-icant role in page layout, but you might find them useful when formatting tabu-lar data with tables. Here is an example of a header cell in a new row of the calendar table:

```
<tr>
  <th>2001</th>
</tr>
```

This code formats the year of the calendar, 2001, as a header cell. So "2001" will appear centered within the cell and in bold. However, the text won't be centered across the entire width of the table because it occupies only the first of three cells in the row. Figure 7-4 illustrates what I'm talking about.

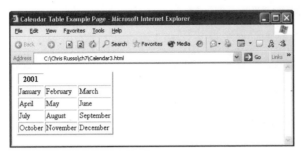

Figure 7-4 The `<th>` tag allows you to automatically place a centered, boldface heading in a cell.

The problem with the table in Figure 7-4 is that the year of the calendar is displayed in the first cell of the first row, and the second and third cells in that row are empty. Why are there other cells, even blank ones, in the row, when there are no additional `<td>` tags in the code? The reason is that every row in a table is automatically sized to the maximum number of cells on any given row. In other words, find the row with the most cells, and that's how many cells will automatically be placed on every row. If on another row, for example, you specify fewer cells, the remaining cells will be empty. This approach may seem a little strange, but it would be difficult for HTML to handle tables any other way.

Spanning Cells

As with most problems in HTML, there is a simple solution to the automatic inclusion of unneeded cells in a table. The concept known as *cell spanning* involves letting one cell flow into another cell, which makes it possible for a cell to merge with adjacent cells and appear as if they are all one big cell. You can span cells vertically across rows using the `rowspan` attribute and horizontally across columns using the `colspan` attribute, leading to some interesting results. You apply the attributes to the number of rows or columns that a cell is to span. For example, to fix the header cell in the calendar table, you need to set the `colspan` attribute so that the cell spans three columns. Here is the new code for this cell:

```
<th colspan="3">2001</th>
```

Lingo   *Cell spanning* is a technique of combining unused cells in a table so that the cells flow together like one big cell.

Figure 7-5 reveals how this code causes the calendar year to span all of the cells in the first row of the table, which results in a perfectly centered table header.

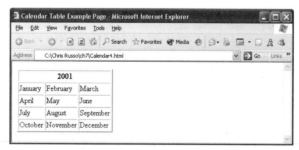

Figure 7-5   The `colspan` attribute allows you to merge cells across columns, making multiple cells appear as one.

The `rowspan` attribute serves a purpose similar to `colspan`, except that it causes cells to merge vertically with cells in adjacent rows. You can even combine the two attributes to merge cells in a rectangular fashion. You will learn later in the chapter that cell spanning plays a role in using tables to control the overall layout of Web pages.

Setting the Size of Tables

One topic worth tackling before you move on to the details of table formatting is the size of a table. The assumption at this point in the chapter is that Web browsers intuitively "know" how to size tables to perfectly fit their content. This assumption isn't far from the truth, although intuitive sizing isn't always a good thing. In general, a Web browser examines the content within a table and attempts to make the table as small as possible. The default size of a table is therefore just large enough to house its content. Although this frequently works out fine, you will want to exert control over the size of your tables in many situations.

The `<table>` tag offers an attribute that allows you to explicitly set the width of a table: `girth`. Just kidding. The real attribute is `width`, and it lets you specify the width of a table in pixels or as a percentage of the width of the displayed page. If you specify pixels, the table is exactly as wide as the number of pixels in the `width` attribute. The only exception is when you set a width that isn't wide enough to hold the table's content. In this case, the table will ignore your specification and adopt a width just wide enough to fit the content. You can think of the width of a table as either the number of pixels specified in the `width` attribute or the minimum number of pixels in width required to fit the content, whichever number is larger. To specify a table width in pixels, you provide a number in the `width` attribute:

```
<table border="2" width="400">
```

> **Tip**   In general, it's a good idea to keep the width of tables under 600 pixels. Most Web users have their screen resolution set to 800×600 pixels, which provides 800 pixels of screen width. When you factor in a Web browser scroll bar and some extra space around the edges of the page, it works out that even the largest tables should be no wider than 600 pixels, and 400 pixels is a much safer maximum width. Keep in mind that you can't accurately predict the resolution of a user's screen, so you're always working from the perspective of what is most common, which currently is 800×600.

This code sets the width of the table to 400 pixels, which means that the table will be 400 pixels wide unless it needs to be made larger to fit its content. The other approach to setting table width is to specify a percentage of the page size instead of a number of pixels in the `width` attribute, as the following code demonstrates:

```
<table border="2" width="60%">
```

Instead of setting the table width to a fixed value in pixels, this code causes the table to take on a width that is a percentage of the entire page width. The primary difference between this approach and the pixel approach is that the table width varies if the page size changes. For example, if the browser window is maximized at a screen resolution of 800×600, the page width will be approximately 800 pixels, so the table width will be 60 percent of that, or 480 pixels. However, if you resize the browser window so that it is only 500 pixels wide, the width of the table is cut to 300 pixels. Because of this variation in table size, the percentage approach to setting the table width is less predictable. On the other hand, it does have the positive effect of allowing the table to scale with the page. This is especially nice if you have a relatively large monitor with a screen resolution higher than 800×600.

Note In case you're curious, there is also a `height` attribute that allows you to set the height of tables, at least in theory. In practice, however, it sometimes yields inconsistent results. Therefore, I encourage you to use it with caution.

You can set the width of individual cells by using the `width` attribute within the `<td>` tag. Actually, you are setting the width of the entire column, because cells in a column must all be the same width. For this reason, you can specify the `width` attribute in the first cell of a column. The exception to this rule is when you have cells that span multiple columns, in which case it is necessary to stipulate the width of each cell.

Digging Deeper into Table Formatting

You can have fun with tables beyond creating them and defining a few cells. There is much more to table formatting than what I've discussed so far. The next few sections explore some of the finer points of table formatting and will no doubt leave you with enough skills to fill your Web pages with dazzling, functional tables.

Aligning Tables

Because tables typically must fit into the context of a complete Web page, it is necessary to consider their alignment, which is relative to other content on the page. Fortunately, the alignment of tables is easily controlled with the `align` attribute of the `<table>` tag. This attribute can be set to one of the following values to control the alignment of a table:

- `left`—aligns the table at the left edge of the Web page.
- `right`—aligns the table at the right edge of the Web page.
- `center`—centers the table horizontally on the Web page.

The `align` attribute also allows you to set the alignment of content within each cell. You can also set the alignment of an entire column by using the `align` attribute with the first cell in a column. Another interesting twist regarding alignment and cells is the `valign` attribute, which lets you set the vertical alignment of cells and rows. The `valign` attribute can be set to one of the following values:

- `top`—positions the cell content at the top of the cell.
- `middle`—positions the cell content at the middle of the cell.
- `bottom`—positions the cell content at the bottom of the cell.

Note In addition to these possible values for the `valign` attribute, Netscape Navigator also supports a `baseline` value that positions a cell at the baseline of the first line of text in the cell. The *baseline* of a line of text is the bottom of the text, excluding any letters that extend down below the others, such as *g* and *y*.

Incidentally, the default value for the `align` attribute is `left`, and the default value of `valign` is `middle`. So skipping these attributes results in content that is left-aligned horizontally and middle-aligned vertically.

To make sure you understand the practical usefulness of table alignment, let's take a quick look at an example. If you recall, I described some of my mountain biking exploits in Chapter 5, "Connecting Pages with Hyperlinks," in a Web page named Tsali (the name of the mountain bike trails). Although that page was formatted reasonably well given your knowledge of HTML at the time, you're now ready to improve its appearance and structure with a table. Here is code that repositions the images and main paragraph on the page:

```
<table align="left">
<tr>
  <td>
  <a href="Jump.jpg"><img src="SmJump.jpg" alt="Here I am
  catching a little air." hspace="10" align="left"></a>
  </td>
  <td>
  <a href="Cruise.jpg"><img src="SmCruise.jpg" alt="Here I am
  cruising by Fontana Lake." hspace="10" align="left"></a>
  </td>
</tr>
<tr align="center">
  <td>
  Catching a little air
  </td>
  <td>
  Cruising Fontana Lake
  </td>
</tr>
</table>
```

You may not quite have the ability to visualize the final product based on HTML code just yet. Basically, this table adds captions for each of the two thumbnail images and aligns the table with the left edge of the screen. The captions appear near the bottom of the code, and take up their own row in the table thanks to the `<tr>` tag. The alignment of the table takes place within the `<table>` tag at the start of the code, and is made possible by the `align` attribute. This alignment causes the main paragraph of text in the page to flow around the right side of the table. Figure 7-6 shows the new and improved tabular format of the Tsali page.

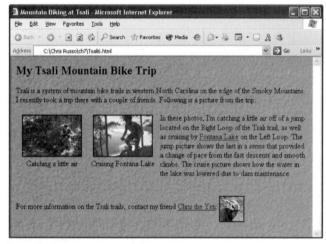

Figure 7-6   The layout of the Tsali page is improved by using a table to add captions to the images and to flow the main paragraph of text around the right of the images.

For the record, I'm jumping ahead a little by showing how to use tables to describe the layout of Web pages. Later in the chapter, you will get a formal introduction to Web page layout with tables in the section titled, "Using Tables for Page Layout." For now, let's continue the discussion of table formatting by venturing into space.

Giving Tables Some Space

Have you ever been in line at a movie waiting for tickets and had someone crowding too close behind you? Maybe I just need more personal space than most people, but having strangers breathing down my neck is not my idea of a good time. The point of this analogy is that tables often like a little breathing room, too. Sure, you could jam a table into a page right up against other content, but why not make it easy for everyone to see what you have to say?

The bad news is that the HTML specification does not provide any attributes for the <table> tag that allow us to accomplish this directly. But before you fall into a depression and start writing dark poetry in HTML, let me remind you that there is always another way. I repeat, because it will come in handy as you continue to develop HTML skills: "There is always another way." In this case, the other approach goes by the cutting-edge name of *pixel shims*.

Lingo   A *pixel shim* is a tiny blank image used to fill space in a Web page.

If you're familiar with carpentry, you know that a *shim* is a small piece of wood used to fill a gap. A good example of using shims in carpentry is window installation in a new house. Because it is virtually impossible to size the window opening down to the millimeter to fit the exact dimension of the window, carpenters don't even bother trying. They shoot for a *rough opening* size that's within a quarter of an inch of the size of the window, which guarantees that the opening won't be too small. When they set the window in the opening, they drive wood shims in the gap and make a tight fit. This same logic applies to pixel shims used in a Web page.

Pixel shims are 1-pixel GIF images that can be resized to fill any rectangular area on the page. You create the shim with the color that looks good to you or even leave the shim transparent so the background of the page shows through. Also, pixel shims can be used to add space around a table. Look at the following revised Tsali page code, which uses pixel shims to spread out the table horizontally:

```
<table align="left">
<tr>
  <td rowspan="2" bgcolor="red">
  <img src="Shim.gif" width="15">
  </td>
  <td>
  <a href="Jump.jpg"><img src="SmJump.jpg" alt="Here I am catching a little
air." hspace="10" align="left"></a>
  </td>
   <td>
  <a href="Cruise.jpg"><img src="SmCruise.jpg" alt="Here I am cruising by
Fontana Lake." hspace="10" align="left"></a>
  </td>
  <td rowspan="2" bgcolor="red">
  <img src="Shim.gif" width="15">
  </td>
</tr>
<tr align="center">
  <td>
  Catching a little air
```

```
</td>
<td>
Cruising Fontana Lake
</td>
</tr>
</table>
```

Before you freak out over the size of this code, understand that I've added
only two new cells in the first row, one at the beginning of the row and one at
the end. The following code is used for both of the cells in the table that contain
a pixel shim:

```
<td rowspan="2" bgcolor="red">
<img src="Shim.gif" width="15">
</td>
```

This code creates a pixel shim that spans two vertical cells, or the entire first
column of the table. The same code is used to span the entire last column of the
table as well. This may sound confusing, but Figure 7-7 should make it clear.

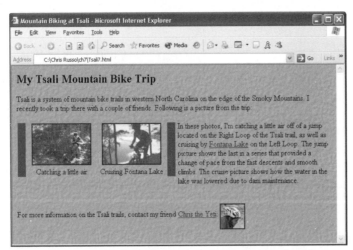

Figure 7-7   Pixel shims are used to add space to the left and right sides of the table in the Web page about
Tsali.

As the figure reveals, I did something interesting in this code: I deliberately
set the background color for the shim cells to a contrasting color so you can see
the effect of the pixel shim on the table. In this case, the code makes the end
column 15 pixels wide. You can't see the pixel shim image in the figure because
this shim is a transparent GIF image, letting the background show through. By
using a transparent GIF for the shim, you can set the background color to any
color you choose, and effectively create extra space in that color. Use this trick
to add extra space virtually anywhere on a page.

Try This!   Change the background color of the cell in the previous example to a different color to see how the transparent pixel shim allows the color to show through.

Individual cell spacing is also worth addressing. The `cellspacing` and `cellpadding` attributes of the `<table>` tag set the internal spacing of cells. The `cellspacing` attribute adds space between cells in a table but does not change the size of the cells themselves. The `cellpadding` attribute, on the other hand, adds space within the walls of a cell, around its content, and on all four sides. Both attributes set the spacing in pixels.

Tip   The default value for the `cellspacing` attribute is two pixels, and the default value for `cellpadding` is one pixel. You can set both attributes to zero to minimize the spacing of cells and pack them tightly together; no spacing or padding is applied to a cell in this case.

Dressing Up Tables with Colors and Images

Previously, I mentioned using the `bgcolor` attribute to set the background color of cells in order to determine how the Web browser is sizing them. This technique is valuable for testing purposes, as well as for setting the background color of cells as part of the design of a page. Using a solid color for a filled area of a page is much more efficient than using an image, because images must be downloaded before they can be displayed. Tables provide the perfect opportunity to use color as a design element by way of the `bgcolor` attribute. Here is an excerpt of code from the Tsali page, which has been modified so that the background color of the cell is set to maroon:

```
<td bgcolor="maroon">
Catching a little air
</td>
```

Tip   In addition to setting the predefined colors in HTML, you can specify custom colors. You'll learn how in Appendix C, "Using Custom Colors."

Thanks to the convenience of HTML, you can extend the `bgcolor` attribute setting across entire rows with the `<tr>` tag. Taking it a step farther, you can use the background color for an entire table by setting the `bgcolor` attribute in the `<table>` tag. It is possible to use the `bgcolor` attribute in several different tags to get different effects; the more detailed tag always overrides the more general tag. In other words, the background color specified in a `<td>` tag will override the background color set in the `<table>` tag. Here is an example of how to create a table that resembles a checkerboard by carefully setting the background color of cells.

```
<table bgcolor="black" width="400" height="400">
<tr>
  <td bgcolor="red"></td> <td></td>
  <td bgcolor="red"></td> <td></td>
  <td bgcolor="red"></td> <td></td>
  <td bgcolor="red"></td> <td></td>
</tr>
<tr>
  <td></td> <td bgcolor="red"></td>
  <td></td> <td bgcolor="red"></td>
  <td></td> <td bgcolor="red"></td>
  <td></td> <td bgcolor="red"></td>
</tr>
<tr>
  <td bgcolor="red"></td> <td></td>
  <td bgcolor="red"></td> <td></td>
  <td bgcolor="red"></td> <td></td>
  <td bgcolor="red"></td> <td></td>
</tr>
<tr>
  <td></td> <td bgcolor="red"></td>
  <td></td> <td bgcolor="red"></td>
  <td></td> <td bgcolor="red"></td>
  <td></td> <td bgcolor="red"></td>
</tr>
<tr>
  <td bgcolor="red"></td> <td></td>
  <td bgcolor="red"></td> <td></td>
  <td bgcolor="red"></td> <td></td>
  <td bgcolor="red"></td> <td></td>
</tr>
<tr>
  <td></td> <td bgcolor="red"></td>
  <td></td> <td bgcolor="red"></td>
  <td></td> <td bgcolor="red"></td>
  <td></td> <td bgcolor="red"></td>
</tr>
<tr>
  <td bgcolor="red"></td> <td></td>
  <td bgcolor="red"></td> <td></td>
  <td bgcolor="red"></td> <td></td>
  <td bgcolor="red"></td> <td></td>
</tr>
<tr>
  <td></td> <td bgcolor="red"></td>
  <td></td> <td bgcolor="red"></td>
  <td></td> <td bgcolor="red"></td>
```

```
<td></td> <td bgcolor="red"></td>
</tr>
</table>
```

Granted, this code segment is a little long, but it's an excellent example of how you can use the bgcolor attribute creatively. Figure 7-8 shows the results of the checkerboard code.

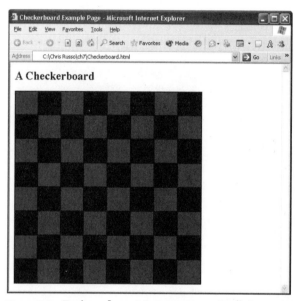

Figure 7-8   The bgcolor attribute can be used to do interesting things, such as create a checkerboard.

In addition to background colors, you can set an image as the background of either a table or its individual cells. The background attribute that sets the background of an entire page is the same one you use to set the background of tables. To use this attribute, simply assign the name of the image. Here is an example of how to set the background of a cell to an image named Marble.gif:

```
<td background="Marble.gif">This is a cell!</td>
```

So, the background image for a table appears behind the table's content. In this example, the Marble.gif image shows up behind the text, "This is a cell!" This is fine, but remember not to use images that compete visually with the table content. Contrast makes text or other content stand out. It's more important for the user to be able to access the information on your Web pages than it is to have that user be impressed with aesthetics, especially ones that introduce too many distracting elements.

Try This!   To make a background image contrast less with the content on a table, try editing the image in an image editing program and altering its brightness. If the table content is dark, add more brightness to the image, and if the table content is light, remove brightness from the image. Also, you can really improve the contrast of an image by softening the image in an image editor, which makes the image appear to be somewhat blurry. This contrasts well with the sharpness of text appearing on top of the image.

Caution   One small caveat regarding a background image for an entire table: Internet Explorer and Netscape Navigator handle table backgrounds differently. Navigator doesn't support a true background image for a table because it places the entire image in each cell. Internet Explorer, on the other hand, sets a single image for the entire table.

Revisiting Borders

Earlier in the chapter, you learned that the border attribute allows you to set the width of a table's border in pixels. Internet Explorer provides an additional attribute of the <table> tag that allows you to fine-tune the border's appearance and the parts of the table it's drawn around. This is the frame attribute, and it can be set to one of the following values:

- above—specifies a border on the top of the table.
- below—specifies a border on the bottom of the table.
- hsides—specifies a border on the top and bottom of the table.
- lhs—specifies a border on the left side of the table.
- rhs—specifies a border on the right side of the table.
- vsides—specifies a border on the right and left sides of the table.
- box—specifies a border on all sides of the table.
- border—specifies a border on all sides of the table—the same as box.
- void—specifies no borders on the table.

Specifying the frame attribute value gives you some degree of control over how the border of a table is drawn. Here is an example from an NHL Hockey Standings Web page that uses the below value to fine-tune the border of a table:

```
<table border="2" frame="below">
<tr>
  <th align="left">Team</th>
  <th>Wins</th>
  <th>Losses</th>
```

```
    <th>Ties</th>
    <th>OT Losses</th>
  </tr>
  <tr>
    <td>Colorado Avalanche</td>
    <td>40</td>
    <td>12</td>
    <td>9</td>
    <td>3</td>
  </tr>
  <tr>
    <td>Detroit Red Wings</td>
    <td>39</td>
    <td>17</td>
    <td>7</td>
    <td>4</td>
  </tr>
  <tr>
    <td>Dallas Stars</td>
    <td>36</td>
    <td>22</td>
     <td>5</td>
    <td>2</td>
  </tr>
  <tr>
    <td>St. Louis Blues</td>
    <td>39</td>
    <td>16</td>
    <td>7</td>
    <td>4</td>
  </tr>
</table>
```

Figure 7-9 shows the impact of the frame attribute on what the NHL Hockey Standings Web page looks like.

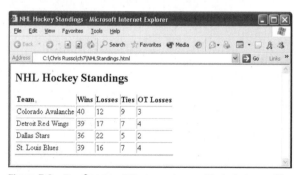

Figure 7-9   The `frame` attribute can be used to include specifics about the exact manner in which a border is drawn around a table.

Using Tables for Page Layout

Tables are great for formatting tabular data, such as that in the Web page with NHL hockey standings. You will also find them useful for laying out the general structure of your pages. Keep in mind that tables allow you to divide an area into rectangular segments. Where a single table might come up a little short, you can nest tables to get more interesting results. The next few sections of the chapter explore using tables for page layout.

Working Out the Design.

Before you design a Web page, sketch the page on paper—not hundreds of words, just the general format of the page and where major elements of the page will reside. For example, if you plan on having a navigation bar with buttons down the left side of the page, show it in the sketch. You may also have a title image in mind that is positioned along the top of the page. From there, you may decide to format the body of the page as two-column text, like a newspaper article. It's all up to you, but by sketching it on paper you can form a better understanding of what you'll need to include in your HTML code.

Another huge benefit of the paper sketch approach to Web page design is that it allows you to visualize the structure of any tables needed to carry out the design. As you've learned, tables can get somewhat tricky at the code level and are often hard to picture.

Putting the Table Together

With your sketch in hand, you'll find the coding of the table pretty straightforward. The most important part is to set a border for all of the tables so you can see what is happening in the browser as you test the layout. (You can remove them when you are finished.) Beyond that, the coding is primarily a process of studying the sketch and creating rows and columns within tables to accommodate the design. Keep in mind that you will probably need to span rows and columns in some situations to get the desired effect. You may even need to nest a table or two within another table. Take a look at this HTML code, which shows an example of a page layout made possible with the creative use of tables:

```
<table width="600" border="1">
<tr>
  <td width="60" rowspan="3">Navigation Bar</td>
  <td>Page Title</td>
 </tr>
<tr>
  <td width="540">
  <table width="540" border="1">
```

```
<tr>
   <td>Column One</td>
   <td>Column Two</td>
</tr>
</table>
</td>
</tr>
<tr>
  <td width="540">Page Footer</td>
</tr>
</table>
```

First, notice that I've set the width of certain parts of the table to specific values. This helps to eliminate any browser inconsistencies when it comes to sizing a table with respect to the current browser window size. Next, notice how spanning the first cell down through all three rows in the table creates the navigation bar. Another table is nested in the second row and used to break up what will be the content area of the page into two columns. Figure 7-10 shows the results of viewing this newly coded table in Internet Explorer.

Figure 7-10   Laying out a page using nested tables is as simple as thinking through a design on paper and then creating a few tables.

Adding the Content

The real fun of seeing a page layout come together is when you add the actual content of the page. The table design you saw in the previous section is an excellent starting point for adding content and building a Web page of your own. Rather than provide you with all the specifics and take the fun out of the experience, I encourage you to take the template I've provided and build your own page from it. Just keep in mind that a navigation bar typically consists of equal-sized images that serve as hyperlinks to other parts of a Web site. Also, you will probably want to use the footer of the page to place a copyright notice identifying the Web page as your own intellectual property. The rest of the creative process is up to you, so have at it!

Tip   The code for this example, as well as all of the examples throughout the book, is available for download from my Web site at the following URL: *http://www.michaelmorrison.com/ cbook_fshtml.html.*

Key Points

■   Tables in HTML are similar to spreadsheets in that they consist of cells arranged in a grid-like structure of rows and columns.

■   The <table> tag is used to create tables, while the <tr> and <td> tags are used to create rows and individual cells within tables, respectively.

■   A border is a thin line drawn around a section of content on a Web page, and is used in conjunction with a table via the border attribute.

■   Header cells can be useful when formatting tabular data with tables and are created using the <th> tag.

■   Cell spanning relies on the rowspan and colspan attributes and allows you to combine cells so that they act as one.

■   A pixel shim is a tiny image that provides a neat trick for filling space within tables.

■   You can dress up tables by taking advantage of their support for background colors and images.

Chapter 8

Graphical Tools and HTML

Yours truly already knew this, but it's worth pointing out that graphical Web development tools have advanced rapidly in the past few years. Today's graphical Web tools blow away the best publishing and multimedia software of only a few years ago. What does this have to do with HTML? Well, HTML is the fundamental language used to develop Web pages, so graphical Web tools must edit and manipulate HTML code.

Although the focus of this book is clearly on coding Web pages with HTML by hand, it's important to learn how graphical Web tools fit into the Web development equation. Even if you choose to become an HTML whiz, you'll no doubt find some of these tools useful in certain situations.

Why Use a Graphical Tool?

In case you haven't noticed, people don't think the way computers do. Computers think of everything in terms of steps and instructions. When you get down to it, everything in a computer boils down to a number. People tend to think in terms of physical things and how they relate to one another, resorting to numbers only when it's absolutely necessary. One of the principal challenges in any computing system is bridging this gap between computer thought and human thought. One situation in which this gap is readily apparent is in HTML code.

The very word *code* reveals that HTML is not something natural to human expression. To get a desired visual effect on a Web page, you have to use HTML to write code that the computer can comprehend and act upon through a Web browser. Even though HTML uses tags that most people understand, a certain degree of thought goes into formatting a page using HTML, as opposed to sketching the same page on a piece of paper.

The ultimate Web development tool would allow you to sketch a page and skip the HTML coding. Supercomputers and artificial intelligence may some day make this a reality. But for now we have graphical Web development tools that help transfer a Web page design from your head to HTML—a format that the computer can understand.

Graphical Web development tools work like a word processor or desktop publishing software. In fact, early Web development tools followed the lead of desktop publishing tools used for printed publications. Just as the word processor of desktop publishing tools allows you to visually lay out a printed page containing images, text, and other visual elements, a graphical Web tool allows you to lay out a Web page with similar elements. These kinds of tools are sometimes referred to as *WYSIWYG*, or What You See Is What You Get. Essentially, what you see on the screen is close to what you will see on the final page. Building a Web page this way is significantly more intuitive than hacking away at HTML code.

Lingo   *WYSIWYG* is a nerdy term used in the desktop publishing community to describe the accurate creation of visual documents. *What you see is what you get* simply means that the tool used to create a document will show the document exactly as it will appear in print or in a Web browser.

Why learn HTML when you can construct Web pages graphically by using a Web development tool? The answer is that no tool can replace the efficiency and accuracy of hand coding HTML. In other words, you'll need to know HTML at some point even if you plan to use a graphical Web development tool religiously. If you plan to be an HTML purist and snub graphical tools for the most part, you will still encounter situations in which a graphical tool can save you time. You have the best of both worlds when you know how to leverage a graphical Web development tool with your HTML coding and understand when each can improve the Web development process.

Getting Acquainted with Graphical Tools

My family has a somewhat tragic and often entertaining history with tools. I'm talking about traditional construction tools such as hammers, saws, ladders, and so on. My uncle lost a few fingers in a strange table saw accident, and I witnessed my dad fall from the attic to the ground floor of his house with a ladder in tow. I've personally crashed and burned while pushing a fully loaded wheelbarrow, so I don't have much room to talk. This is just a theory, but it may be that if my family spent a little more time getting acquainted with tools, we would all be safer for it. This brings us to graphical Web development tools, which I want to acquaint you with before you run out and hurt yourself.

When I talk about graphical Web development tools, I'm referring to HTML-based tools, such as Microsoft FrontPage and Macromedia DreamWeaver. But they are not the only graphical tools available for Web development. Imaging tools are other development tools that you'll find useful in creating Web pages with images. They allow you to create and edit images and image maps. When you couple them with a graphical Web-page-design tool, you have a complete Web development toolkit that goes a long way in helping you create compelling Web pages. A handy set of tools will allow you to spend more of your time focusing on the design of pages. The next few sections explore some of the popular tools that you can use to build Web pages.

Image-Editing Tools

I have a friend named Keith whose eyes appear red in every photograph taken of him. I've pondered the possibility of a demonic influence at work, but the truth is that red-eye in photographs is caused by the reflection of the camera's flash off the retina of the eye. I'm not sure why some people are more prone to photographic red-eye than others, so I'll continue to look into the notion of a demonic influence on my friend. I mention the red-eye problem because software can now easily correct it in digital photographs. The software that makes this magical feat possible is the image-editing tool.

With the transition from traditional cameras to digital ones, image-editing tools have become very popular. You no doubt have an image-editing tool already if you own a digital camera. They become important for Web development because they allow you to resize, crop, and otherwise manipulate images for your Web pages. Most image-editing tools also support multiple image file formats such as (Graphics Interchange Format) GIF, (Joint Photographic Experts Group) JPEG, and (Portable Network Graphics) PNG. Some comprehensive image-editing tools offer powerful image manipulation features such as the automatic removal of red-eye, along with many other special effects.

Here are several popular image-editing tools to consider using for your Web pages:

- Adobe Photoshop
- CorelDRAW
- Paint Shop Pro
- Microsoft Photo Editor

These image-editing tools are arranged roughly in order of most feature-packed to least feature-packed. Of course, this also means that they are in order of decreasing price, so your desire to have loads of features will likely be offset by the depth of your pockets. Of course, additional features require additional memory, so make sure that your computer is equipped to handle a high-end graphics tool before making the investment. Adobe Photoshop is without a doubt the king of image-editing software and is clearly the tool of choice for professional artists and designers who work with digital images every day.

The power and flexibility inherent in Photoshop comes at two significant costs: a steep learning curve and a big dent in the wallet. I'm not saying that you can't work through a few tutorials and get up to speed with Photoshop in a reasonable amount of time, but it's definitely a more complex tool than the others I've listed. On the other hand, there isn't much you can't do in Photoshop, which is why it's so widely used by professional artists, photographers, and Web designers. To learn more about Photoshop, visit the Adobe site on the Web at *http://www.adobe.com/*.

Note   Adobe recently released a slimmed-down version of Photoshop called Photoshop Elements that is geared toward people who want a more economical, easier-to-use alternative to Photoshop. Photoshop Elements is considerably cheaper than Photoshop and has a much shorter learning curve.

CorelDRAW is another high-end professional graphics tool with loads of image-editing features. CorelDRAW rivals Photoshop in some ways, including cost, so you should probably check it out if you're considering a big investment in an image-editing tool. You can find out more about CorelDRAW by visiting the Corel Web site at *http://www.corel.com/*.

Another popular Microsoft Windows graphics tool is Paint Shop Pro by Jasc Software. It originated as a shareware graphics software package that evolved into a full-blown retail application. This shareware history is what made it popular among those of us who couldn't afford expensive graphics software.

In keeping with its shareware roots, an evaluation version of Paint Shop Pro is available from the Jasc Software Web site at *http://www.jasc.com/*. The program includes a variety of image-editing features that come in handy for prepping images for the Web. The Paint Shop Pro software package also includes a tool called Animation Shop that allows you to create animated GIF images. Animated GIF images can be tricky to create without the help of a good tool, and Animation Shop is just the one to simplify the process.

The final image-editing tool I feel compelled to mention is Microsoft's Photo Editor, which ships standard with most versions of Windows. Although Photo Editor is certainly limited when compared to its commercial counterparts, I have to tell you that I use it almost every day. The reality is that Photo Editor is extremely simple and extremely fast, which are two important considerations for me. Before you spend any money on an image-editing tool, make sure you try Photo Editor first to see how well it meets your needs. If it comes up short in a few important areas, you can safely consider buying a fancier tool. Even so, you may still find yourself using Photo Editor for quick image adjustments such as resizing and cropping images.

Image Map Tools

In Chapter 6, "Visual Navigation with Image Maps," you learned how valuable a graphical tool can be in creating image maps. It is extremely tedious to create image maps by hand in HTML. You'll find that an image map tool will help a great deal, regardless of whether you're creating pages with a graphical Web page tool or by hand in straight HTML code. I already showed you how to use the built-in image map features in FrontPage in Chapter 6. Now I'd like to unveil another handy tool designed solely for creating and editing image maps: CuteMAP.

CuteMAP is a tool by GlobalSCAPE that allows you to create image maps graphically, freeing you from calculating and coding the areas of an image map by hand. Figure 8-1 shows the familiar skateboard image example from Chapter 6 as viewed in CuteMAP.

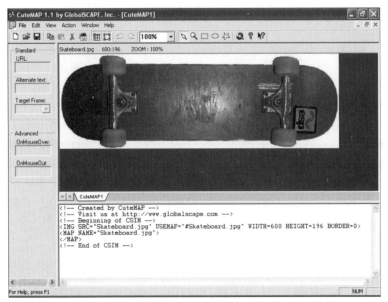

Figure 8-1 The CuteMAP image map tool allows you to create image maps graphically.

When you create a project in CuteMAP, the program prompts you to select an image to use as the basis for the image map. The image is then displayed in the CuteMAP window, along with the HTML code. That CuteMAP displays the HTML code is significant because it allows you to cut and paste image maps into your own Web pages. It's also educational because you can see the HTML code being generated as you work through the creation of an image map.

If you elect not to use a full-featured Web design tool such as FrontPage, which includes a built-in image map tool, I highly recommend CuteMAP for your image map creation needs. To find out more about CuteMAP, visit the Globalscape Web site at *http://www.globalscape.com/*.

Note   The CuteMAP image map tool is available for the Windows platform only. However, there are a few image map tools available for the Macintosh platform. For example, Macromedia Dream-Weaver for the Mac includes a built-in image map tool. You might also visit your favorite Macintosh shareware Web site and search for additional image map tools if these don't suffice.

Web Page Design Tools

If you start creating complex Web pages with only a text editor, you will find Web design exceedingly tedious and messy. You might want to consider using a graphical Web page design tool to avoid some of the drudgery of HTML coding and to allow you to focus on the visual aspects of your pages. Many people have the attitude that graphical tools allow you to be blissfully ignorant of HTML. But it's not a good idea to limit yourself to only graphical tools if you plan to create Web pages with any flair.

Graphical Web design tools such as Microsoft FrontPage give you the freedom to build Web pages visually, resorting to HTML only when necessary. You learned in the previous section that coding image maps can be tiresome. Another facet of Web design that isn't particularly entertaining in straight HTML code is creating tables. You learned in Chapter 7, "Organizing Pages with Tables," that coding tables in HTML by hand isn't necessarily difficult, but using a graphical design tool can make the process much smoother and more intuitive. Figure 8-2 shows how it is possible to visually create a table in FrontPage.

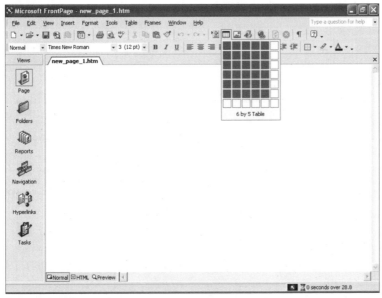

Figure 8-2 FrontPage allows you to create tables by dragging the mouse and visually indicating the number of rows and cells.

Try This!   For a more automatic approach to creating tables from existing data, you can create Web pages directly from Microsoft Excel spreadsheets. Follow these steps to create a Web page from a spreadsheet:

1   Open the .xls spreadsheet file in Excel.

2   Select Save as Web Page from the File menu.

You will learn later in the chapter that FrontPage also makes it possible to view the HTML code for a Web page. This is helpful if you are using only the table and image mapping features of FrontPage. You can use FrontPage to create just the tables and image maps, and then copy and paste the code generated by FrontPage into your hand-coded HTML files. This is a reasonable trade-off between graphical and non-graphical Web page design. It avoids the hassle of manually coding highly visual Web elements in HTML while still giving you complete control over your Web pages.

If I've convinced you to consider using a graphical Web design tool, you'll be glad to know that there are numerous options. Here are three more popular ones:

- Microsoft FrontPage
- Adobe GoLive
- Macromedia DreamWeaver

I found it easier to distinguish the price and target user of each product than to fairly compare their respective features. In truth, any of these tools will likely serve your purpose well into the future because they are all quite powerful.

FrontPage and GoLive are professional-quality Web design tools that are simple enough that beginning Web designers can get started quickly. Be aware that GoLive offers more features than FrontPage and costs twice as much. FrontPage also comes bundled with several Microsoft Office suites. If you are an Office user, you might already have FrontPage as part of Office. There are benefits to using FrontPage with Office because of its integration with other Office applications. For more information about FrontPage, visit the FrontPage Web site at *http://www.microsoft.com/frontpage/*. To learn more about GoLive, visit the Adobe Web site at *http://www.adobe.com/*.

Just as Adobe Photoshop offers a high-end, high-price solution for image editing with Photoshop, Macromedia DreamWeaver offers a high-end answer in a graphical Web design tool. DreamWeaver quickly became the Web design tool of choice for many professional Web designers a few years ago, and it is still going strong. If you are an aspiring professional Web designer, you might want to consider spending the money for DreamWeaver. Short of that ambition, you might be better served with FrontPage, GoLive, or some other Web design tool.

Keep in mind that GoLive and DreamWeaver are available for both Mac and Windows, but FrontPage is available for Windows only. There are many other Web design tools; I've highlighted only the most popular ones.

HTML Editors

The last type of Web tool I want to mention is an HTML editor—the one tool that you can't live without. So far I've assumed that you're using a no-frills text editor such as Windows Notepad to code your Web pages. Although Notepad or some other text editor is certainly suitable for coding Web pages, there are options that offer significant benefits.

HTML editors are special text editors designed specifically for editing HTML code. They offer benefits such as *context-sensitive highlighting,* a fancy way of saying that the HTML code is colored differently to help distinguish tags from other types of content. I've listed two popular HTML editors that you might consider if you go beyond a simple text editor such as Notepad.

- GlobalSCAPE CuteHTML

- Macromedia HomeSite

In addition to serving as more powerful options to traditional text editors, these HTML editors are also great educational tools. They help you write HTML code, which helps you get acquainted with tag usage. As an example, look at Figure 8-3, which shows how CuteHTML allows you to place an image on a Web page using an intuitive dialog box.

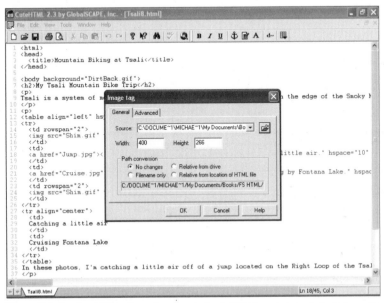

Figure 8-3 The CuteHTML editor allows you to "write" HTML code by entering information about an HTML element in a dialog box.

HomeSite and CuteHTML aren't technically graphical Web design tools. They don't support WYSIWYG Web page editing, but they do provide graphical features that improve the development of HTML code. For example, CuteHTML includes a visual table creation feature similar to the one you saw in FrontPage. Figure 8-4 shows how tables are created using this feature in CuteHTML.

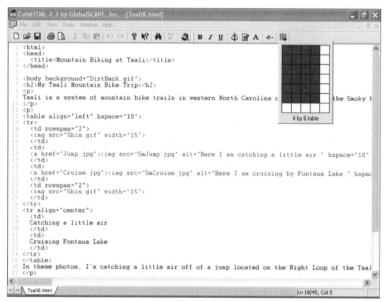

Figure 8-4 Creating tables in CuteHTML is as simple as dragging the mouse to indicate the number of rows and columns.

HomeSite and CuteHTML aren't the only HTML editors out there. Rather than give you a long list of HTML editors, I'm simply giving you an idea of what is possible with these kinds of tools. By all means, look around for other options. If you consider HomeSite, visit the Macromedia Web site at *http://www.macromedia.com/*. Learn more about CuteHTML by visiting the GlobalSCAPE Web site at *http://www.globalscape.com/*.

Note   Like the CuteMAP image map tool you learned about earlier in the chapter, CuteHTML is available for the Windows platform only.

Working with HTML in FrontPage

Because Microsoft FrontPage is perhaps the most prevalent graphical Web design tool among beginning and intermediate Windows users, I want to explore how to carry out a few tasks that you'll find useful even if you aim to be an HTML purist. By HTML purist, I mean that you decide to stick with hand coding your Web pages in a text editor or HTML editor so that you have maximum control over what goes in them. Here are a few common HTML coding chores that I find useful to carry out within FrontPage, even when I'm coding pages by hand:

- Previewing Web pages
- Creating tables
- Creating image maps
- Publishing Web pages

The next few sections describe how to use FrontPage to make each of these Web design tasks easier to manage. If you don't have FrontPage and you intend to use a different graphical Web design tool, you can rest easy knowing that you can probably perform similar steps in your tool of choice for a similar result. If you're hardcore about HTML coding and avoiding all graphical tools, more power to you. But I recommend that you continue reading just to find out what you might be missing.

Using Different Views

In an attempt to accommodate both beginner and advanced Web page designers by providing both a low-level and a high-level approach to editing Web pages, FrontPage offers several different views of a page. You can edit the page using a WYSIWYG editor that displays the page more or less as it will appear in a browser, or you can edit the HTML code directly. The WYSIWYG view in FrontPage is considered the Normal view because most users will avoid HTML coding at all costs. But not you! You can also use Preview, the view that allows you to see the page exactly as it will appear in a Web browser.

To summarize, here are the three views supported in FrontPage:

- Normal
- HTML
- Preview

These views are displayed as tabbed panes within the main area of the FrontPage workspace. Figure 8-5 shows the Tsali mountain bike Web page as viewed in the Normal view in FrontPage.

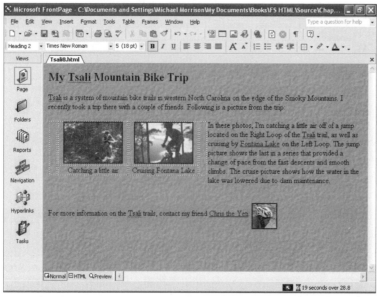

Figure 8-5 The Normal view in FrontPage provides a WYSIWYG editor that displays a Web page in a form that resembles its final browser appearance.

As you can see in the figure, the Tsali Web page is displayed roughly as it will appear in a Web browser. The obvious difference is the outline around the table, which is necessary for you to see the table for editing purposes. To change the view and edit the Web page as straight HTML code, click the HTML tab below the page. Figure 8-6 shows the HTML view of FrontPage, which allows you to directly edit the HTML code for the Web page.

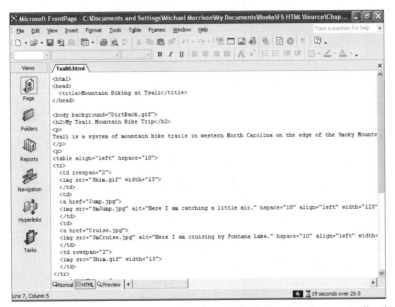

Figure 8-6   The HTML view in FrontPage provides an HTML editor that allows you to directly edit the HTML code for a Web page.

The other view in FrontPage is Preview, which allows you to see a page as it will appear in a browser. Its advantage is that you view the page directly in FrontPage, so you don't have to run a Web browser separately. To switch to Preview, click the Preview tab below the Web page. Figure 8-7 shows the Preview view in FrontPage and displays a page as it will appear in a Web browser.

The neat thing about the views in FrontPage is that you can quickly switch between them by clicking the tabs below the view window. This makes it possible to try out different things in the HTML view and quickly see the results in the Preview view. And if you want to use the WYSIWYG editor to help create a table or an image map, you can hop over to it and then jump back to the HTML view to see the resulting HTML code. I encourage you to experiment with the views in FrontPage and get a feel for how they let you build and test Web pages.

Try This!   Open one of the example Web pages from the previous chapter in a graphical Web design tool such as Microsoft FrontPage. Try making changes to the Web page using the graphical editor, and then switch to text view to see how the tool generates the appropriate HTML code.

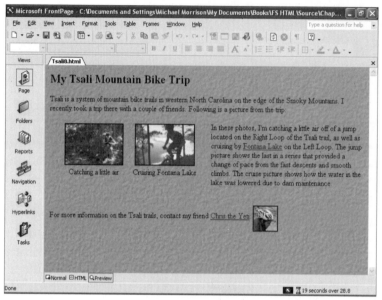

Figure 8-7 The Preview view in FrontPage allows you to see a Web page as it will appear in a Web browser.

Note   Most graphical Web design tools, including FrontPage, generate HTML code that seems unnecessary. These tools typically require special tags to carry out some of their more advanced features, which you may or may not be interested in using. If you avoid using these features, you can typically avoid the automatic insertion of the complex-looking code. Regardless of how careful you are, some of this code may end up in your pages. You can decide to ignore it or delete it by hand in the HTML view.

Creating Tables

As you learned earlier in the chapter, creating a table in FrontPage is straightforward, thanks to the visual table creation feature that allows you to click and drag the mouse to determine the number of rows and columns in a table. You already saw what this looked like, so I'll spare you another figure. What I haven't mentioned is that it's also possible to enter content in a table in FrontPage using the WYSIWYG editor.

For example, if you want to create a table to catalog your monthly budget for an internal family Web site, you would first create a table by clicking the Table button, then dragging to define the dimensions of the table. After creating the table, make sure you are in the Normal view. You will see the outline of the table with rows and columns delineated. Click in each cell of the table and start typing away to add the budget content. Keep in mind that you can highlight cells and format the text using the FrontPage menus and toolbars. Once you're finished entering the budget numbers, you should have a page that is similar to the one in Figure 8-8.

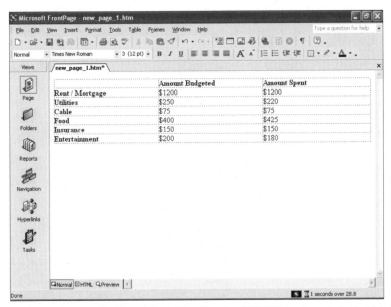

Figure 8-8 Because the Normal view of FrontPage is a WYSIWYG display, entering text into table cells is simply a matter of selecting the cell and typing.

The interesting aspect of the table creation process is when you pop over to the HTML view and take a look at the HTML code generated for the table, as shown in Figure 8-9. Of course, the most exciting part of creating any Web page is seeing the finished result, which is possible by simply switching to the Preview view, as shown in Figure 8-10.

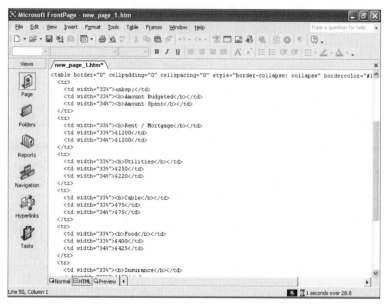

Figure 8-9 The HTML view provides a means of studying or modifying HTML code generated by FrontPage for the newly-created table.

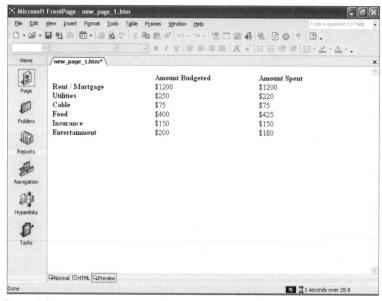

Figure 8-10 The Preview view displays the newly created table in all its glory.

Previously, I mentioned that the multiple views of FrontPage can be used in conjunction to provide a powerful Web development environment. This table creation example serves as a great demonstration of this point.

Creating Image Maps

Like tables, image maps can be a pain to code by hand in HTML. For this reason, I strongly recommend using a graphical Web design tool such as FrontPage to create and edit image maps. You learned how to work with image maps in FrontPage in Chapter 6, "Visual Navigation with Image Maps." Note that the same use of the multiple FrontPage views comes in handy with image maps as well as with tables.

Publishing Your Pages

One last facet of FrontPage, and most graphical Web design tools for that matter, is the publication of pages to the Web. In Chapter 2, "Your First HTML Web Page," you created your first Web page and published it to the Web using the Microsoft Web Publishing Wizard. Tools such as FrontPage eliminate the need for the Web Publishing Wizard by including a built-in feature for publishing Web pages. The advantage is that you complete the design, test, and publication phases of Web site development from within the same application. In other words, with a tool such as FrontPage, you can quickly publish pages after editing them without using any other tool or utility. You will learn much more about publishing pages using FrontPage and other software utilities in Chapter 9, "Publishing Pages on the Web."

Key Points

- All Web designers have preferences for certain tools they find useful based on how those tools mesh with their HTML coding efforts.

- Building a Web page with the assistance of a graphical design tool can sometimes be more straightforward than hacking away at HTML code in a text editor.

- WYSIWYG (what you see is what you get) refers to a design tool's ability to display a Web page exactly as it will appear in a Web browser.

- Image-editing tools are important for Web development because they allow you to resize, crop, and otherwise manipulate images for your Web pages.

- A graphical design tool can make the process of creating tables much smoother and more intuitive.

- HTML editors are special text editors designed specifically for editing HTML code and offer features such as context-sensitive highlighting.

- If you already use Microsoft Office, then you may find FrontPage an excellent option for incorporating a Web design tool into your HTML coding.

Publishing Pages on the Web

Just as digital photography gives us an opportunity to become our own photo finishers, the Web allows us to become our own printing press operators. In fact, the growth of self-publishing is one of the most significant contributions of the Web. Never before has it been possible for people with modest means to present their ideas to the entire world. Granted, I'm using the word "ideas" rather loosely, because there are plenty of personal Web pages floating around that are devoid of much meaningful thought. Even so, I'm all for empowering individuals regardless of how they choose to use that power. In this chapter, you exercise your power to self-publish by learning how to publish your own Web pages on the World Wide Web.

Web Publishing Basics

In guiding you through the creation of your first Web page, Chapter 2, "Your First HTML Web Page," addressed Web publishing by quickly showing you how to publish the page. Although you covered the steps required to use a specific Web publishing tool, I glossed over the details of the Web publishing process.

Now it's time to dig deeper into Web publishing and find out what's really happening when you make your presence known on the Web. Let's start off by reviewing two important terms from Chapter 2:

- **Web client**   A Web browser that displays Web pages after receiving them from a Web server
- **Web server**   A special computer on the Internet that delivers Web pages to Web clients

The relationship between a Web client and a Web server is pretty simple: The client (Web browser) asks the Web server for a certain Web page, and the server obliges by delivering the page to the client. This relationship is important to Web publishing because you must understand how and where to place your Web pages to make them accessible by Web users. More specifically, you must copy your pages to a Web server, allowing your pages to be viewed by anyone with a Web browser.

You probably don't have a Web server sitting around the house. So, your first task is to choose whether you will install Web server software on a computer with a permanent Internet connection or use a Web hosting service. Most likely you'll be using a Web hosting service unless you are developing a business Web site, and the business plans to house its own Web server. You might also have the capability to publish Web pages through your Internet service provider (MSN, America Online, Earthlink, or others).

Note   One type of permanent Internet connection is the cable modem, which is very popular. It is technically possible to install a Web server on a computer with a cable modem connection and run a Web site, but most cable Internet providers don't allow it. That's because it can result in problems if too many people browse your pages at once. If you're considering bending the rules and running a Web site over your cable modem anyway, keep in mind that if everyone ran a Web site using a cable modem connection, the connection speed would likely slow to a crawl.

Although Web pages are typically stored on the hard drive of a Web server computer, the actual development of the pages takes place on your local computer. If you are hosting your own Web server, then your local computer may perform both the development and the distribution functions. When you're ready to publish the pages on the Web, you copy them to a Web server.

You learned in Chapter 2 how this is accomplished on the Windows platform with Microsoft's Web Publishing Wizard. If you aren't using a Windows computer or don't have access to the Web Publishing Wizard, you can use an

FTP (File Transfer Protocol) program to send the Web page files to a server using FTP. Some popular Windows FTP programs are WS_FTP and CuteFTP. For the Macintosh, Fetch is a popular FTP program. You can also use a graphical Web development tool such as Microsoft FrontPage or Macromedia DreamWeaver, which both include built-in publishing features.

Lingo   If you recall from earlier in the book, *FTP* stands for File Transfer Protocol and is a technology that allows you to send and receive files over the Internet.

A potential source of confusion regarding publishing Web pages is that Web servers often aren't computers that you will see and interact with. Don't get me wrong—a Web server looks like a normal computer. But you usually have no idea where the Web server for your Web site is located, especially if you use a Web hosting service. Do you know the exact location of the phone company's central office that services your phone line? Probably not.

Note   If you're working on a business Web site, there may actually be a Web server in your building. In this case, you may be able to walk up and interact with it—perhaps against the wishes of the network administrator. However, most individuals and many smaller companies can't justify the expense of the permanent Internet connection that is required for Web servers.

The same situation applies with Web servers because it really isn't important where the Web server is physically located. In lieu of knowing its physical location, you interact with a Web server by using its *Internet address*.

Lingo   An *Internet address*, or *IP address*, is basically an online version of a mailing address.

When you publish pages using the Web Publishing Wizard, an FTP program, or a graphical Web development tool, you must specify the Internet address of the Web server for your Web site. Your Web hosting service will have provided the address to you. If you have your own domain name, you will enter it as the address of the Web server. For example, when I modify my personal Web site, I specify the Web server as *http://www.michaelmorrison.com* (Figure 9-1). The Web publishing software (FrontPage in this case) will then ask for a user name and password, which I must enter so that I can publish the updated pages.

Figure 9-1   The Publish Destination window of Microsoft FrontPage prompts you to enter the address of the Web server for the Web site being published.

If you have a Web site as part of your AOL (America Online) Internet account, you will specify *http://members.aol.com* as the address of the Web server. You then enter your AOL user name/ID and password, and the pages are published. The AOL Web server automatically stores the pages in the appropriate location within the AOL Hometown community. I will go into more detail regarding AOL as a Web hosting service in the next section of this chapter.

The goal of this section isn't to give you a detailed play-by-play analysis of how the Web publishing process works for a specific Web server or Web publishing program. There are so many different possible configurations that it is virtually impossible to discuss them all. Instead, I want to present you with the fundamentals of Web publishing so you can successfully publish your Web pages with any tool on any Web server. Let's move on and take a look at the options available for hosting your Web pages.

Finding a Good Home for Your Web Pages

There are some hard questions that enter into the picture when you face the important decision of where to place your Web pages. Here are the major options, listed in order of decreasing cost, that are available to you, the Web page owner:

- Host your own Web server ($$$$)
- Pay for a Web hosting service ($$$)
- Use the Web hosting service built into your Internet account ($$)
- Store the pages on your local hard drive only ($)

Of course, decreasing cost corresponds with decreasing power and flexibility. The old adage, "You get what you pay for," definitely holds true for Web hosting. Notice that at this point I haven't made any recommendations regarding how you should host your Web pages, regardless of how much money you have buried in the backyard. But I will. Rest assured that the majority of individual Web page designers can safely rule out two of the options on this list.

Hosting Your Own Web Site

If you're struggling on the dating circuit and looking for a way to impress a potential mate, I can think of no better way than hosting your own Web server. Whereas luxury cars were the status symbols of the eighties and nineties, the new millennium has ushered in information management as a status symbol. As you show your date around your house, think about the captivating effect that the whirring hard drive of a Web server will have as you casually say, "And this is the server room." Trust me, if you've got a tricked out Mercedes, ditch it and get a Web server!

Truthfully, I have serious doubts that anyone but an aspiring e-business tycoon will have the need for his or her own Web server. Hosting your own Web server involves setting up a separate computer and paying a hefty monthly fee for a dedicated Internet connection. Such a connection isn't cheap, so unless you have money to burn you might want to look for another option. It's worth pointing out again that it is technically possible to use a broadband connection such as a cable modem or DSL connection to run your own Web server, but most broadband ISPs don't allow it.

On the upside, if you do have money to burn, a Web server of your own provides the most flexibility, because you can use it however you wish. Practically speaking, this means you can install any kind of special server software, such as custom Common Gateway Interface (CGI) scripts, that a traditional Web hosting service might not allow. Web hosting services tend to be very hesitant to try new things because network stability is a huge issue for them.

Paying for a Web Hosting Service

If you've ruled out the possibility of running your own Web server, then the next option you might consider is paying for a Web hosting service. This type of Web hosting service is different from your normal Internet account in that it is solely used for hosting Web pages. Literally thousands of companies offer Web hosting services, and their prices and service levels vary considerably. These are a few popular Web hosting services:

- Earthlink (*http://www.earthlink.net/*)
- Yahoo! (*http://website.yahoo.com/*)
- Hosting.com (*http://www.hosting.com/*)
- VeriSign (*http://www.networksolutions.com/*)
- WestHost (*http://www.westhost.com/*)

Note   A *domain name* is a unique name that identifies your Web site to the world. Although you can host your Web site as part of someone else's domain name, it's pretty cool to have a name that's all your own. For example, I own the domain names *michaelmorrison.com* and *michaelmorrison.net*. Domain names are somewhat like real estate because only so many of them are available. If you have a domain name in mind, I encourage you to spend a little money and register it now, assuming it's still available. To see if your domain name is available, visit VeriSign at *http://www.networksolutions.com/*, Register.com at *http://www.register.com/*, or EasyDNS at *http://www.easydns.com/*. All three companies allow you to perform domain name searches and register new names.

Try This!   Visit some of the Web hosting services mentioned in this section and do some comparison shopping to compare price against features for each service.

Having your own domain name is one of the factors that will likely affect the type of Web hosting you choose. For example, most Internet services that include built-in Web hosting don't allow you to use your own domain name. Instead, you store your Web site within a folder on the domain of the Internet provider. There's nothing wrong with your Web site having another domain name, other than that it isn't quite as succinct. And, of course, it doesn't carry the prestige of having your own dot-com.

Note   The primary parameter that affects Web hosting services is the amount of space available for Web pages. In other words, you should note the amount of storage space provided when comparison shopping among Web hosting services. Keep in mind that text takes up little space, so the space issue mainly comes into play if you're using a large number of photos or multimedia files, such as videos.

If you do decide to pay for a Web hosting service, you can expect to pay somewhere in the range of U.S.$10 to U.S.$75 per month. If you don't plan on doing any e-commerce on your site, you can easily come in on the low end of this price range. The monthly cost moves to the high end of the range when you have shopping cart features and process credit cards. Also, don't forget that there is a fee associated with registering a domain name, which you will learn about later in the chapter.

Hosting with Your Internet Account

For the majority of people who simply want a presence on the Web, the best option is to use free Web features that accompany most Internet accounts. For example, my cable modem Internet account includes 10 MB of free Web space that I can use to store a Web site. However, like most Internet services, mine doesn't allow customers to use domain names of their own. This means that Web sites appear as a folder beneath the Internet service's domain. This isn't as slick as having your own domain name, but it may serve your purposes just fine. And you can't beat the price!

Try This! Visit the Web site for your Internet service provider, or give them a call, and find out if you have any free Web space included with your account. If you do, you'll also want to find out from them how they recommend you publish pages to their Web server.

One point to keep in mind about using Web features built into your Internet account is that your Internet service provider may require you to use a standard template for your pages. This is certainly a reasonable approach for some people because it makes creating Web pages simple. On the other hand, because you're reading this book, I would guess that you're looking for a more hands-on approach that gives you the flexibility to modify and improve upon simple designs. For this reason, you will probably want to look for an option that allows you to create your own pages and then transfer them directly to the Internet service's Web server. Most Internet service providers support this option for people who, like you, are on their way to becoming HTML gurus.

Foregoing Web Hosting Entirely

If you're the kind of person who wants the utmost in privacy and is secretive to the point of compulsion, then you might consider foregoing Web hosting entirely. In this scenario, you'd create your Web pages and keep them on your local hard drive. Of course, the drawback is that you will be the only person to see your Web pages—unless you call your friends and family over to check out the pages directly on your own computer. Realistically, this isn't much of an option, because then your pages aren't really part of the World Wide Web. Nonetheless, I want you to know that I'm leaving no stone unturned in terms of giving you options for your Web pages.

Obtaining a Domain Name

Several times throughout the chapter I've alluded to the fact that you can register your own domain name and host your Web site in style. A certain air of mystery surrounds domain names and where they come from, so please allow me to take you behind the scenes and reveal the tricks of the domain name trade.

In reality, obtaining a domain name is a straightforward process. The only trick is making sure that the name is available before attempting to register it; you'd be surprised how many domain names are already taken. To find out if your domain name is available, visit one of the following Web sites:

- VeriSign (*http://www.networksolutions.com/*)

- Register.com (*http://www.register.com/*)

- EasyDNS (*http://www.easydns.com/*)

These Web sites all offer a search page that allows you to enter the name of your domain and see if it's available. Figure 9-2 shows the VeriSign domain name search page.

Figure 9-2   You can enter a domain name and check its availability on the home page of the VeriSign Web site.

Unfortunately, you'll probably find that your name is already taken. There isn't much you can do about this except try a different extension such as .net or .org, instead of .com. Keep in mind that domain names are essentially leased properties, which means that they can expire and become available again. This happened with my domain name, *michaelmorrison.com*. When I first tried to register it a few years ago, it was taken. I kept checking the status every few months—a seemingly futile effort—and I couldn't believe it the day the name came up as available. Apparently the previous owner didn't renew, so the name went back on the block.

Note   As of this writing, the available Internet domains are .com, .net, .org, .tv, .biz, .info, and .ws, as well as a bunch of country- and locale-specific extensions.

Try This! Using one of the domain name services mentioned in this section, go check and see if the domain name for your personal name is available. Or, if you aren't so concerned about having a site based upon your name, try a domain name for your business or some other name that you might like to own.

Once you've found a domain name, you can register it on one of the registration Web sites mentioned previously by entering information about yourself and paying the registration fee. Registration fees are calculated on a yearly basis, which means that you pay to reserve the domain name for years at a time.

The minimum amount of time you can reserve a domain name is one year, and the cost varies according to where you register the name and what domain name extension you are registering. There are domain name companies out there who offer special deals, such as providing discounts if you register a name for multiple years. You also may consider at some point registering a name for one of the new domains, such as .biz or .tv.

Note   The registration fees for domain names come down considerably if you're willing to register a name for a longer period of time. The longest time frame you can register a domain name is currently 10 years, which results in a considerable yearly discount.

Once you've registered your domain name, you'll need to inform your Web hosting service so it can take the appropriate steps to associate your Web pages with the domain name. Most Web hosting services will register the name for you as part of the hosting setup process if you want to handle everything in one step. However, it's important to read the fine print before committing to a Web hosting service, because some of them charge you a fee to move an existing domain name to them. Additionally, some Web hosting services have been known to register a new domain name to themselves, even when you're paying for it. The bottom line is that you need to do your homework and take on a "buyer beware" attitude when exploring Web hosting and domain name options.

Keep in mind that it's a good idea to register the name even if you aren't ready to build the Web site yet. For example, you could register your domain name and wait to build your Web pages until you finish reading this book. The significance of registering now is that your domain name is safe and secure, and you don't have to worry about someone else beating you to the punch.

Note   I'd like to point out that I don't have any affiliation with Web hosting services—or any other Internet-related services for that matter. I encourage you to do your own research to find the service solution that best meets your needs.

Selecting Web Publishing Software

Once you've decided how to host your Web site and maybe even registered a domain name, you'll need to consider the software you plan to use to publish the finished Web pages on the World Wide Web. There are two main types:

- FTP clients
- Graphical Web development tools

These terms should look familiar to you because they appeared earlier in the chapter. Graphical Web development tools are complete software environments that support every phase of Web development from HTML editing to Web page publishing. Regardless of whether you use the HTML editing features of a graphical Web development tool, you might find such a tool useful for publishing pages you've created by hand in HTML. FrontPage is a good example of a Web development tool that makes it easy to publish Web pages.

In addition to FTP clients and graphical Web development tools, you can also use a special Web publishing tool such as the Microsoft Web Publishing Wizard to publish your Web pages. As you learned in Chapter 2, the Web Publishing Wizard is essentially an FTP client designed solely for transferring Web pages to a Web server. For more information about using the Web Publishing Wizard, please refer to the step-by-step Web publishing procedure in Chapter 2.

Key Points

- It's not difficult to take Web pages that you've created on your local computer and transfer them to a Web server for the entire world to see.

- The relationship between a Web client and a Web server involves the client (Web browser) asking the Web server for a certain Web page and the server obliging by delivering the page to the client.

- Although you can certainly pay for a Web hosting service, your existing Internet service may already include enough Web space for you to publish your Web pages.

- If you want to improve your status among your geeky friends, you'll definitely want to register your own domain name for your Web site.

- Domain names are kind of like prime real estate because once a particular name is taken, it rarely changes hands; if your chosen domain name is available, it's a good idea to go ahead and register it.

- If you don't rely on a Web development environment to publish your Web pages, you can upload the pages to a Web server using a File Transfer Protocol (FTP) tool.

Gathering Information with Forms

If you ever filed your taxes prior to the widespread use of computers for tax filing, you certainly have an appreciation for how much of a pain paper forms can be. Although they serve as a reasonably efficient way to gather information in a standard manner, they are nonetheless still a headache for those of us prone to handwriting errors. They also waste an awful lot of paper. HTML offers a modern alternative to paper forms that makes it possible to create Web pages that retrieve information from a person.

HTML forms are roughly equivalent to paper forms in that they allow you to enter information and send it to a Web server for processing. In many cases, a form is designed so that the information is sent to an e-mail address. The recipient examines the information and decides what to do with it. This chapter explores the inner workings of forms and how they are created, along with how you can put them to good use in your Web pages.

Understanding Forms

The whole premise behind a Web page is that you have information that you'd like to share with the world. You code it in HTML, and people view it by using a Web browser. The central idea is that you share information with others. You probably didn't realize that the Web also works the opposite way: People can share information with you through your Web pages. This is possible thanks to *forms*, which are collections of data entry fields that you include in your Web pages. When people visit the page, they enter information into the form, and the information is subsequently collected and delivered to you. You can process the information you received and perform wondrous things—such as storing it in a database or processing it as part of an online poll.

Lingo   *Forms* are collections of data entry fields in a Web page that allow people to enter information, which is subsequently collected and delivered to you.

If you've ever ordered anything off the Web, you've probably encountered forms. They are used regularly in online shopping carts when you enter your shipping address and payment information. Another common use of forms is in personalizing Web sites to suit your own unique tastes. Figure 10-1 shows the Edit Profile page on the MSN Web site, which uses a form to allow you to enter information about yourself.

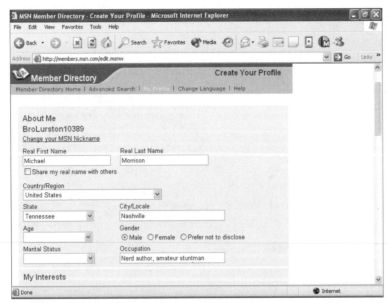

Figure 10-1   The MSN Edit Profile page uses a form as the basis for collecting personal information from MSN members.

Notice that on the MSN Edit Profile page, you type text in several text boxes. You also choose from a few drop-down menus, which are identified by the small arrows on the right of each box. For example, the Country/Region and

State fields use drop-down menus to allow you to select from existing choices. If you scroll down the page, there is a Save button, which is extremely important because it is used to submit the form data. The form gathers the information entered in the boxes and uses that data to establish your personal profile. This is an excellent use of a form, showing how one can be used in practical situations.

The *boxes* on the MSN form are referred to as *controls*, which come in various types. You will learn about the different form controls later in the chapter, but I want to take a quick moment to show you how to use a few of them in the context of a real form. To create a form, use the `<form>` tag, which requires several attributes to function properly. One is the `action` attribute, which determines what happens to the information entered on the form. There are a couple of other important `<form>` attributes, but let's jump ahead and look at code for a form:

```
<form enctype="text/plain" action="mailto:me@tailspintoys.com"
method="post">
Name:
<input type="text" name="username"/><br>
City, State:
<input type="text" name="userlocation"/><br>
Comments:
<textarea name="comments" rows="3" columns="40" wrap="">Type
your comments here!</textarea><br>
<input type="submit" value="Finished"/>
<input type="reset" value="Start Over"/>
</form>
```

Lingo   *Controls* are user interface components such as text fields and check boxes that are used to gather information in forms.

This code represents a simple form for a *guest book* that you might want to add to your Web site. A Web guest book works much like a printed guest book in that people enter their name, address, and possibly a few comments about your Web site. Figure 10-2 shows what this form looks like in action.

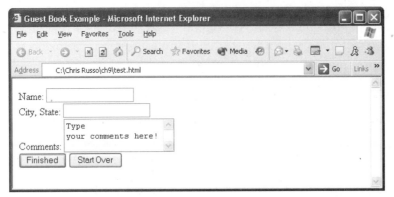

Figure 10-2   This guest book form is an example of a simple form that could use a little layout help.

Tip   The code for this example, as well as all of the examples throughout the book, is available for download from my Web site at the following URL: *http://www.michaelmorrison.com/ cbook_fshtml.html.*

As you can see in the figure, I opted for function over fashion by not adding any additional HTML code to improve the layout. The result: The form isn't pretty, but it works.

To modify this form for your own purposes and take it for a test spin, just follow these steps:

1   Substitute your e-mail address in the `action` attribute of the `<form>` tag.

2   Open the form Web page in a Web browser.

3   Fill out the form.

4   Click Finished.

After following these steps, the form data will be delivered to you by e-mail. Most Web browsers warn you before sending information for processing by a form. This is primarily a security precaution in case you've entered sensitive information, such as credit card numbers or your age. Also, the e-mail message containing the form data displays your e-mail address as the return address. Depending on who you are submitting it to, you might not want to reveal your e-mail address. The only alternative is to cancel the form submission. Figure 10-3 shows the security message that pops up when you submit a form in Internet Explorer.

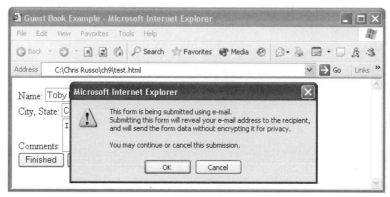

Figure 10-3   When you submit a form, as a security precaution most browsers will prompt you before sending along the information.

The guest book form sends the form information to you by e-mail, the simplest way to process the data. Figure 10-4 shows how the form information is formatted and stored in an e-mail message.

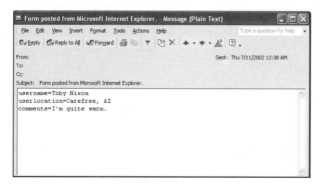

Figure 10-4   When a form is designed for processing as e-mail, information in it is carefully packaged into an e-mail message.

The e-mail in the figure highlights an important aspect of forms: Information in forms always consists of pairs of names and values. For example, in the guest book example there are three named properties that have been assigned a value. More specifically, the username property has been assigned the value Toby Nixon. Not surprisingly, this is the text the user entered in the form control named username.

Look at the form's HTML code, and you'll see that there's a control with its name attribute set to username. This technique of associating values with named controls is how form information is packaged and delivered in e-mail. It is also how information from a form is delivered to special programs that perform additional processing, as you will learn in the next section.

Don't worry if the HTML code for the guest book form doesn't make complete and total sense yet. I primarily wanted to give you a glimpse of the code for a form so that you would have a basic understanding of what goes into one.

Processing Forms with Scripts

In the guest book example form, the *form action* was set to send the form data to an e-mail address. Although this is perfectly fine for retrieving information from the user, there are many situations in which it's beneficial to process the information using a special program called a *script*. For example, the popular auction site eBay uses a Smart Search form to allow you to perform powerful searches for auction items. This search form relies on a script to carry out the search, based on the search criteria entered in the form.

Lingo   A *form action* determines what happens when the user submits a form for processing. You specify what kinds of actions are available for use with a form when you create the form.

Even though you aren't going into the details of creating your own *Common Gateway Interface* (CGI) scripts, it's worth a look at how you might use existing CGI scripts to process your forms. It turns out that there are a lot of free CGI scripts on the Web that you can use in your Web pages. First, let's take a look at how a script is used in the context of a form.

Note   Scripts used in forms are typically referred to as *CGI scripts*, because they are designed to adhere to a Web communication standard known as the Common Gateway Interface. CGI scripts are usually written in a programming language called Perl.

Using Scripts

As I mentioned previously, the `<form>` tag has an attribute named `action`. The `action` attribute was used in the guest book example to identify the e-mail address that is to receive the form information. The `action` attribute is actually more flexible than this and can be used to specify a script for processing a form. Check out the following line of code, which shows how you might process a form using a CGI script named StoreIt.cgi:

```
<form action="http://www.tailspintoys.com/cgi-bin/StoreIt.cgi">
```

In this code, the `action` attribute is set to the URL of the CGI script. When you click the Finished button for the form, the form information is delivered to the StoreIt.cgi script to be processed. The specifics of this processing are up to the script, which is why you need knowledge of a programming language such as Perl or C++ to create your own scripts. But it's also possible to use scripts that someone else has written. For example, check out the following code:

```
<form method="post"
action="/cgi-bin/demos/visitorbook/visitorbook.cgi">
```

This is the starting `<form>` tag for a CGI script that acts as a powerful guest book, which stores the guest information in a database rather than delivering it by e-mail. Of course, the visitorbook.cgi script is responsible for handling the details of storing the information in the database. This software is named Visitor-Book LE, and is made available by FreeScripts.com (*http://www.freescripts.com/*). Figure 10-5 shows what the demo form for this script looks like as you enter information into the guest book.

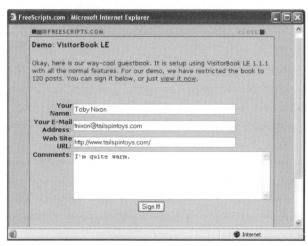

Figure 10-5   The VisitorBook LE CGI script stores form information in a database and includes a demonstration form for testing the script.

In the `<form>` tag that establishes the visitorbook.cgi script as the processor for the guest book form, the script is stored several directories beneath a directory named `cgi-bin`. This is a common directory on most Web servers and is used to store CGI scripts. In many cases, using a CGI script is as simple as placing the .cgi file in the `cgi-bin` directory and referencing the file in the `action` attribute of the `<form>` tag. Now that you have a basic understanding of how scripts are used, let's see where you can find them.

Finding Scripts

If you're the type of person who gets up at the crack of dawn on Saturdays to hunt for yard sale bargains, you'll do well when it comes to finding free CGI scripts. Good CGI scripts are even easier to find than something useful at a yard sale.

Here are several Web sites that I highly recommend visiting to find all kinds of interesting CGI scripts:

- The CGI Resource Index: *http://cgi.resourceindex.com/*
- ScriptSearch.com: *http://www.scriptsearch.com/*
- Matt's Script Archive: *http://www.scriptarchive.com/*
- FreeScripts.com: *http://www.freescripts.com/*
- CGI City: *http://www.icthus.net/CGI-City/*

Most of the CGI scripts available on these Web sites are free for you to use. Just make sure that you credit the author appropriately if the documentation for the script mentions it. Often, script authors simply ask you to notify them of your site so they can provide a link to it; they see it as a feather in their cap that someone is using their script. It's essentially a win-win situation.

Try This! Visit some of the script Web sites mentioned in this section, and see if you can find any interesting scripts for use in your own Web pages. Keep in mind that scripts are designed to do a lot more than just process forms, so you might find some scripts that carry out some surprisingly useful tasks outside of forms.

Borrowing Scripts

Unless you're running your own Web server, you may find that your Web hosting service doesn't allow the use of custom CGI scripts. There are a number of reasons why it might impose this restriction, the most important being the security risk of having a custom application running rampant on its servers. Some Web hosting services offer CGI scripts, which is ideal because the scripts are probably free and guaranteed to work with the Web server. If your Web hosting service doesn't allow custom scripts and doesn't offer any scripts that serve your needs, consider using a *form hosting service*.

Lingo A *form hosting service* is a special service that handles forms for Web sites and provides the CGI scripts that process the forms.

When you use a form hosting service, you typically use both a form and a CGI script that is stored at the service.

Here are several form hosting services that you might consider for your form processing needs:

■   Response-O-Matic: *http://www.response-o-matic.com/*

■   Responders.com: *http://www.responders.com/*

■   FormSite.com: *http://www.formsite.com/*

■   HostedScripts.com: *http://pages.hostedscripts.com/*

Most of these services are free. They may be worth checking into if you plan to use forms throughout your Web pages and you can't host your own scripts. On the other hand, if you don't mind receiving form information by e-mail with no frills, you can forego scripts completely. It's ultimately up to your individual needs.

Getting to Know Form Controls

As you now know, forms consist of entry fields such as text boxes and check boxes, as well as buttons. These form elements are called controls, and they are the building blocks of forms. A form without any controls is not a form; it's kind of like a sentence without words. There are several different controls that you can use in the creation of forms. Each is designed to collect a certain type of information from the user.

Here are the controls available for you to use in creating forms:

■   Text box

■   Password box

■   Text area

■   Check box

■   Radio button

■   Menu

■   Button

The next few sections examine these controls in more detail, including how to use them in forms. After learning more about them, you will create a complete form that shows how they work in a practical application.

The Text Box and Password Box Controls

The text box and password box controls allow the user to enter one line of text. The only difference between the two controls is that the password box control hides the typed text by showing bullet-characters instead of the real characters. This allows you to enter confidential information such as passwords without someone being able to look over your shoulder and see what you've typed. However, no other security is employed by the password box control, so the Web page is not inherently secure and could be vulnerable to hackers.

Note   Information on a Web page that is not secure is transmitted in an unencrypted form that Web hackers could feasibly view. Secure Web pages are encrypted, which means that even if someone hacks into the information, he or she won't be able to read it without a considerable amount of skill, patience, and ingenuity. A secure Web page is like the newer cordless telephones that encrypt a conversation digitally before sending it between the handset and the base. This prevents nosy people with scanner radios from eavesdropping on their neighbors' conversations.

You use the `<input>` tag to create both text boxes and password boxes. Each control is differentiated by the `type` attribute of the `<input>` tag, which you set to either `text` or `password`. In addition to the `type` attribute, most form controls also have `name` and `value` attributes for identifying the name of the control and its initial value, if any. This name/value pair is delivered to the Web server upon submitting a form and, if a CGI script was named in the `action` attribute, this name/value pair is processed by that script. Here is an example of creating a text box control using the `<input>` tag:

```
<input type="text" name="username" value=""/>
```

This code might be used to create a text box that allows someone to enter a user name for access to a Web site. It might also make sense to add a password box:

```
<input type="password" name="userpass" value=""/>
```

Notice that the type of the control is set to `password` in this example, and the name of the control is assigned a unique value (`userpass`). Also, the `value` attribute in both controls is set to empty (indicated by the pair of double quotes), which results in the controls having no initial values. This is actually the default setting of the `value` attribute, but I set it explicitly to show you how it's done.

Two other attributes are of interest with respect to text boxes and password boxes: `size` and `maxlength`. They establish the size of the box in characters and the maximum number of characters that can be entered in the box. More specifically, the `size` attribute determines how many characters can be *seen* in the box on the screen, while the `maxlength` attribute determines how many characters can be *entered* in the box. Here are the text box and password box examples with the `size` and `maxlength` attributes set:

```
User Name:
<input type="text" name="username" value="" size="12"
maxlength="12"/><br>
Password:
<input type="password" name="userpass" value="" size="8"
maxlength="8"/>
```

In this code, the text box is 12 characters in size and the password box is only 8 characters in size. Figure 10-6 shows how these two controls look when added to an empty form.

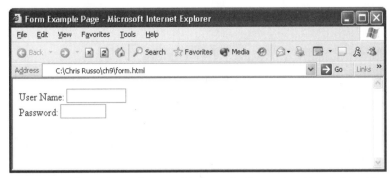

Figure 10-6   The text box and password box controls allow you to retrieve text input from the user in a form.

If you want to allow the user to enter more than a single line of text, a text box is not your best option. However, there is a form control that handles this chore, which you will learn about next.

The Text Area Control

For those occasions when you want to allow the user to enter several lines of text, the text area control is the control of choice. It can accommodate several lines of text and automatically adds scroll bars if the user enters more text than can visibly fit in the control. To create a text area control, use the `<textarea>` tag along with a few attributes.

The familiar `name` attribute is used to name the control, and the `rows` and `cols` attributes set the size of the control. The value of the `rows` attribute should be set to the number of lines of text that can fit in the control, while the `cols` attribute specifies the maximum width of text in the control, in characters. An additional attribute, `wrap`, causes the text to automatically wrap to the next line when the user types beyond the width of the control. It isn't necessary to assign an actual value to the `wrap` attribute.

The text area control is unique among form controls because it doesn't use the `value` attribute. And, unlike the other form controls, the text area control requires a closing `</textarea>` tag to complete the control in HTML code. This allows you to initialize the text in the control by placing text between the starting and closing `<textarea>` tags. Here is an example of how to create a text area control that is initialized with a short sentence:

```
<textarea name="comments" rows="4" cols="40" wrap="">
Please enter your comments here.
</textarea>
```

This code could be used to create a comment box on a form that gives the user room to enter several lines of text. Specifically, the text area control is set up so that it can accommodate four lines of text with each line 40 characters wide. This control is shown in Figure 10-7.

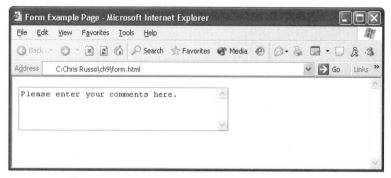

Figure 10-7   The text area control allows the user to enter multiple lines of text that you can retrieve.

> **Note**   A text area control can hold up to 32,700 characters, which is quite a lot of text. If you have a chatty aunt who is typing that much information into a form on a family Web site, you may need to just give her a call instead of communicating by form.

The Check Box Control

If you need to prompt the user for a response that has an answer of *Yes* or *No* or *True* or *False*, you might consider using a check box control. It displays a simple box that the user can click to select or clear. The `<input>` tag is used to create check box controls, along with the familiar `type`, `name`, and `value` attributes. For check box controls, set the `type` attribute to `checkbox`. There is also a `checked` attribute that you can use to indicate that a check box control should be initially selected. You don't need to set a specific value for the `checked` attribute.

Keep in mind that the only information displayed for a check box control is the check box, even if you set the `value` attribute. The significance of the `value` attribute is that it's delivered to the Web server when a form is submitted if the control has been checked. If you don't set the `value` attribute, a value of "on" is sent to the Web server if the control is checked, which indicates that the check box control has been turned on. Although this works fine if you are using a check box control by itself, it presents a problem if you are using the control as part of a group. You will learn about check box grouping shortly. For now, take a look at this code, which creates a single check box control:

```
<input type="checkbox" name="emaillist" checked=""/>
Check the box to join our e-mail list.
```

In this code, a check box control prompts users to join an e-mail list. Notice that the actual text prompt is entered just after the `<input>` tag. Figure 10-8 shows what this control looks like in action.

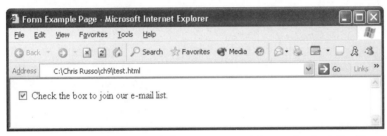

Figure 10-8   The check box control allows you to prompt the user for simple Yes/No or True/False information.

As previously mentioned, it's possible to group several check boxes as a set. This is useful if you have multiple pieces of related information that you want the user to be able to turn on and off on a form. When you use check box controls in a group, specify the same value for the `name` attribute for all of the controls, and then set unique values for the `value` attribute of each control. When the user makes his or her selections and submits the form, each of the checked values is passed along to the server. Here is an example of how you might use several check box controls in a group:

```
<input type="checkbox" name="addons" value="sunroof"/>Sun roof
<input type="checkbox" name="addons" value="alloywhls"/>Alloy wheels
<input type="checkbox" name="addons" value="heatseats"/>Heated seats
<input type="checkbox" name="addons" value="abs"/>ABS
<input type="checkbox" name="addons" value="spoiler"/>Rear spoiler
```

This code creates a set of check box controls that might be handy on a car shopping Web page, where the potential buyer enters add-ons for a new car. Figure 10-9 shows what these controls look like in a form.

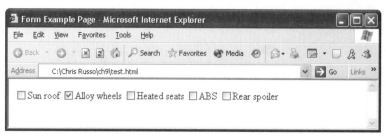

Figure 10-9   Multiple check box controls can be used as a set to prompt the user for multiple pieces of information.

The Radio Button Control

Although you can select multiple pieces of information from a group of options presented in check box controls, you may want to limit the selection to one item in certain situations. This is where the radio button control comes into play. It is designed for use in groups, but you can select, or turn on, only one control at any given time. The radio button control got its name from old car stereos that had a row of buttons you could set to different radio stations. The trick was that when you pushed one button it would automatically release the previously pushed button, so that only one button was pushed at a time. If you've never seen this type of car stereo, be thankful because they weren't very user-friendly.

You create a group of radio button controls in the same manner that you create groups of check box controls. As with check box controls, you create a radio button control using the `<input>` tag. However, you must set the `type` attribute to `radio`. To create a group of radio buttons, make the `name` attribute for each control the same, and then provide unique values for each `value` attribute. You can set the `checked` attribute for one of the controls if you'd like it to be set initially. The idea behind a group of radio buttons is to have just one of them set, so it's a good idea to set one of them initially as a default selection using the `checked` attribute.

Like check box controls, radio button controls appear on the page as individual graphical icons, with no text. To make each control meaningful to the viewer, you need to include text next to it. Here is an example of the code required to create a group of radio buttons:

```
<input type="radio" name="size" value="s"/>Small
<input type="radio" name="size" value="m" checked=""/>Medium
<input type="radio" name="size" value="l"/>Large
<input type="radio" name="size" value="xl"/>Extra large
```

This code creates a set of controls that might be useful in allowing the user to select a pizza size for an order on a pizza delivery Web page. Figure 10-10 shows what these radio button controls look like in a form.

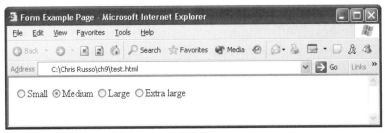

Figure 10-10 The radio button control allows you to create groups of mutually exclusive items—a fancy way of saying that only one item in a group can be selected at a time.

The Menu Control

The menu control accomplishes roughly the same task as the radio button control; it allows the user to select from a group of options. But the items associated with a menu control appear in a drop-down list that the user reveals by clicking the arrow, much like the menu that appears when you click File or Edit in a desktop application. Also, a single menu control houses all of the items that a user can select. You don't have to do anything special to associate them as a group, as you do with the check box and radio button controls.

> **Note** HTML menu controls are identical to the graphical user interface controls, known as combo boxes and drop-down lists, found in operating systems such as Windows.

To generate a menu control, use the `<select>` tag to first create the menu. It's important to use the `name` attribute with this tag to give the menu a name that will be associated with the menu selections when the form is processed. You can also specify the height of the unopened menu, in lines of text, by using the `size` attribute. By default, menus are one line of text, meaning that only one item is visible in the menu when it is not opened.

The other attribute you might use with the menu control is the `multiple` attribute, which specifies that multiple items in the menu can be selected, as opposed to allowing one item only to be selected at a time. Here is an example of how you might start a simple menu with the `<select>` tag:

```
<select name="color">
```

Now that wasn't too difficult, was it? The next step in setting up a menu is to create the individual menu items, using the `<option>` tag and its `value` attribute. The `value` attribute of the `<option>` tag assigns a unique name to each menu item. The following code reveals how to put together a complete menu:

```
Select a color:
<select name="color">
```

```
<option value="red">Fire engine red</option>
<option value="yellow">Canary yellow</option>
<option value="blue">Ocean blue</option>
<option value="green">Forest green</option>
<option value="black">Black onyx</option>
<option value="gray">Gun metal gray</option>
<option value="white">Pearl white</option>
</select>
```

The first thing to notice about this code is that the phrase *Select a color:* is added before the `<select>` tag to indicate the purpose of the menu. The `<option>` tags are used within the starting and ending `<select>` tags to identify each of the items in the menu.

Tip   The `size` attribute of the `<select>` tag can be used to make an unopened menu larger. The default size of 1, for example, means that the menu shows one line of text only. Of course, all menus open to reveal a drop-down list upon being clicked.

Figure 10-11 shows a menu control after it's been clicked.

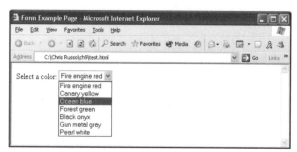

Figure 10-11   When you click a menu control, it opens to reveal a drop-down list of items that can be selected.

The Button Controls

The form controls you've learned about are important in establishing a means of retrieving information from the user. Yet none of them provides control over the entire form. Here's where the button controls come into play. You can use two types of form buttons: Submit and Reset. It's important for every form to have a Submit button, which sends the form data to the Web server for processing. The Reset button, on the other hand, is used to reset a form to its default setting. It's the equivalent of obtaining a new piece of paper when you're filling out a paper form. Although it's not as critical as the Submit button, you'll want to include a Reset button on your forms as a convenience to the user.

You create a Submit button by using the `<input>` tag and setting the `type` attribute to `submit`. Set the text that will appear on the button by setting the `value` attribute. Here is an example of creating a Submit button:

```
<input type="submit" value="Place Order"/>
```

This example might apply to an order entry form where the user clicks the Submit button to enter an order in an online store. To add a Reset button to the same form you use the `<input>` tag again, but this time you set the `type` attribute to `reset`. Here's an example of how you might code the Reset button:

```
<input type="reset" value="Start Over"/>
```

You can see that the Reset button is created the same way as the Submit button is. Figure 10-12 shows how both buttons appear within a form.

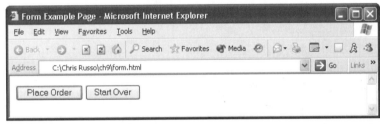

Figure 10-12   The Submit and Reset buttons allow you to submit a form for processing and reset the form controls to their default values, respectively.

To make your button controls spiffier, use the `style` attribute with the `<button>` tag. The `style` attribute uses style sheet settings to alter the buttons' appearance. You will learn about style sheets in Chapter 12, "Style Sheet Basics," so for now I'll show you just enough to jazz up the form buttons. The `<button>` tag is necessary for creating buttons with a custom appearance. When you use the `<button>` tag to create Submit and Reset buttons, you must set the `type`, `name`, and `value` attributes all to either `submit` or `reset`. The button text is placed between starting and ending `<button>` tags. If this all sounds a bit confusing, then hopefully the following clears things up:

```
<button type="submit" name="submit" value="submit"
style="font:18pt Helvetica; background:green">Place Order
</button>
<button type="reset" name="reset" value="reset"
style="font:18pt Helvetica; background:red">Start Over
</button>
```

This code uses the `<button>` tag and `style` attribute to customize the font and background color of the Submit and Reset buttons.

Finally, you can customize the appearance of buttons with images. Just as you place the text of a button between the starting and ending `<button>` tags, you can place an image between these tags. The following code demonstrates how you might add an image to a Submit button:

```
<button type="submit" name="submit" value="submit"
style="font:18pt Helvetica; background:green">
<img src="Order.gif">Place Order
</button>
```

This code is similar to that of the previously customized Submit button. In fact, the only difference is the addition of the `<img>` tag between the starting and ending `<button>` tags. Adding an image to a button control is that simple!

Creating Forms

We've finally gotten to the point of actually creating a complete form that can do something useful. The form you will create in this section is a feedback form that allows your Web site visitors to leave detailed information about your site by way of the form. In addition to reinforcing what you've learned throughout the chapter, it should serve as a practical example of how to create complete forms with different types of form controls.

Establishing the Form's Action

As you may recall, forms are created by using the `<form>` tag and a few attributes to describe the form. The `action` attribute is important because it determines how a form is processed. The `action` attribute is often set to a CGI script that resides on your Web server. If you don't have access to a CGI script and want to receive form information by e-mail, set the `action` attribute to your e-mail address by preceding the address with the word `mailto` followed by a colon. You will see how this is accomplished soon.

You also need to be concerned with the `method` attribute of the `<form>` tag. The `method` attribute determines how information entered in the form is delivered for processing. If you specify `post` for this value, the data will be delivered to the CGI script or e-mail address specified in the `action` attribute.

The other setting you can use for the method attribute is `get`, which sends the form information to the Web server as part of the URL for the Web page with the form. This *get* technique is commonly used by search engines. It's why you often see a huge line of jumbled text in the address bar of your browser when you perform a search. For the purpose of this chapter, we're going to stick with the *post* approach to processing form information.

If you opt to have data delivered to an e-mail address, I recommend using one other attribute of the `<form>` tag: `enctype`. This attribute allows you to specify how the data is formatted for processing. In the case of e-mail, it's good to format the information as plain text; just set the `enctype` attribute to `text/plain`. The result of this setting is that the information will appear directly in the body of the e-mail message in plain text.

Here is the complete `<form>` tag for the feedback form:

```
<form enctype="text/plain" action="mailto:me@tailspintoys.com"
method="post">
```

> **Tip** Don't forget to plug in your own e-mail address in the `action` attribute.

Of course, this form isn't of much use without controls, which are discussed next.

Laying Out the Controls

The heart of any form is the controls used to obtain information from the user. The feedback form is no different in this regard. The first step is to find out what kind of feedback the user would like to provide. You want to know if this is a happy or irate user. That's a good opportunity to use a set of radio buttons, as the following code demonstrates:

```
What is the nature of your comment?<br>
<input type="radio" name="nature" value="praise" checked=""/>Praise
<input type="radio" name="nature" value="suggestion"/>Suggestion
<input type="radio" name="nature" value="problem"/>Problem
<input type="radio" name="nature" value="complaint"/>Complaint
```

This code creates a set of radio buttons to find out the nature of the user's comment. Notice that I've cleverly made the Praise button the default option, which might give the user a hint that positive feedback is preferred and expected. It's also important to find out what specifically the user wants to leave feedback about. This is a great place to use a menu, as the following code reveals:

```
What specifically would you like to comment on?<br>
<select name="specific">
<option value="website">Web site</option>
<option value="company">Company</option>
<option value="products">Products</option>
<option value="services">Services</option>
<option value="other">Other</option>
</select>
```

There's nothing tricky about this code; it's just a basic menu with several items to select from. Now that you have some information about the feedback, you can give the user an opportunity to leave detailed comments with a text area. The following code shows how the text area is created:

```
Please enter your comments below:<br>
<textarea name="comments" rows="6" cols="60"
wrap=""></textarea>
```

As you can see, the text area gives the user room to enter six lines of text that are 60 characters wide. Of course, if you run across a particularly verbal person, the text area will automatically use scroll bars to allow for more text.

You're not likely to encourage anonymous feedback, so the next step is obtaining contact information, including the user's name, e-mail address, phone number, and fax number. Text box controls work well for this, but it's somewhat difficult to line up the controls properly with labels to the left of them. For this reason, a table comes in handy as a layout tool for aligning the text box controls, as the following code shows:

```
How can we get in touch with you?<br>
<table>
<tr>
  <td>Name:</td>
  <td><input type="text" name="name" size="40"/></td>
</tr>
<tr>
  <td>E-mail:</td>
  <td><input type="text" name="email" size="40"/></td>
</tr>
<tr>
  <td>Phone #:</td>
  <td><input type="text" name="phone" size="20"/></td>
</tr>
<tr>
  <td>Fax #:</td>
  <td><input type="text" name="fax" size="20"/></td>
</tr>
</table>
```

The purpose of the table in this code is to align the controls with each other, greatly improving the table's appearance. This will be clearer when you see the end result of the form.

The last piece of necessary information is the site visitor's preference about being contacted quickly in response to his or her feedback. This requires a Yes or No answer, so a check box control is the obvious choice. The following code shows how a check box control is used to obtain this information:

```
<input type="checkbox" name="asap"/>Please contact me as soon as
possible regarding this feedback.
```

No control is complete without a Submit button. And while you're adding a Submit button, you might as well throw in a Reset button so that the user can clear the form. Here are these two buttons for the feedback form:

```
<input type="submit" value="Submit Feedback"/>
<input type="reset" value="Start Over"/>
```

That concludes the controls for the feedback form. You had already learned the ins and outs of each one, so this section was pretty straightforward.

The Complete Form

Before you move on to test the feedback form, it's worthwhile to see the HTML code for the complete form. It shows all of the different form controls together and in context. Here is the complete code for the feedback form:

```
<form enctype="text/plain" action="mailto:me@tailspintoys.com"
method="post">
<p>
What is the nature of your comment?<br>
<input type="radio" name="nature" value="praise"
checked=""/>Praise
<input type="radio" name="nature" value="suggestion"/>Suggestion
<input type="radio" name="nature" value="problem"/>Problem
<input type="radio" name="nature" value="complaint"/>Complaint
</p>
<p>
What specifically would you like to comment on?<br>
<select name="specific">
<option value="website">Web site</option>
<option value="company">Company</option>
<option value="products">Products</option>
<option value="services">Services</option>
<option value="other">Other</option>
</select>
</p>
<p>
Please enter your comments below:<br>
<textarea name="comments" rows="6" cols="60"
wrap=""></textarea>
</p>
<p>
How can we get in touch with you?<br>
<table>
<tr>
  <td>Name:</td>
  <td><input type="text" name="name" size="40"/></td>
```

```
</tr>
<tr>
  <td>E-mail:</td>
  <td><input type="text" name="email" size="40"/></td>
</tr>
<tr>
  <td>Phone #:</td>
  <td><input type="text" name="phone" size="20"/></td>
</tr>
<tr>
  <td>Fax #:</td>
  <td><input type="text" name="fax" size="20"/></td>
</tr>
</table>
</p>
<p>
<input type="checkbox" name="asap"/>Please contact me as soon as
possible regarding this feedback.
</p>
<p>
<input type="submit" value="Submit Feedback"/>
<input type="reset" value="Start Over"/>
</p>
</form>
```

Granted, most of this code is repeated from the control layout section, but it helps to see all the code together. Note that the paragraph tags (<p> </p>) are used to provide space between each section of the form. I know you're itching to see the completed form in a Web browser, so let's take it for a test drive.

Try This! Insert your own e-mail address in the `action` attribute of the `<form>` tag for the feedback form so that you can test the form and receive the resulting e-mail.

Testing the Form

As you know, the feedback form is designed to obtain information from a visitor to your Web site and pass it along to you by e-mail. Figure 10-13 shows the feedback form as it first appears when you open the page in a Web browser.

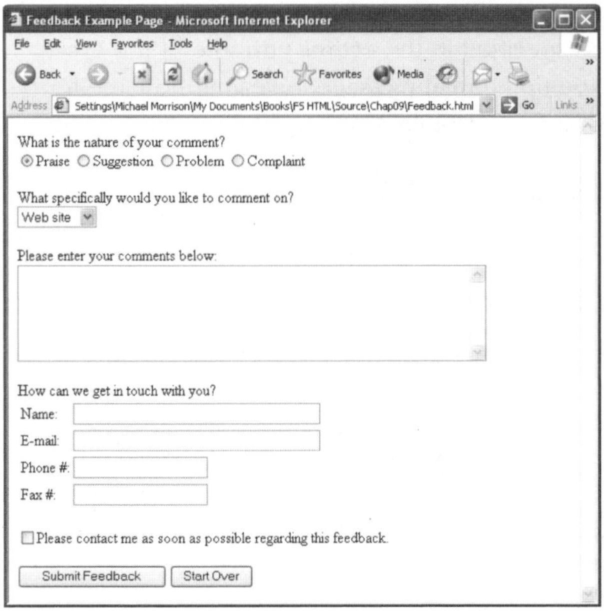

Figure 10-13   Visitors to your Web site leave feedback that is sent to you by e-mail.

I took the liberty of filling out the form and submitting it by clicking Submit Feedback. The information I entered is shown in Figure 10-14.

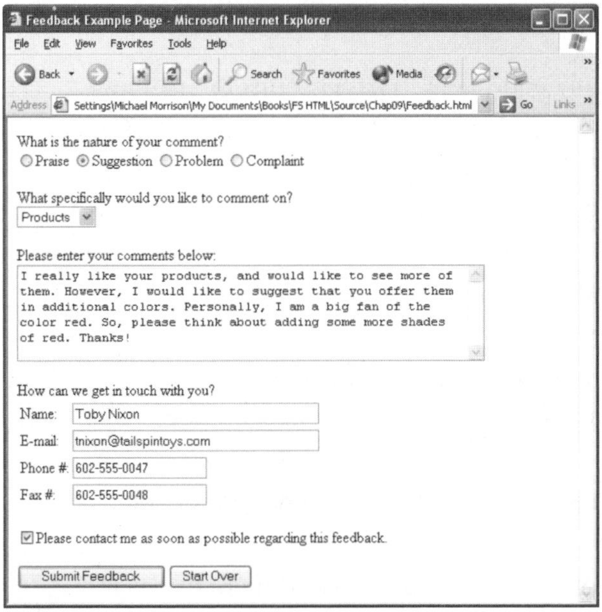

Figure 10-14   Using the feedback form is as simple as entering information and clicking Submit Feedback.

After the feedback is submitted, it's packaged into an e-mail message and delivered to the e-mail address specified in the `action` attribute of the `<form>` tag. Figure 10-15 shows the resulting e-mail message, revealing how the form information is combined with form control names to yield name/value pairs.

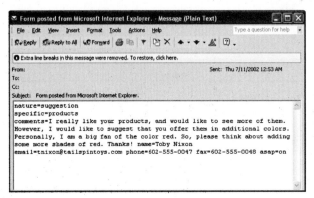

Figure 10-15   The information in the feedback form is packaged into an e-mail message and delivered to you.

To use this form on your Web site, simply change the e-mail address in the `action` attribute of the `<form>` tag to your own. You're now set to receive feedback from visitors to your site.

Key Points

- Forms in HTML are roughly equivalent to paper forms in that they allow you to enter information. Unlike paper forms, however, you send them to Web servers for processing.

- Controls are user interface objects placed on forms to gather information from the user.

- The simplest way to handle the submission of form data is to have it sent to an e-mail address.

- To perform advanced form processing, you'll need to use a CGI script, which is a special program that processes form data and does something useful with it.

- A form's action determines what a form does when the user submits the form data for processing.

- Forms can be as simple or as complex as you need them to be, and you can perform as little or much processing as necessary on the resulting form data.

Chapter 11

Dynamic HTML

In years past, it was expected that you needed complex, heavy-duty programming tools to create interactive software applications, not to mention substantial knowledge of intricate programming languages. But the advent of Web scripting means that you can create interactive Web pages with relative ease. This chapter will explore the technologies involved in Web scripting and will show you how to use them to add interactivity to your Web pages. You will find out that the merger of HTML and other Web tools make up what's known as DHTML, which you learned in Chapter 1, "An Introduction to HTML, DHTML, and XML," stands for *Dynamic HTML*. You will also create some of the most interesting Web pages covered in the entire book.

The Least You Need to Know About Scripts

In DHTML, *scripts* are used to access styles and content of elements in a Web page. To develop your own custom scripts, you'll need to use a scripting language such as JavaScript or VBScript. Instead of teaching you a scripting language—which would be definitely beyond the scope of this chapter—I'll bestow upon you some short scripts that you can use in your own Web pages. Script programming isn't terribly hard to learn, but I'd wait to tackle it until after you get comfortable with HTML.

Lingo *Scripts* are small programs that are embedded directly in Web pages, and that typically interact with or manipulate content on the pages.

Scripting Languages

The two main scripting languages in use are JavaScript and VBScript. Netscape originally developed JavaScript as a scripting version of Sun Microsystems' popular Java programming language. Likewise, Microsoft created VBScript as a scripting version of their popular Visual Basic programming language. JavaScript and VBScript perform essentially the same tasks, so the selection of a language has more to do with your programming background (if any) than the language. In other words, if you've used BASIC, you may find VBScript easier to learn. The one downside to VBScript is that it's supported in Internet Explorer only, while JavaScript is supported in several browsers.

In this chapter, you'll use JavaScript to create DHTML Web pages. Again, don't worry too much about the details of each script; I'll point out the important parts to give you a feel for how they work. You may be surprised at how simple some scripts can be. If you happen to have any experience with the Java or C++ programming languages, you'll find JavaScript somewhat familiar.

Using Scripts in Web Pages

As you might guess, there's a special HTML tag used to add scripts to Web pages. The `<script>` tag encapsulates scripting code. Some older Web browsers don't support scripts, so you have to perform a little trick when including script code in the `<script>` tag. Just enclose the script code inside an HTML comment, as the following example demonstrates:

```
<script language="JavaScript">
<!-- Hide the script from old browsers
alert("Hello!");
// Stop hiding the script -->
</script>
```

In this code segment, the `<!--` code that signifies the start of a comment is used just before the single line of script code. Following the script code is the `-->` code that ends the comment. The script code displays an alert message of Hello! as shown in Figure 11-1.

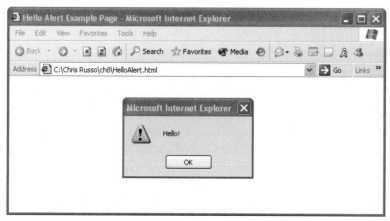

Figure 11-1 The Hello Alert Example Web page shows how to create a simple script that displays an alert message.

In addition to appearing in the `<script>` tag, you can also take advantage of scripting code directly in the attributes of traditional HTML tags. You will learn how to do this in the next section, which introduces you to event handling.

Tip The code for this example, as well as all of the examples throughout the book, is available for download from my Web site at the following URL: *http://www.michaelmorrison.com/ cbook_fshtml.html.*

Responding to Events

The primary way that a DHTML Web page provides interactivity is by responding to actions taken by the user. For example, if the user clicks the mouse button or presses a key on the keyboard, the page might respond by changing the appearance of text on the page. A user interaction such as a mouse click or key press is known as an *event,* and the process of a script taking action based on an event is known as *event handling.* You associate event-handling script code with elements on a Web page using special attributes.

Lingo An *event* is a user interaction such as a key press or mouse click that a script might want to know about and respond to. When a script responds to an event, the process is known as *event handling.*

Here are some of the commonly used event attributes that come in handy in DHTML and when they occur with respect to a Web page element:

- `onload`—Browser loads the element.
- `onkeydown`—User presses a key.

- onkeyup—User releases a key.

- onclick—User clicks the element with the left mouse button.

- ondblclick—User double-clicks the element with the left mouse button.

- onmousedown—User presses either mouse button while the mouse pointer is over the element.

- onmouseup—User releases either mouse button while the mouse pointer is over the element.

- onmouseover—User moves the mouse pointer into the boundaries of the element.

- onmousemove—User moves the mouse pointer while the pointer is over the element.

- onmouseout—User moves the mouse pointer out of the boundaries of the element.

As you can see, you use event attributes to handle common user input events such as mouse clicks and key presses. You associate script code with an event by assigning the event attribute to the script code, like this:

```
<h2 onclick="this.style.color = 'blue';">
I turn blue when clicked.
</h2>
```

In this example, you assign script code to the onclick event attribute, which means that the code runs in response to the user clicking the left mouse button on the text. The script code sets the color of the text to blue. So, interactivity is added to normally bland text by changing the color of the text in response to a mouse click.

Getting to Know the Document Object Model

In the script event example in the previous section, you saw what will happen when the user initiates the following script code with the click of the mouse button:

```
this.style.color = 'blue';
```

It's fairly easy to see that the color style property of the text is being set, but the code is a little strange looking because it has a few pieces of information you haven't seen before. The color style property is preceded by the code this.style., specifying that the color is for this text element. The style part of this code identifies the style attribute in which the color property is typically used. For example, the following code clarifies how a color style property is usually set using *cascading style sheets* (CSS), which is the basis for changing text styles in script code:

```
style="color:blue"
```

Lingo *Cascading Style Sheets*, or *CSS*, is a technology used to inject advanced style and for-matting into Web page content. You learn a great deal more about CSS in Chapter 12, "Style Sheet Basics," but for now it's important to understand that CSS is used in scripts to control the appear-ance of Web page content.

This code is different from the earlier example because it applies to HTML content, as opposed to script code. The reason for showing you this code is to illustrate the correlation between style properties and scripting. You now know why the `color` property in the script code is preceded by the word `style`, but you may not have known that the word `this` means that a script applies to the current element. By appending the `style.color` code to `this`, you are saying that you want to set the `color` property of the `style` attribute for the given text element. If I've thoroughly confused you, just understand that script code is capable of manipulating any part of a Web page. Therefore you must clearly identify the element to which an attribute or property applies.

Exposing the pieces of content on a Web page as objects that can be refer-enced in script code is performed in a Web browser by the *Document Object Model*, or *DOM*. The DOM essentially creates a programmatic interface around all of the content in a Web page, making it possible for any part to be accessed and modified with script code.

Lingo The *Document Object Model*, or *DOM*, provides a programmatic interface for accessing parts of a Web page, which allows you to select and apply dynamic styles to individual elements on a page.

The DOM consists of a hierarchy of objects that describes every bit of con-tent in a Web page. When referencing content in script code, you identify the hierarchy of DOM objects by separating each object with a period (.). That's why I punctuated the words `this`, `style`, and `color` with periods in the previous example; `color` is part of the `style` object, while `style` is part of the `this` object.

To give you an example of how to reference an object using the DOM, take a look at the following example code:

```
alert(window.location);
```

This code shows how to display the URL of the current Web page in an alert window. The word `location` specifies a property of the `window` object that stores the current Web page's URL. Figure 11-2 shows the results of this Web page.

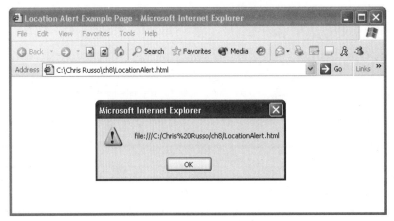

Figure 11-2   The Location Alert Example Web page shows how to display the URL of the current Web page in an alert window.

Your head is probably spinning from all this talk of objects and the DOM, so I won't go into more detail. I don't expect you to become a DOM expert in the span of a few minutes. My main goal is to lay down a few ground rules so when you see scripts during the remainder of the chapter, you won't totally be in the dark.

Working with Dynamic Styles

Earlier in this chapter, you learned that you can handle events that are created in response to user interactions such as mouse clicks and key presses. Event attributes represent perhaps the easiest way to add dynamic styles to Web pages. Here is an example of how to change the color of text when the user clicks it with the mouse.

```
<h3 onclick="this.style.color = 'red';">Click me, I dare you!</h3>
```

This code is similar to the example you saw earlier in the chapter, but I wanted to show it to you again now that you have a better understanding of script code. Here is a more dramatic example showing how to apply a dynamic style whenever the mouse pointer is dragged over text:

```
<div onmouseover="this.style.fontSize = '20pt';
this.style.color = 'green'">
Drag the mouse over me to see me get larger and turn green with envy.</div>
```

In this example, the font size of the text increases to 20 points, and the color changes to green. This code is interesting because changing the font size increases the amount of space that the text occupies.

To better understand how dynamic styles work, take a look at the following code. It includes the two style examples you just saw, along with another awesome dynamic style:

```
<html>
<head>
  <title>Dynamic Styles Example Page</title>

  <script language="JavaScript">
  <!-- Hide the script from old browsers
  function StartRainbow() {
    window.setInterval("Rainbow()", 100);
  }

  function Rainbow() {
    if (rainbow.style.color == 'red')
      rainbow.style.color = 'green';
    else if (rainbow.style.color == 'green')
      rainbow.style.color = 'blue';
    else if (rainbow.style.color == 'blue')
      rainbow.style.color = 'yellow';
    else if (rainbow.style.color == 'yellow')
      rainbow.style.color = 'orange';
    else if (rainbow.style.color == 'orange')
      rainbow.style.color = 'purple';
    else
      rainbow.style.color = 'red';
  }
  // Stop hiding the script -->
  </script>
</head>

<body style="background-color:white" onload="StartRainbow()">
  <h1>Dynamic Styles Example Page</h1>

  <h3 onclick="this.style.color = 'red';">Click me, I dare you!</h3>
  <div onmouseover="this.style.fontSize = '20pt';
  this.style.color = 'green'">
  Drag the mouse over me to see me get larger and turn green
  with envy.</div>
  <div id="rainbow">
  This text appears in a rainbow of colors.
  </div>
</body>
</html>
```

Given your limited knowledge of scripting, this Web page is admittedly quite ambitious. However, the script code isn't too hard to understand and can always be entered into your pages verbatim without understanding every detail.

Try This!   Try a different font size (larger!) and maybe even a different color for the second sentence in the example ("Drag the mouse..."). Take note of how easy it is to get different dynamic effects just by tweaking a few values.

In addition to the two style examples you worked through earlier, this page includes a dynamic style that yields an animated rainbow effect. Near the bottom of the code you'll notice a `<div>` tag with its `id` attribute set to `"rainbow"`. The script code in the head of the page uses this identifier to reference the `<div>` text and change its color every 1/10 of a second (100 milliseconds). Two *script functions*—small self-contained scripts—are defined in the `<script>` tag for the page.

Lingo   *Script functions* are self-contained chunks of script code that carry out different tasks and can be reused throughout a Web page.

The `StartRainbow()` function sets a timer for the page that calls the other function, `Rainbow()`, every 1/10 of a second. The `Rainbow()` function checks the current color of the text and then sets it to another color. If you picture this code running every 1/10 of a second, you can visualize the animated rainbow effect. The script code begins, thanks to the `onload` event attribute in the `<body>` tag, which is set so that the `StartRainbow()` function runs when the page is loaded.

Note   One neat aspect of the script code in the Dynamic Styles Example Web page is that you can enter the code into your own Web pages and apply it to virtually any text. All you do is set the `id` of the text element to `"rainbow"`. You also need to make sure that you paste the script code into the head of the Web page.

Figure 11-3 shows the Dynamic Styles Example Web page when it's first being loaded in Internet Explorer.

Figure 11-3 The Dynamic Styles Example Web page demonstrates several different techniques for using dynamic styles.

When you click the first line of text, it changes to red. When you drag the mouse pointer over the second line of text, it becomes larger and turns green. The animated rainbow effect on the third line of text is somewhat difficult to capture in a figure. So Figure 11-4 shows the Dynamic Styles page after I clicked, dragged, and otherwise interacted with the page.

Figure 11-4 After clicking and dragging the mouse pointer over text in the Dynamic Styles Example Web page, you can see the changes in the appearance of the text.

Manipulating Dynamic Content

Just as dynamic styles allow you to alter the style of Web content based on user interactions or script code, you can also change the content of elements on a Web page. For example, you can change the text in a paragraph or even change the source file of an image. For images, the key to changing the content is the src attribute. Here is an example of how to change the source of an image when the mouse pointer moves over the image:

```
<img src="Candles.jpg"
onmouseover="this.src = 'CandlesHilite.jpg';"
onmouseout="this.src = 'Candles.jpg';">
```

This code demonstrates how to change an image when the mouse pointer moves over and out of the image boundary. Notice that the code this.src is used to access and set the src attribute of the image element.

To alter the content of text elements, you set the innerText attribute as opposed to the src attribute used for images. Here is an example of an entertaining little paragraph that's altered dynamically:

```
<p style="font-size:14pt" onmouseover="this.innerText = 'Stop
it!';" onmouseout="this.innerText = 'Thank you.';">
I dare you to drag the mouse here.
</p>
```

In this example, the content of the paragraph changes when you move the mouse pointer into or out of the boundary of the paragraph. The this.innerText reference is used to set the content for the paragraph.

To get a feel for how these dynamic content examples fit into the context of a real Web page, take a look at the following code:

```
<html>
<head>
  <title>Dynamic Content Example Page</title>
</head>

<body style="background-color:white">
  <h1>Dynamic Content Example Page</h1>

  <p>
  <img src="Candles.jpg"
  onmouseover="this.src = 'CandlesHilite.jpg';"
  onmouseout="this.src = 'Candles.jpg';">
  Drag the mouse over the candles to see them flare up.
  </p>
```

```
<p style="font-size:14pt" onmouseover="this.innerText = 'Stop
it!';" onmouseout="this.innerText = 'Thank you.';">
I dare you to drag the mouse here.
</p>
</body>
</html>
```

This code describes a page named Dynamic Content that includes the two examples you just saw. Figure 11-5 shows what this Web page looks like when opened in Internet Explorer.

If you drag the mouse pointer over the image, the candles appear to flare up as shown in Figure 11-6.

Likewise, if you drag the mouse pointer over the second paragraph of text, the text changes. Figure 11-7 shows how the text in the paragraph changes in response to dragging the mouse pointer over it.

Try This! Changing an image dynamically is a great way to get unique effects on a Web page. Try changing the candle images in the example page to a picture of a person's face. A good example might be an image of a person with a straight face. Then find a second image and write the code so that when you drag the mouse over the straight face it changes to a person who is smiling.

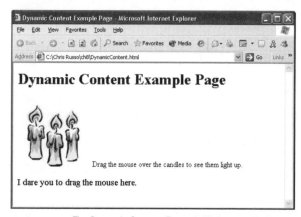

Figure 11-5   The Dynamic Content Example Web page displays an image of candles and a paragraph of text when it's first opened.

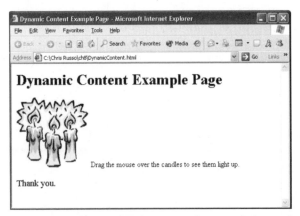

Figure 11-6   When you drag the mouse pointer over the image, the candles appear to flare up.

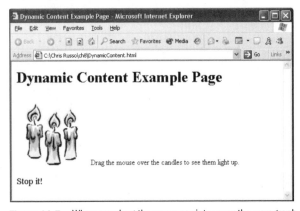

Figure 11-7   When you drag the mouse pointer over the paragraph of text, the text changes.

Fun with Dynamic Positioning

If you really want to add excitement to your Web pages with DHTML, how about dynamically altering the position of elements? That's right, it's possible to use script code and CSS style properties to change the position of elements so that they animate and move around on the page.

You can use CSS styles to position images and text so they appear in an exact location on the page. This type of positioning is known as *absolute positioning*. If you position an element using absolute positioning, you can easily alter its position on the page using script code. Here is an example of an image that's positioned using absolute positioning:

```
<img id="glider" style="position:absolute; top:100px; left:0"
src="IncRat.jpg">
```

Lingo   *Absolute positioning* allows you to position HTML content at precise locations on a Web page. *Dynamic positioning* involves altering the position of content once a page has already been loaded.

This image uses absolute positioning and will be displayed at a position 100 pixels down from its parent element on the left edge of the parent. The parent element is the tag in which the `<img>` tag resides, such as a `<p>` tag or even the `<body>` tag. If the parent is the body of the Web page, the image will appear 100 pixels down from the top of the page along the left edge of the page. Notice that the image has its `id` attribute set to `"glider"`. The `id` attribute is necessary so that script code can access the image and alter its position. Here is an example Web page containing script code that animates this image by making it appear to glide across the page:

```
<html>
<head>
  <title>Gliding Image Example Page</title>

  <script language="JavaScript">
  <!-- Hide the script from old browsers
  function StartGlide() {
    window.setInterval("Glide()", 50);
  }

  function Glide() {
    glider.style.pixelLeft += 5;
    if (glider.style.pixelLeft >= document.body.offsetWidth)
      glider.style.pixelLeft = 0;
  }
  // Stop hiding the script -->
  </script>
</head>

<body style="background-color:black" onload="StartGlide()">
  <p>
  <h1 style="color:white; text-align:center">Gliding Image
  Example Page</h1>
  <h3 style="color:white; text-align:center">Watch out for the
  rat!</h3>
  </p>
  <img id="glider" style="position:absolute; top:100px; left:0"
  src="IncRat.jpg">
</body>
</html>
```

This code is structured like the code in the Dynamic Styles Example Web page earlier in the chapter. For example, the script code in this page sets up an interval timer that runs a script function again and again. The script function increases the pixelLeft property of the image, causing it to move across the page from left to right. Figure 11-8 captures the image during its glide across the page.

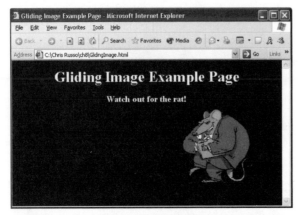

Figure 11-8 The Gliding Image Example Web page shows how to dynamically alter the position of an image by using script code and CSS style properties.

I have glossed over some details in the Gliding Image Example Web page, but it's another example of script code that you can use in pages of your own. In this case, it allows you to move content around dynamically.

The Practical Side of DHTML

Throughout this chapter, I've shown you how to do some neat things with DHTML; you can now spice up your Web pages with a bit of interactivity. However, most of the examples are aesthetic or cute interactive effects, as opposed to practical uses to improve the functionality of your pages. The next two sections remedy this with a couple of examples of Web pages that use DHTML to solve practical problems. Keep in mind that the examples would be virtually impossible to create without DHTML or another more complicated custom programming solution, such as Java.

Displaying an Animated Ad Banner

As you may know, many Web sites make their money from advertising. The ad-based business model of most of these Web sites has been questioned following the Great Dot-Com Fallout of 2000, but the fact remains that ads play an important role on the Web. You may not be able to put ads on your Web pages to obtain millions of dollars in venture capital, but you may find other uses for advertising that can still add value to your Web pages.

As I'm sure you've seen, most online ads appear as horizontal images known as *ad banners*, usually sized at 468×60 pixels. Although you could easily slap an ad banner on a Web page with an <img> tag, why not use DHTML to create an animated ad banner that rotates between several different images? Using a little script code, you can create an animated ad banner without much effort.

Lingo An *ad banner* is a special image, usually sized 468x60 pixels, that is displayed on a Web page as an advertisement. There are also vertical ad banners that are similarly sized but oriented vertically instead of horizontally.

Take a look at the following code for the Ad Banner Example Web page, which demonstrates how to create a DHTML ad banner:

```
<html>
<head>
  <title>Ad Banner Example Page</title>

  <script language="JavaScript">
  <!-- Hide the script from old browsers
  var bannerNum = 1;

  function linkBanner() {
    window.alert("You just clicked Ad Banner " + bannerNum +
    ".");
  }

  function rotateBanner() {
    if (++bannerNum > 3)
      bannerNum = 1;
    banner.src = "Banner" + bannerNum + ".jpg";
    window.setTimeout('rotateBanner();', 3000);
  }
  // Stop hiding the script -->
  </script>
</head>

<body style="background-color:white"
onLoad="window.setTimeout('rotateBanner();', 3000);">
  <h1>Ad Banner Example Page</h1>

  <p style="text-align:center">
  <a href="javascript:linkBanner();">
  <img id="banner" style="border:none" src="Banner1.jpg">
  </a>
  </p>
</body>
</html>
```

Not surprisingly, the Ad Banner Example Web page uses the same `<img>` tag that you saw earlier in this section. The page rotates through three different ad banner images, stored in image files named Banner1.jpg, Banner2.jpg, and Banner3.jpg. If you want to add more ad images, modify the following line of code in the `rotateBanner()` script function:

```
if (++bannerNum > 3)
```

This code checks to see if the number of the banner that's displayed is greater than 3. If so, the next line of code sets the current banner number back to 1:

```
bannerNum = 1;
```

If you want to expand the number of ad banner images to 5, for example, you change the `if` code to:

```
if (++bannerNum > 5)
```

Hey, you're now a script programmer! Seriously, you've learned some of the details about the inner workings of scripts and, more importantly, you've learned how to modify scripts to suit your own purposes.

Try This!   Replace the images in the Ad Banner example to create an ad banner of your own. The ad banner can be for a real business or maybe a personal ad for yourself—be creative!

Figure 11-9 shows the Ad Banner page as it first appears upon opening in Internet Explorer.

Figure 11-9   The Ad Banner Example Web page begins by displaying the first ad banner image.

The timer in the Ad Banner Example Web page is set so that the ad banners rotate every 3 seconds (3000 milliseconds). After waiting approximately 3 seconds, the ad banner changes to the second image, as shown in Figure 11-10.

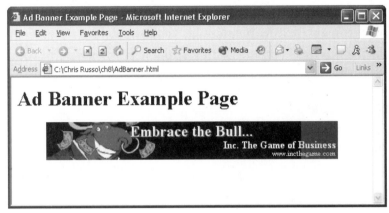

Figure 11-10 After approximately 3 seconds, the second ad banner image is displayed on the Ad Banner Example Web page.

If you click an ad banner image, an alert message displays the number of the current banner. Figure 11-11 shows the alert message for the third ad banner.

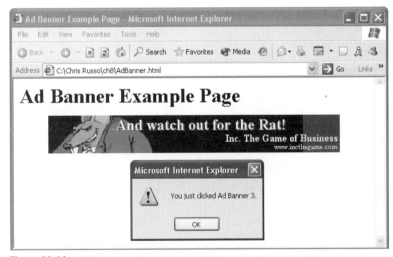

Figure 11-11 Clicking an ad banner image displays an alert message.

One interesting aspect of the Ad Banner Example Web page is what happens when an ad banner image is clicked. Keep in mind that the whole point of ad banners is to provide a link to another Web site. The linkBanner() script function displays an alert message in response to a click on an ad banner. For a real ad banner, you would probably change this code so that a link is followed to the URL of a different page. Here is what this script code might look like.

```
if (bannerNum == 1)
  window.location = 'http://www.incthegame.com/about.htm';
else if (bannerNum == 2)
  window.location = 'http://www.incthegame.com/game.htm';
else if (bannerNum == 3)
  window.location = 'http://www.incthegame.com/rules.htm';
```

The URLs shown in this code are for my financial board game Web site, and relate to the ad banner images in the Ad Banner Example page. Substitute your own URLs when creating animated ad banners.

Displaying Random Quotes

The Quotable Quotes Example Web page displays a randomly selected quote, and is a good example of how to vary the appearance of a Web page so that it looks different when visited repeatedly. The code for the Quotable Quotes Example Web page follows.

```html
<html>
<head>
  <title>Quotable Quotes Example Page</title>

  <script language="JavaScript">
  <!-- Hide the script from old browsers
  function getQuote() {
    // Create the arrays
    quotes = new Array(4);
    sources = new Array(4);

    // Initialize the arrays with quotes
    quotes[0] = "When I was a boy of 14, my father was so " +
    "ignorant...but when I got to be 21, I was astonished " +
    "at how much he had learned in 7 years.";
    sources[0] = "Mark Twain";
    quotes[1] = "Everybody is ignorant. Only on different " +
    "subjects.";
    sources[1] = "Will Rogers";
    quotes[2] = "They say such nice things about people at " +
    "their funerals that it makes me sad that I'm going to " +
    "miss mine by just a few days.";
    sources[2] = "Garrison Keilor";
    quotes[3] = "What's another word for thesaurus?";
    sources[3] = "Steven Wright";

    // Get a random index into the arrays
    i = Math.floor(Math.random() * quotes.length);

    // Write out the quote as HTML
    document.write("<dl>\n");
    document.write("<dt>" + "\"<i>" + quotes[i] + "</i>\"\n");
    document.write("<dd>" + "- " + sources[i] + "\n");
```

```
      document.write("<dl>\n");
    }
    // Stop hiding the script -->
    </script>
</head>

<body style="background-color:white">
    <h1>Quotable Quotes Example Page</h1>

    <p>
    Following is a random quotable quote. To see a new quote, just
    reload this page.
    <br>
    <script language="JavaScript">
    <!-- Hide the script from old browsers
    getQuote();
    // Stop hiding the script -->
    </script>
    </p>
</body>
</html>
```

I apologize for the length of this code, but if you look carefully you'll see that a lot of it consists of the four quotes available for display on the page. Once you get past the shock of the code size, the script code for the page is relatively simple to understand.

After creating an array, or list, of quotes and their sources, the `getQuote()` script function picks a random number and uses it to select a quote to be displayed. The quote is formatted on the page by the HTML code that is generated by the `getQuote()` function. Notice that the standard `document.write()` function is used to generate the HTML code that formats the quote. This script function is powerful because by using it, you can dynamically generate HTML code at any point in a Web page.

Figure 11-12 shows the Quotable Quotes Example Web page as it appears in Internet Explorer. To view a different quote, simply click the Refresh button in your Web browser, and the page reloads.

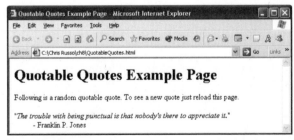

Figure 11-12   The Quotable Quotes Example Web page displays a randomly selected quote.

Keep in mind that you can easily modify the Quotable Quotes Example Web page to include your own quotes or other Web content that you want to display randomly. You can also increase the number of quotes available for display by adding more entries in the `quotes` and `sources` arrays in the code. I realize that some of this script code might be intimidating. Just understand that the best way to learn how to use DHTML is to take something that works and experiment with making modifications to it. If you use the Quotable Quotes page as a starting point, I guarantee you will be able to alter the script and create your own interesting variation on the idea without much trouble. And if you make mistakes along the way, so be it. Any time you learn something new, you're likely to make mistakes. The trick to getting past mistakes in script code is to be patient and carefully analyze the code you've entered. You can always remove code to simplify a script until you get it working and then add new code one piece at a time to make sure each piece works. Experiment and have fun with DHTML.

Key Points

- Dynamic HTML, or DHTML, represents a combination of technologies that make it possible to insert scripts into Web pages, giving you the ability to dynamically manipulate content on the page.

- The two main scripting languages in use are JavaScript and VBScript, with VBScript being supported in Internet Explorer only, while JavaScript is supported in several browsers.

- The `<script>` tag allows you to embed script code in a Web page.

- Event handling involves using a script to respond to a user interaction such as a mouse click or key press, which are *events*.

- The *Document Object Model*, or DOM, is a feature most Web browsers have that allows scripts to access parts of a Web page and apply styles to them.

- It is often beneficial to organize script code into a script function so that it can be reused more easily throughout a Web page.

- Dynamic positioning enables you to change the position of content on a Web page after the page loads.

- DHTML provides a neat way to improve on an online ad campaign by using rotating ad banners.

Part III

Adding Style to Your Pages

Part III is all about style, as you learn how to use style sheets to dramatically improve the appearance of Web pages. You begin by learning the fundamentals of style sheets and how they work. You then move on to learn how to format text and position content on a Web page using styles. As if using styles isn't enough to make your pages more exciting, this part concludes by showing you how to incorporate multimedia, including sound and video clips, into your Web pages.

Chapter 12

Style Sheet Basics

One limitation of HTML is that it doesn't provide a very thorough means of formatting text and other Web content. For example, you are limited in how detailed you can get with font sizes, text styles, and general document layout with HTML. However, a technology known as cascading style sheets (CSS) makes it possible to carry out all kinds of interesting formatting and layout tasks in Web pages. CSS allows you to create style sheets that control the appearance of Web content, and are the recommended means of formatting Web pages for viewing.

This chapter introduces you to style sheets and defines their role in improving Web pages' appearance. Along with learning the basics of style sheets, you will also learn several techniques for introducing style sheets into your Web pages. This chapter doesn't cover the gamut of style sheets, but it is a good start. Chapter 13, "Using Styles to Format Text," covers the details of various styles.

What Are Style Sheets?

As you've seen throughout this book, you can create Web pages that use different colors for text, borders, and the background. Altering the color of a piece of Web content is a formatting task that applies only to how the content looks when viewed in a Web browser. Consequently, you should make a clear distinction between the information in a Web page and the formatting code used to describe its appearance. The benefit of dividing formatting code from content in a Web page is that it makes the Web pages easier to alter and maintain. For example, consider the following code, which sets the color of several paragraphs of text to green:

```
<h3>Rules</h3>
<p><font color="green">
Q : Can I sell employees to other players, transfer them
between businesses, or turn them back in to the Employee Pool
for money?
</font></p>
<p>
A : No, you cannot sell employees to other players or
transfer them between different businesses. Employees can be
turned back in to the Employee Pool (laid off) but you don't
receive any money.
</p>

<p><font color="green">
Q : What happens if I land on the Corporate Headhunter space
and I can't use all of the employees I receive?
</font></p>
<p>
A : The employees must be returned to the Employee Pool.
</p>
```

Tip   The code for this example, as well as all of the examples throughout the book, is available for download from my Web site at the following URL: *http://www.michaelmorrison.com/cbook_fshtml.html.*

This code is part of a Frequently Asked Questions (FAQ) Web page for a financial board game called *Inc. The Game of Business* that I co-created. If you look closely, you'll notice that each question is formatted to appear in a green font. This is accomplished using the `<font>` tag and the `color` attribute, and it helps to distinguish the questions from the answers when the page is viewed. Figure 12-1 shows the *Inc. The Game of Business* FAQ page as viewed in Internet Explorer.

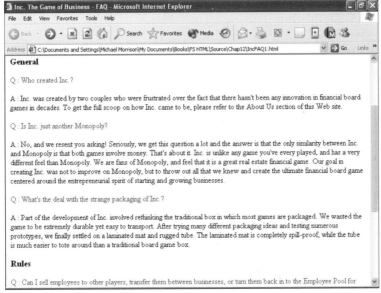

Figure 12-1   The Inc. The Game of Business FAQ page uses the `<font>` tag to set the color of different paragraphs of text.

It's very difficult to discern the different colors in the black and white figure, but you can see how the questions and answers are arranged on the page. A subtle problem arises when the page expands to contain additional questions and answers. The `<font>` tag must be applied to each of the questions repeatedly. It's easily handled in HTML code, but what if you decide to change the color of the questions to blue or use a different font for the questions? In either of these situations, you would have to go through the HTML code and make changes to each question because the formatting code, `<font>`, is tightly linked to the content of the page—the question text.

Style sheets offer a solution that links formatting code with Web page content. You define specific styles that can then be used to format Web page content. They can apply to an entire Web page, to specific portions of a page, to specific tags, and even to specific instances of a tag. In short, style sheets offer a great deal of flexibility. They accomplish this by maintaining an arm's length of distance between themselves and the Web page content. To understand how this works, consider the following code that simplifies the FAQ page with a simple style sheet:

```
<style>
  p.question { color:green }
</style>
```

This code contains a simple style sheet that establishes a specific *class* of
`<p>` tag named `question`. Any time a `<p>` tag is used and its `class` attribute is set
to `question`, the text in the paragraph will be displayed in green.

Lingo   A *class* is a grouping of content within a particular tag so that it can have a style applied
to it.

Here is an example of how this style sheet is used in the FAQ Web page
code:

```
<h3>Rules</h3>
<p class="question">
Q : Can I sell employees to other players, transfer them
between businesses, or turn them back in to the Employee Pool
for money?
</p>
<p>
A : No, you cannot sell employees to other players or
transfer them between different businesses. Employees can be
turned back in to the Employee Pool (laid off) but you don't
receive any money.
</p>

<p class="question">
Q : What happens if I land on the Corporate Headhunter space
and I can't use all of the employees I receive?
</p>
<p>
A : The employees must be returned to the Employee Pool.
</p>
```

Notice that in this code, the `<font>` tag is mysteriously absent. Instead,
the `class` attribute of the `<p>` tag for each question paragraph is now set to
`question`. No additional formatting code is present in the question paragraphs.
More importantly, the style of the paragraph is set in one place—the style sheet.
So, if you want to change the appearance of the question paragraphs, you
change the `p.question` style in the style sheet. This reveals how style sheets
make it possible to separate formatting code from Web page content and
ultimately improve the organization of information in Web pages.

This brings us to the question of the day: What is a *style sheet?*

Lingo   A *style sheet* is a collection of formatting rules for a Web page.

Style sheets consist of individual styles that apply to parts of a Web page.
You can specify a style sheet directly within a Web page using the `<style>` tag,

as the FAQ page demonstrated, or in a separate document that is referenced by a Web page. You can also apply styles individually throughout a Web page.

The formal name for style sheets is *cascading style sheets* (*CSS*), which refers to the manner in which styles cascade from one HTML tag to another. This means that if you apply a style sheet to a tag that has child tags, the styles will apply to both the parent and child tags, cascading from the parent to the children. In addition, if you specify a style for a tag, such as the <p> paragraph tag, the style will apply to all paragraphs. However, you can still use the class approach shown earlier in the FAQ example to override general styles with a specific style for a certain class of tags.

Don't worry at this point if style sheets seem a little complicated. I've thrown a lot at you quickly to immerse you in style sheets so you can see them in context. Let's take a short step back to reconsider the significance of style sheets and why you need to add them to your Web design knowledge base. Keep in mind that you've been liberally using HTML formatting tags to dress up your Web pages so they have more impact. Style sheets are designed to replace these HTML formatting tags (<font>, <big>, <small>, and so on) with a more unified approach to styling Web pages. Not only is it a good idea to start using style sheets instead of HTML formatting tags, it's also eventually going to be a necessity.

The *W3C* has already ruled that most HTML formatting tags are obsolete, which means that at some point browsers may stop supporting them. This isn't a likely scenario when you consider how many Web pages rely on such tags, but you could take it as a warning sign that style sheets represent the future of Web page formatting. HTML formatting tags won't be phased out in browsers any time soon, but style sheets are quickly becoming the standard for formatting Web pages.

Lingo   The *World Wide Web Consortium*, or *W3C*, is the governing body that oversees Web technology standards such as HTML and CSS.

Try This!   Visit the W3C Web site at *http://www.w3.org/* for all kinds of detailed technical information about the technologies that make the Web work.

The Essentials of Style

You've already learned a great deal about style sheets, even if it felt like a cyclone hit you. In this section, I want to take things more slowly and lay the ground rules for style sheets, which will prove invaluable as you progress. Let's begin with the structure of a style. Look at this example of a style that is used to format a heading:

```
h1 { font-weight:bold; font-size:14pt; color:orange }
```

In this example, a style is created for the `<h1>` tag that sets the font weight, size, and color for the heading. The `font-weight`, `font-size`, and `color` names in the style are style properties. Each style property is separated from its respective value by a colon (`:`), and individual properties within a style are separated by semicolons (`;`). All of the style properties are enclosed in braces (`{}`), which are preceded by the name of the tag that the style applies to.

The `<h1>` style is an example of a style that is declared in a style sheet using the `<style>` tag, as the following code demonstrates:

```
<style>
  h1 { font-weight:bold; font-size:14pt; color:orange }
</style>
```

The style section of a Web page must be included in the head of the page, as the following code shows:

```
<head>
  <title>A Stylish Web Page</title>

  <style>
    h1 { font-weight:bold; font-size:14pt; color:orange }
  </style>
</head>
```

As you can see, this code shows how a style sheet is created for a single Web page. Later in the chapter, you'll learn how to create a style sheet in a separate file so that it can be shared among multiple Web pages.

It's also possible to create styles directly in HTML code without using a formal style sheet (`<style>` tag). Here is an example of how to apply a style directly to a piece of HTML code:

```
<h1 style="font-weight:bold; font-size:14pt; color:orange">
Part I
</h1>
```

In this code, the same style that you saw previously is created and applied to a specific instance of the `<h1>` tag. The difference between the two style approaches is that the first created a style as part of a style sheet that applies to all `<h1>` tags, while the second approach created a style that applied to only the specific instance of the `<h1>` tag. In the latter example, any other `<h1>` tags in the Web page would be unaffected by the style, which applies to only that particular

`<h1>` tag. In coding the two different tags, the primary difference is that one uses `<style>` tags and the properties are enclosed in braces, while the other uses the `style` attribute and encloses its properties in quotes. How the style properties are described remains the same, although the latter approach of applying a style directly to a tag will override any styles assigned using the first approach.

Although the standard technique used to describe styles is to create a listing of style property/value pairs, you can group some style properties together. Here is an example of how to describe a font by grouping font style properties:

```
h1 { font:bold 14pt "Helvetica" }
```

In this example, the font style for the `<h1>` tag is created using a single property name (`font`) and several property values listed one after the other. The only required values for the `font` property are the font size and font family. Keep in mind that this code is equivalent to the following code, which specifies each font property individually:

```
h1 { font-weight:bold; font-size:14pt; font-family:"Helvetica" }
```

It's easy to see how the compact approach to defining font properties is easier to read and understand than spelling out each property individually. Remember that you can still use other style properties in addition to the `font` property, as the following code demonstrates:

```
h1 { font:bold 14pt "Helvetica"; color:orange }
```

In this example, the text color for the `<h1>` tag is set, in addition to the font styles shown in the previous example.

At this point I could go on and on about how to create different types of styles, but that's the focus of the next chapter. Right now it's more important to learn how styles are applied to Web pages.

Applying Styles to Web Pages

Although styles are powerful and enable you to describe how Web content is formatted for viewing, they wouldn't be very useful without a way to apply them to Web pages. In other words, it's important to have a way of pointing out the Web page content affected by each style you create. You've already seen two approaches—now we're going to explore some other options available to you in applying styles to your Web pages.

Internal Style Sheets

When you create a style or set of styles and enclose it within the `<style>` tag in the head of a Web page, you are basically saying that the styles apply to the

page as a whole. This collection of styles within a Web page is known as an
internal style sheet because it's defined directly within the page that it styles.
Internal style sheets are always created using the <style> tag, and they must
appear in the head of a Web page. Individual styles in an internal style sheet
apply to the entire Web page, but they do not affect any other Web pages.

Lingo   An *internal style sheet* is a set of styles that is placed directly within a Web page.

Here is an example of an internal style sheet:

```
<head>
  <title>Inc. The Game of Business - FAQ</title>

  <style>
    h3 { background:green; color:white; font-style:italic;
    font-weight:bold }
    p.question { color:green; font-style:italic;
    font-weight:bold }
  </style>
</head>
```

As you may have guessed, this is the internal style sheet for the *Inc. The
Game of Business* FAQ Web page that you saw earlier. Actually, this style sheet
is more interesting than the first one you saw. In addition to including more formatting for the <p> tag, it includes a style for the <h3> tag, which is used in the
Web page to divide the questions and answers into groups. Notice that the
background style is also set, which determines the background color of all <h3>
tags in the page. Figure 12-2 shows the resulting Web page as seen in Internet
Explorer.

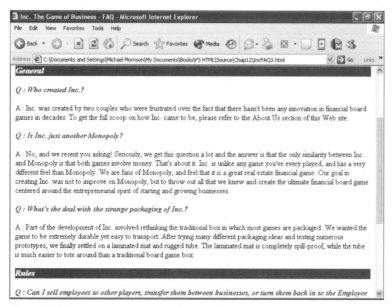

Figure 12-2 The Inc. The Game of Business FAQ page relies on an internal style sheet to format portions of its text content.

This style sheet is a good example of how such internal style sheets fit into the overall structure of Web pages. Specifically, it shows how an internal style sheet is formatted with the `<style>` tag that appears in the head of the page beneath the familiar `<title>` tag.

External Style Sheets

Like internal style sheets, external style sheets define styles that you apply to a Web page. However, *external style sheets* are contained in separate files, apart from the Web page to which they are applied. The primary advantage to using external style sheets is that you can apply styles to multiple Web pages. For example, if you create a Web site and you want all of the pages to look similar, you could create an external style sheet that describes styles for the different tags used in the pages. These styles would specify the font, colors, and other formatting details of the Web pages. The pages themselves wouldn't contain any style information except a reference to the style sheet.

Lingo An *external style sheet* is a set of styles that is placed in its own file, separate from a Web page document.

External style sheets typically help you organize your Web pages and apply styles consistently because they allow you to describe styles in one place and apply them to multiple Web pages. If you decide to change the style of a Web site, you simply change the style sheet. This is much more efficient than going to each page to update the styles. But if you want to apply styles to only a single Web page, then you might as well stick with an internal style sheet.

The code for external style sheets is no different than that for internal style sheets. For example, the following code contains an external style sheet that defines the same styles you saw in the previous section in an internal style sheet:

```
h3 { background:green; color:white; font-style:italic;
font-weight:bold }
p.question { color:green; font-style:italic; font-weight:bold }
```

This code must appear in a file named with a .css file extension, which is the standard extension used for cascading style sheets. Assuming that you place this code in a file named IncStyles.css, use the following code to reference the style sheet from a Web page:

```
<link rel="stylesheet" type="text/css" href="IncStyles.css">
```

Hold on—the <link> tag doesn't sound very familiar. That's because the <link> tag is something you haven't encountered so far. But it's not hard to use. The <link> tag is used to *link* the .css style sheet with a Web page, and is somewhat similar to the <a> tag that you learned about back in Chapter 5, "Connecting Pages with Hyperlinks." The rel attribute in the <link> tag says that the link references a style sheet to be applied to the document. The type attribute specifies the type of link content, in this case a cascading style sheet. The href attribute is the most important element for this discussion because it identifies the file name of the external style sheet. When you reference your own style sheets, href is the only attribute you need to change.

Note The <link> tag is an all-purpose tag used to reference different kinds of external files from a Web page.

Just as internal style sheets must appear in the head of a document, the reference to an external style sheet must also appear there. This is an example of how a <link> tag is placed in the head of the FAQ Web page you've been working with:

```
<head>
  <title>Inc. The Game of Business - FAQ</title>

  <link rel="stylesheet" type="text/css" href="IncStyles.css">
</head>
```

The best way to understand this code is to visualize the external style sheet being copied and pasted in the Web page where the `<link>` tag appears.

Classes of Styles

Styles are surprisingly flexible in how they can be applied to different portions of a Web page. In addition to applying a style to all instances of a given tag in a page, you can also establish a *style class* that applies to a class of tags. A class of tags is simply a subset of a particular tag. For example, you could organize the paragraphs in the FAQ Web page according to question paragraphs and answer paragraphs. Using style classes, you could create a different class for each type of paragraph. Here is an example of how to create a style class for a question paragraph:

```
p.question { color:green; font-style:italic; font-weight:bold }
```

The code shows that a style class is created by specifying the style as the tag name (p) followed by a period, and then the class name, `question`. This means that all `<p>` tags of class `question` will have the specified style. To identify a paragraph as a question paragraph, you use the `class` attribute of the `<p>` tag to identify the name of the class:

```
<p class="question">
Q : Can I sell employees to other players, transfer them
between businesses, or turn them back in to the Employee Pool
for money?
</p>
```

In this code, the class of the paragraph is set to `question` by using the `class` attribute, which means that the `p.question` style will be used to style the paragraph when it's displayed in a Web browser. Keep in mind that any other paragraphs coded with the `<p>` tag will not have the style applied unless they specify the same class information.

Styling Individual Tags

Creating an *individual style* involves assigning a special identifier to a tag that uniquely identifies the tag in the Web page. This identifier is then used in the style sheet to create a style that applies to the tag only.

Lingo   An *individual style* is a style that is applied to a particular type of tag in a Web page.

Here's an example of how to create a style that applies only to the copyright information on the FAQ Web page:

```
p#copyright { text-align:center; font-size:8pt }
```

This code shows how an individual style is created by specifying the style as the tag name (p) followed by a number symbol (#), and then the unique identifier for the tag, `copyright`. In other words, the number symbol (#) is used to associate the unique name of the style with a particular tag. To apply the individual style to a tag, you use the `id` attribute of the tag to specify the unique identifier, as the following code demonstrates:

```
<p id="copyright">Inc. The Game of Business
(c)1998 Gas Hound Games</p>
```

In this code, the `id` attribute of the `<p>` tag is used to specify the unique identifier for the individual style. Figure 12-3 shows the resulting Web page containing this individual style; pay close attention to the copyright notice near the bottom of the browser window.

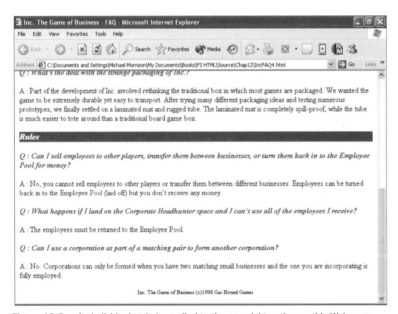

Figure 12-3   An individual style is applied to the copyright notice on this Web page.

Note   In addition to allowing you to style individual tags, the unique identifier used with an individual style is also important when it comes to scripting a Web page using a scripting language such as JavaScript or VBScript. Please refer back to Chapter 11, "Dynamic HTML," for more information about scripting.

Local Styles

Although style sheets provide the most organized approach to applying styles to Web pages, it's possible to apply styles to tags on an individual basis throughout the HTML code for a Web page. This kind of style is known as a *local style*. Local styles are coded in Web pages using the `style` attribute, which is supported by most HTML tags. When using the `style` attribute, you can specify styles in the same way that you specify them in style sheets, except you enclose them in quotation marks instead of braces.

Lingo   A *local style* is a style that is applied to a specific tag in a Web page.

Here is an example of applying a local style to a heading:

```
<h3 style="background:green; color:white; font-style:italic;
font-weight:bold">Rules</h3>
```

This is actually the same style you saw in the previous external style sheet, except in this case it's applied to a specific `<h3>` tag instead of all `<h3>` tags. Local styles allow you to style individual tags, which can be useful in situations in which you want to establish a unique style for a specific tag. It's still perfectly fine to have a style sheet for the same Web page. In this case, the local style will override any styles in the style sheet that apply to the same tag.

Linking with Style

Have you had enough of styles? Of course not! I'd like to show you one other interesting technique related to the application of styles. I'm referring to *link styles*, which are styles that apply specifically to hyperlinked text in a Web page. Link styles are similar to other styles in that they declare specific style information, but they apply to hyperlinks only. You can apply styles to the unique aspect of a hyperlink known as a *hyperlink state*.

Lingo   A *link style* is a style that is applied to hyperlinked text in a Web page.

The following hyperlink states correspond to link styles:

- `link`—the link has not been visited.
- `visited`—the link has been visited.
- `active`—the link has just been clicked.
- `hover`—the mouse pointer is hovering over the link.

You create a style for one of these hyperlink states by specifying the anchor tag name (a), followed by a colon (:), followed by the name of the hyperlink state. For all link states, the tag name is a, because hyperlinks are defined using the `<a>` tag. Here is an example of how to set a style for the hover state:

```
a:hover { background:green; color:white }
```

This code shows how simple it is to set a style for a hyperlink state. Follow the same pattern for the other hyperlink states: `a:link`, `a:visited`, and `a:active`. Link styles are powerful because they affect all of the hyperlinks in a Web page. Figure 12-4 shows the effect of the hover link style, as the mouse pointer is held over an e-mail hyperlink.

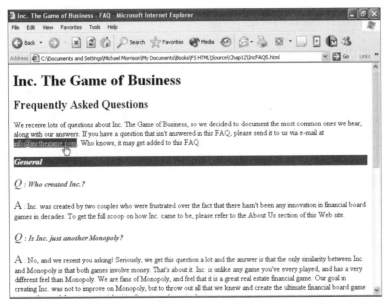

Figure 12-4   Link styles allow you to set styles for the different states of a hyperlink, such as dragging the mouse cursor over a link.

Try This!   It's important to actually test out a page that uses the link styles mentioned in this section, because you have to see them in action to appreciate how they add impact to hyperlinked text.

Styles and Custom Style Tags

Custom style tags are not custom in the sense that you get to make up your own tag names. Instead, you use one of two generic tag names, div or span, and then customize them with attributes. The benefit is that they allow you to structure your Web pages carefully according to the meaning of the content, which goes a long way toward separating the formatting of your pages from the content. If you recall, this is a desirable goal in all Web pages.

Lingo *Custom style tags* are special HTML tags that you use to identify and format content in your Web pages according to your own rules.

Custom style tags also make it easier to use style sheets with your Web pages because the content is organized according to specific tags. So, although custom style tags have structural and organizational benefits, they are also significant in styling your pages. Styles and custom style tags may not get you into the National Gallery, but they can certainly help you create more organized and visually appealing Web pages.

Before launching into the creation and use of custom style tags, you need to understand the difference between the two main types of HTML tags: *block-level tags* and *inline tags.*

Lingo *Block-level tags* are tags that usually start a new line in a Web page and often contain other tags. *Inline tags* are tags that usually do not start a new line in a Web page, and can only contain text or other inline tags.

The best example of a block-level tag is the `<p>` tag, which contains text content as well as other tags. Other examples of block-level tags include the `<body>`, `<table>`, and `<h1>`, `<h2>`, and so on heading tags.

Inline tags differ from block-level tags in that they are typically more concise and apply to smaller pieces of content. Examples of inline tags include the `<b>`, `<i>`, `<font>`, and `<img>` tags.

The significance of block-level and inline tags here is that you must determine whether a custom HTML tag is a block-level tag or an inline tag when you create it. The `<div>` tag is used to create custom block-level tags, and the `<span>` tag is used to create custom inline tags. The next two sections will show you how to create custom block-level and inline tags.

Creating Custom Style Tags

Custom HTML tags affect style sheets because you can use them to apply styles to a Web page in a controlled manner. For example, you can create several custom style tags that have their own styles; using these tags throughout a Web page achieves a high degree of organization and formatting, while still separating formatting code and content.

Creating Custom Block-Level Tags with `<div>`

You just learned that one of the uses of the `<div>` tag is to create custom block-level tags. The custom aspect of the `<div>` tag comes into play when you classify a specific type of `<div>` tag. This might be confusing, so let's look at a practical example. Here is the style code for a custom block-level tag that you could use to represent a question in the FAQ Web page:

```
div.question { color:green; font-style:italic;
font-weight:bold }
```

This code creates a style for a custom question tag. The style is specified by using the `div` tag name followed by a period, and then by the name of the custom style tag, `question`. Keep in mind that this doesn't mean you've created a custom style tag named `<question>`; instead, you've created a custom *classification* of the `<div>` tag named `question`. The bottom line is that you have a custom style tag that you can use to mark up questions in an FAQ Web page. More important is that the questions will be styled according to the `div.question` style in the style sheet.

Notice that the style code for the custom style tag is similar to that of the earlier example of creating a style class. Style classes require an existing HTML tag such as the `<p>` paragraph tag, however, whereas the `<div>` tag is more generic and can be used to mark up virtually any content.

Creating Custom Inline Tags with `<span>`

Just as the `<div>` tag allows you to create custom block-level tags, the `<span>` tag allows you to create custom inline tags. If you recall, inline tags are used to mark up smaller sections of content, and don't allow you to nest block-level tags within them. Inline tags are typically used to mark up individual words or phrases. For example, the `<b>` tag is used to bold a section of text and typically doesn't apply to more than a few words. Custom inline tags are created the same way as custom block-level tags, except that you use the `span` tag name instead of `div`. The following example demonstrates how to create a simple custom inline tag:

```
span.qna { font-size:150% }
```

In this example, a custom style tag is created that has the class name `qna`, which stands for *Question and Answer*. The `qna` tag is used to mark up the letters Q and A that appear in the questions and answers in the FAQ Web page. More specifically, the font size of the text enclosed by the custom tag is increased to 150 percent. This makes the text larger, which improves the appearance of the FAQ page, as you will see in the next section.

Putting Custom Style Tags to Work

You now understand that a custom style tag created with the generic <div> or
<span> tags is really just a style class associated with one of the two generic tags.
You use these custom style tags the same way that you used style tags earlier in
the chapter—by specifying the name of the style class in the class attribute of
the appropriate tag, <div> or <span>. Study this example to clear up any confusion about how custom style tags are used:

```
<div class="question">
<span class="qna">Q</span> : What happens if I land on the
Corporate Headhunter space and I can't use all of the
employees I receive?
</div>
<p>
<span class="qna">A</span> : The employees must be returned
to the Employee Pool.
</p>
```

In this example, the custom question style class is used with the <div> tag
to mark up the question paragraph. Even though you're using the <div> tag to
carry out the coding specifics of the custom style tag, the net effect is that a Web
browser considers the question style class to be its own unique tag. Contrast
this code to the answer paragraph that appears just after the question paragraph,
which is still marked up using the traditional HTML <p> tag. Along with adding
more meaning to the question paragraph, the custom question tag also applies
the appropriate style to the question paragraph.

This code also demonstrates inline custom tags by specifying the qna style
class with the <span> tag. In this case, the <span> tag is used to mark up the individual Q and A letters in the FAQ content, which then presents them in a larger
font when displayed. Again, the benefit of this tag is not just that it applies a
style to the inline content, but that it also adds meaning to the content. In other
words, you can read the code and immediately see that the Q and A letters are
related to questions and answers because they are marked up with the qna custom style tag. Figure 12-5 shows the FAQ Web page as it appears with these custom style tags applied.

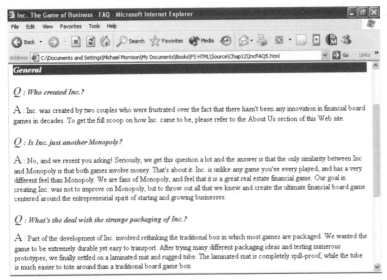

Figure 12-5   Custom style tags can be used to improve the structure of Web pages and to apply styles to Web content more effectively.

Key Points

- Style sheets dramatically improve the organization of Web content and provide a clean approach to formatting content for display in a Web browser.

- Style sheets support a richer set of formatting styles than you could ever achieve purely through HTML formatting tags.

- Style sheets are made possible by cascading style sheets (CSS), which allow you to control the appearance of Web content and are the recommended means of formatting Web pages for viewing.

- The two main types of style sheets are internal style sheets and external style sheets, and they differ only in where they are stored: inside a Web page or in an external file with a .css file extension.

- You must use the `<link>` tag to associate an external style sheet with a Web page.

- A style class allows you to apply styles to a group of tags with ease.

- Link styles allow you to change the appearance of hyperlink text, such as the color of the text when the mouse drags over a hyperlink.

- For the utmost in styling flexibility, you can create custom tags using the `<div>` and `<span>` tags that allow you to add a high degree of organization and style control over your Web pages.

Chapter 13

Using Styles to Format Text

You may not realize it, but a great deal of research has gone into making computer screens easier on the eye. Much of this research focuses on fonts and how they can help people read computer screens with the same efficiency as they read a printed page. Microsoft's ClearType technology emerged from this research and is used in the Microsoft Reader eBook software. But you don't have to go to the same lengths to make your Web pages more readable; you can use style sheets to alter the appearance of text and make it easier to read for those who visit your Web pages.

This chapter presents the different styles used to format text with cascading style sheets (CSS) styles. You'll learn interesting ways to enhance your Web pages and gain a better appreciation of styles. In the previous chapter, you saw a few text formatting styles, but you didn't dig very deep into learning how flexible they are. This chapter takes a closer look at text formatting styles and how to use them.

Assessing CSS Text Styles

A significant goal of CSS is to carefully format the appearance of text. Not surprisingly, you can use several different text-related styles. CSS has no formal organization of text styles, so I've come up with the following general categories:

- **Font styles**   set the font for text.

- **Dress styles**   set the foreground color, background color, and background image of text.

- **Space styles**   control the spacing of text.

- **Alignment styles**   position text on a page.

- **Other styles**   perform text formatting tasks that don't fit into the other categories.

These categories are sufficient to organize CSS text styles and clarify their role in text formatting. In other words, I created these categories to provide structure to the CSS text styles. The remainder of this chapter explores each category and how to use the styles within it.

Working with Font Styles

If you've ever heard of Courier, Arial, Times New Roman, or Wingdings, then you probably have some experience with *fonts*. You can use several different font style properties to fine-tune the appearance of your text. Table 13-1 shows these properties and the part of a font that they format.

Lingo   A *font* establishes, sometimes dramatically, the appearance of text.

Table 13-1   Font Style Properties

Property	Characteristic
font	Style, variant, weight, size, and family of a font as a single property
font-style	Style of a font
font-weight	Thickness of a font
font-size	Size of a font
font-family	Family of a font
font-variant	Normal or small caps

You can specify several font styles at once using the `font` property, which serves as a convenience property for describing a font using a single property. For example, the `font` property allows you to list values for each of the individual font properties as a single property value, thereby eliminating the need to use the individual font properties. You will learn how to use the `font` property to group font styles a little later in this chapter.

Setting Individual Font Properties

You can use most of the font style properties to set individual aspects of a font, such as its size or weight. The `font-style` property sets the style of a font to `normal` or `italic`. The default setting for the `font-style` property is `normal`, resulting in a font without any special style. Here is an example of how to use the `font-style` property:

```
<p style="font-style:italic">This is italic text.</p>
```

This code sets the font style for a short paragraph of text to `italic`, which means that all of the text in the paragraph will appear in italics.

Tip   If you don't specify a style property, the default setting will prevail.

The `font-weight` property sets the weight, or thickness, of a font, which can be set to any one of the following values: `normal`, `light`, `bold`, `bolder`, `100`, `200`, `300`, `400`, `500`, `600`, `700`, `800`, or `900`. The default value of the `font-weight` property is `normal`, which results in a font with a normal weight. Here is an example of how to use the `font-weight` property:

```
<p style="font-weight:bold">This is bold text.</p>
```

This code sets a paragraph of text so that it appears in a bold font. The values `100` through `900` set the font weight based on `100` being very light and `900` being very bold. A value of `400` results in `normal`, and a value of `700` equals `bold`. Not all fonts can be weighted across this entire range, so the browser will select the next most appropriate weight.

The `font-size` property sets the size of a font and can be specified in several different units: points (`pt`), inches (`in`), centimeters (`cm`), or pixels (`px`). The sky is the limit in selecting font sizes. Here are a few examples of how to use the `font-size` property:

```
<p style="font-size:12pt">This is 12 point text.</p>
<p style="font-size:0.75in">This is 0.75 inch text.</p>
<p style="font-size:20px">This is 20 pixel text.</p>
```

Note   When you use a font in a word processor, the font size is expressed as a number, such as 12 or 14. This number specifies the font size in points. So a value of 12 is a 12-point font.

Each of these examples sets the font size using a different unit. The first line of code specifies the size in points, the second line uses inches, and the last line expresses the font size in pixels. No unit is preferred over the others, but being consistent throughout a Web page certainly helps eliminate confusion.

The most important font style property is font-family, which sets the family, or *face*, of a font. For example, Times New Roman, Courier, and Helvetica are all font faces. Here are a few examples of how to use the font-family property:

```
<p style="font-family:Courier">This is Courier text.</p>
<p style="font-family:Helvetica">This is Helvetica text.</p>
<p style="font-family:Arial">This is Arial text.</p>
```

These examples show how you can use different font names with the font-family property to set the family of a font for several paragraphs of text. When you choose a font whose name consists of several words, such as Times New Roman, you must enclose the name in single quotes, like this:

```
<p style="font-family:'Times New Roman'">This is Times New Roman text.</p>
```

It's important to understand that there are no guarantees that a user will have a particular font installed on his or her system. If you specify a font that isn't available, the Web browser will find the best match. If you're thorough and want to make a contingency font plan, you can identify several fonts that serve as alternates if the preferred font isn't available. Here is an example of specifying a backup font using the font-family property:

```
<p style="font-family:Courier, Arial">This is Courier text that
will display as Arial if the Courier font isn't available.</p>
```

In this example, the Courier font is the primary font, which means that it will be used if it's available. If it can't be found, the Arial font will be applied to the paragraph. You can list additional fonts if you want more backup fonts. Just be sure to separate the font names with commas.

Use the font-variant property to set a font so that the text is displayed in small caps. The only values for the font-variant property are normal (the default value) or small-caps. Here is an example of how to use the font-variant property:

```
<p style="font-variant:small-caps">This is small-caps text.</p>
```

A small-cap font displays all lowercase characters in uppercase, but not as large as typical uppercase characters; uppercase characters are unaffected. This code establishes a small-cap font for a paragraph of text; all lowercase characters in the paragraph will be displayed as small uppercase characters.

Setting Font Properties as a Group

If you've ever benefited from a group discount at a retail store, you might appreciate the capability of grouping several font properties together as one. The `font` property allows you to specify a complete font by listing the different individual parts of one after the `font` property name. Here is an example of how to use the `font` property:

```
<p style="font:italic bold small-caps 12pt Courier">This is
italic, bold, small-caps, 12 point, Courier text.</p>
```

This code shows how you can specify several font property values as part of the single `font` property. The `font` property is a convenience property and has no significant style features of its own. The `font` property does have some rules, however. The order in which property values are coded is important. With the exception of the `font-family` value, any single value can be specified for the `font` property; the value for `font-family` must always be preceded by the value for `font-size`. To ensure correct handling of the value parameters when multiple values are coded, specify the values in this order: `font-style`, `font-variant`, `font-weight`, `font-size`, and `font-family`.

Putting the Font Styles Together

I've shown you many code snippets that demonstrate how to use font style properties, but you've yet to see any results. Here is the code for a Font Styles Web page that combines each of the previous font style examples into a single page:

```
<html>
<head>
  <title>Font Styles Example Page</title>
</head>

<body style="background-color:white">
  <h1>Font Styles Example Page</h1>
  <p style="font-style:italic">This is italic text.</p>
  <p style="font-weight:bold">This is bold text.</p>
  <p style="font-variant:small-caps">This is small-caps text.</p>
  <p style="font-size:12pt">This is 12 point text.</p>
  <p style="font-size:0.75in">This is 0.75 inch text.</p>
```

```
<p style="font-size:20px">This is 20 pixel text.</p>
<p style="font-family:Courier">This is Courier text.</p>
<p style="font-family:Helvetica">This is Helvetica text.</p>
<p style="font-family:Arial">This is Arial text.</p>
<p style="font-family:Courier, Arial">This is Courier text
that will display as Arial if the Courier font isn't
available.</p>
<p style="font:italic bold small-caps 12pt Courier">This is
italic, bold, small-caps, 12 point, Courier text.</p>
</body>
</html>
```

Tip   The code for this example, as well as all of the examples throughout the book, is available for download from my Web site at the following URL: *http://www.michaelmorrison.com/cbook_fshtml.html.*

Although the Font Styles page isn't designed to simulate the layout of a real Web page, it nonetheless helps you visualize the application of each font style property. Figure 13-1 shows the Font Styles Web page example as viewed in Internet Explorer.

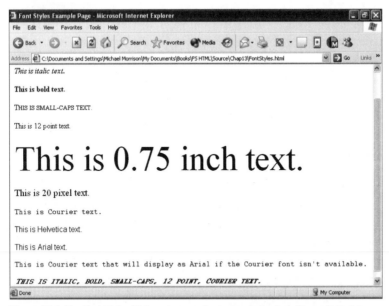

Figure 13-1 The Font Styles Web page example demonstrates how to use font styles.

Dressing Up Text with Style

It wasn't much more than a decade ago that a color monitor was a luxury for most computer users. Now we all take the rainbow of colors on our screen for granted. I propose a Color Appreciation Day to celebrate how far we've come in a few short years. If you're not into that, then at least consider using a few style properties to inject some color into your Web pages. Here are several CSS style properties that control the foreground and background colors as well as set images as backgrounds:

- `color` sets the foreground color of text.
- `background-color` sets the background color for text.
- `background-image` sets the background image for text.
- `background-repeat` determines how the background image for text is placed.
- `background` sets the background color, image, and repeat (tile) for text as a single property.

The `color` property sets the foreground color of text and accepts a standard color name as its value. The following standard colors are supported by the `color` property:

black	white	red	green
blue	yellow	gray	navy
olive	maroon	purple	teal
lime	fuchsia	aqua	silver

Here is an example of how to use the `color` property:

```
<p style="color:red">This is red text.</p>
```

This code displays a paragraph of red text. You can also use custom colors in addition to standard colors. (To learn more about custom colors, see Appendix C, "Using Custom Colors.")

The `background` properties in the property list are used to alter the background that appears behind text. The `background-color` property sets the background color for the paragraph and accepts the same colors as the `color` property. Here is an example of how to use the `background-color` property:

```
<p style="color:yellow; background-color:gray">This is yellow
text with a gray background.</p>
```

This code formats the style of a paragraph so that the text is yellow on a gray background, which provides a decent amount of contrast. Contrast is important when setting the `color` and `background-color` properties because a page can be difficult to read without it.

The `background-image` property displays an image behind text. The image is stored in a file using the GIF, PNG, or JPEG image format. To specify the file for the background image, enter the property value using the following form:

```
background-image:url(ImageFile)
```

When using the `background-image` property, replace the text *ImageFile* with the name of the actual image file. Here is an example of how to use the `background-image` property to set a background image for a paragraph of text:

```
<p style="color:black; background-image:url(Lattice.gif)">This
is black text with a lattice image background.</p>
```

In this example, the background image of the paragraph is set to the image file Lattice.gif. By default, the background image is tiled, or repeated, to fill the entire background of a paragraph or other Web element. The `background-repeat` property can alter the manner in which a background image is tiled. It can be set to one of the following values: `repeat`, `repeat-x`, `repeat-y`, and `no-repeat`. Obviously, the default value of the `background-repeat` property is `repeat`. The `no-repeat` value displays the background image only once. The `repeat-x` and `repeat-y` values duplicate an image only in the X or Y direction, respectively. Here is an example of how to use the `background-repeat` property to ensure that the background image is not repeated:

```
<p style="color:black; background-image:url(Lattice.gif);
background-repeat:no-repeat">This is black text with a
non-repeating lattice image background.</p>
```

In this code, the `background-repeat` property is set to `no-repeat` so that the background image isn't tiled. The image will appear only once behind the paragraph text.

Tip   It's possible to set both the `background-color` and `background-image` style properties, which results in the background image being displayed over the background color. The background color will show through if there are any transparent areas within the background image.

The `background` property is used to specify the different background properties as a single property. Here is an example of how to use the `background` property to combine several background properties and simplify the code for applying background styles:

```
<p style="color:maroon; background:url(Brick.gif) repeat">This
is maroon text with a repeating brick image
background.<br><br><br><br></p>
```

The extra line breaks in this example are there to make the paragraph larger vertically, which provides more room for the repeating background image. To get a feel for how the color and background-related properties affect the appearance of a real Web page, take a look at the following code for the Dress Styles Web page example:

```
<html>
<head>
  <title>Dress Styles Example Page</title>
</head>

<body style="background-color:white">
  <h1>Dress Styles Example Page</h1>
  <p style="color:red">This is red text.</p>
  <p style="color:yellow; background-color:gray">This is yellow
  text with a gray background.</p>
  <p style="color:black;
  background-image:url(Lattice.gif)">This is black text with a
  lattice image background.</p>
  <p style="color:black; background-image:url(Lattice.gif);
  background-repeat:no-repeat">This is black text with a
  non-repeating lattice image background.</p>
  <p style="color:maroon; background:url(Brick.gif)
  repeat">This is maroon text with a repeating brick image
  background.<br><br><br><br></p>
</body>
</html>
```

This Web page contains the color and background style code samples that you've seen throughout this section. Figure 13-2 shows the Dress Styles Web page example as viewed in Internet Explorer.

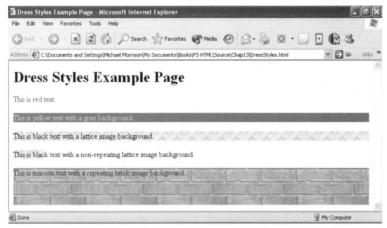

Figure 13-2 The Dress Styles Web page example demonstrates how to use color and background styles to dress up Web content.

Altering the Spacing of Text

You can use a style property to control the amount of space between characters of text, which can yield interesting stylistic effects. You can also use a style property to control the amount of space that appears before any text on the first line of a paragraph of text—the indentation of a paragraph. Here are the two style properties that alter the character spacing and indentation of text:

■   letter-spacing adjusts the spacing between text characters.

■   text-indent sets the indentation for the first line of text in a paragraph.

Both of these properties can be specified in units you are now familiar with: points (pt), inches (in), centimeters (cm), or pixels (px). Keep in mind that the amount of space identified by these units determines the spacing between characters—relative to *normal* spacing—when you're using the letter-spacing property, and the width of the indentation of a paragraph when used with the text-indent property. Here are several examples of how to alter the letter spacing of paragraphs with this property:

```
<p style="letter-spacing:0">The letters in this sentence are
separated normally.</p>
<p style="letter-spacing:4px">The letters in this sentence are
separated by normal spacing plus 4 pixels.</p>
<p style="letter-spacing:0.25cm">The letters in this sentence
are separated by normal spacing plus 0.25 cm.</p>
```

> **Tip**   Concerned about how your Web pages will look on a variety of screen sizes and resolutions? You might want to shy away from using the px unit of measurement. A pixel is not an absolute size and varies according to the size and resolution of the user's screen. It's safer to use traditional units of measure such as in, cm, mm, or even pt, which automatically scale to different screen sizes and resolutions.

Notice that the first example uses a value of zero for letter-spacing, which is the default value for the property. By comparing the letter spacing of the other examples, you can get an idea how other values will affect the spacing.

> **Tip**   To tighten the spacing between characters, set the letter-spacing property to a negative value.

Try This! You can use the letter-spacing property to space out the letters in a heading for an interesting visual effect. For example, try using spaced characters for your name as the heading for a personal resume Web page.

Here are a couple of examples of using the text-indent property to indent paragraphs of text.

```
<p style="text-indent:0">This paragraph has a normal text indent.</p>
<p style="text-indent:0.5in">This paragraph has a text indent
of 0.5 inches.</p>
```

The first use of the text-indent property contains the default property value of zero, which results in a paragraph with no indentation. The second example indents the text one-half inch.

You're no doubt curious about how these letter spacing and text indent examples look in a real Web page. The following code for the Space Styles Web page example shows these styles in the context of a complete Web page:

```
<html>
<head>
  <title>Space Styles Example Page</title>
</head>

<body style="background-color:white">
  <h1>Space Styles Example Page</h1>
  <p style="letter-spacing:0">The letters in this sentence are
  separated normally.</p>
  <p style="letter-spacing:4px">The letters in this sentence
  are separated by normal spacing plus 4 pixels.</p>
  <p style="letter-spacing:0.25cm">The letters in this sentence
  are separated by normal spacing plus 0.25 cm.</p>
  <p style="text-indent:0">This paragraph has a normal text indent.</p>
  <p style="text-indent:0.5in">This paragraph has a text indent
  of 0.5 inches.</p>
</body>
</html>
```

This Web page uses the letter spacing and text indent style code that you've learned about in this section. Figure 13-3 shows the Space Styles Web page example as viewed in Internet Explorer.

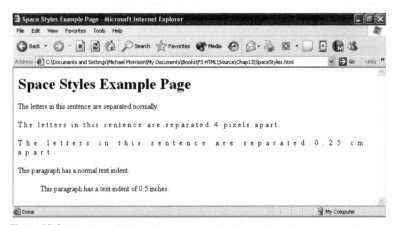

Figure 13-3 The Space Styles Web page example demonstrates how to control the spacing of text.

Using Styles for Text Alignment

Just as spacing is important to obtain a desired text appearance, alignment is also a key element. However, you can't fully understand alignment without knowing how margins affect a text element. The following style properties determine the alignment and margins of text:

- `text-align` positions text horizontally.
- `margin-top` sets the top margin of text.
- `margin-right` sets the right margin of text.
- `margin-bottom` sets the bottom margin of text.
- `margin-left` sets the left margin of text.
- `margin` sets the top, right, bottom, and left margins of text as a single property.

The next two sections demonstrate how to use these properties to control the alignment and margins of text.

Aligning Text

It's easy to align text on a Web page with the `text-align` property's `left`, `right`, and `center` values. Here are a few examples of these property values:

```
<p style="text-align:left">This paragraph is left-aligned.</p>
<p style="text-align:right">This paragraph is right-aligned.</p>
<p style="text-align:center">This paragraph is centered.</p>
```

This code is straightforward in that the `text-align` style property is set to different values to align the paragraph differently in each example.

Adjusting the Margins

I mentioned previously that margins affect text alignment. This is because they limit the area where text can appear. For example, if you set a 1-inch margin along the left side of a page, text can't appear in that margin. So, left-aligned text will appear at the margin as opposed to along the left edge of the page. Here is an example of setting the left and right margins for a paragraph of text using the `margin-left` and `margin-right` properties:

```
<p style="background-color:silver; margin-left:25px; margin-right:25%">
This paragraph has a left margin of 25 pixels
and a right margin of 25%.</p>
```

In this code, you'll notice that I ignored my prior advice against mixing units when specifying the size of style properties. I just wanted to demonstrate the use of two different units without showing you two different examples. The interesting aspect of this code is that the right margin is specified as a percentage. When you specify a margin as a percentage—25 percent in this case—it is based upon the width or height of the entire Web page. This approach allows margins to shrink and grow in relation to the size of a Web page, instead of committing them to a specific value. This is a good example of a technique you can use to design Web pages so that they scale well across different computers, since there is some variety in terms of the screen sizes and monitor resolutions out there.

In addition to the `margin-left` and `margin-right` properties that set the side margins, the `margin-top` and `margin-bottom` properties set the top and bottom margins for a paragraph. Here is an example of setting the top margin for a paragraph:

```
<p style="background-color:silver; margin-top:40px">This
paragraph has a top margin of 40 pixels.</p>
```

In this example, the top margin is set to 40 pixels, which means that above the paragraph, there will be an invisible border 40 pixels high.

Most of the time you will use the individual margin properties to set margins one at a time. However, if you should ever want to set several margin properties at once, you'll want to take a look at the `margin` property. The `margin` property can be used in three different ways; the appearance of the Web page will change depending on how many pieces of information you list for the property's values:

- If one size value is specified, that size applies to all four margins.

- If two size values are specified, the first applies to the top and bottom margins and the second applies to the left and right margins.

- If all four size values are specified, they apply to the top, right, bottom, and left margins, in that order.

To understand how the `margin` property works, look at the following example, which sets all of the margins for a paragraph to a single value:

```
<p style="background-color:silver; margin:10% 20%">This paragraph
has a margin of 10% on all sides.</p>
```

In this example, the top and bottom margins are set to 10 percent, while the left and right margins are set to 20 percent. Keep in mind that this margin style is equivalent to margins of 10%, 20%, 10%, and 20% for the four different margins (top, right, bottom, and left).

Putting the Text Alignment Styles Together

Like the text styles you've learned about so far, the text alignment styles make more sense once you see them in action. The following code shows how the text alignment styles are used within the context of a Web page:

```
<html>
<head>
  <title>Alignment Styles Example Page</title>
</head>

<body style="background-color:white">
  <h1>Alignment Styles Example Page</h1>
  <p style="text-align:left">This paragraph is left-aligned.</p>
  <p style="text-align:right">This paragraph is right-aligned.</p>
  <p style="text-align:center">This paragraph is centered.</p>
  <p style="background-color:silver; margin-left:25px;
  margin-right:25%">This paragraph has a left margin of 25
  pixels and a right margin of 25%.</p>
  <p style="background-color:silver; margin-top:40px">This
  paragraph has a top margin of 40 pixels.</p>
  <p style="background-color:silver; margin:10%">This paragraph
  has a margin of 10% on all sides.</p>
</body>
</html>
```

The Alignment Styles Web page shows the result of all the text alignment example code that you've learned about. Figure 13-4 shows the Alignment Styles Web page as viewed in Internet Explorer. You can easily see the effect of the margin settings by resizing the Web browser and noticing how the margins change in size.

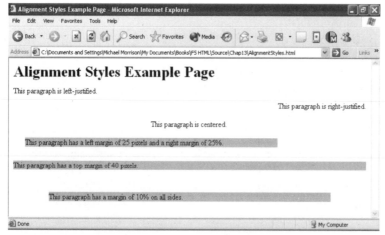

Figure 13-4 The Alignment Styles Web page demonstrates the result of code that aligns paragraphs of text in various ways.

Digging into the Bag of Style Tricks

Earlier in the chapter, I mentioned that some text styles don't fit into any single category. These rogue styles are interesting, so let's see how they might affect your text formatting plans. Consider the following styles for your bag of text formatting tricks:

- `text-decoration` sets the highlight of text.

- `text-transform` sets the case of text to lowercase or uppercase.

- `cursor` sets the mouse pointer icon when the mouse pointer hovers over a paragraph.

The `text-decoration` style property does exactly what its name implies—it decorates text. Use it to set the highlight of text to one of the following values: `underline`, `overline`, or `line-through`. Here are a few examples that demonstrate how to use the `text-decoration` style:

```
<p style="text-decoration:underline">This text is underlined.</p>
<p style="text-decoration:overline">This text is overlined.</p>
<p style="text-decoration:line-through">This text is struck out.</p>
```

These examples are straightforward, showing how to apply each of the different text decoration values to a paragraph.

You might find the `text-transform` property a little more interesting because you can change text to lowercase or uppercase without having to retype all of it by hand. If you ever need to display text in all lowercase or uppercase, the `text-transform` property makes it easy. The values you can use with the `text-transform` property are: `none`, `lowercase`, `uppercase`, and `capitalize`.

The `none` value is the default value because it doesn't alter text in any way. The `capitalize` value capitalizes the first letter of every word in a paragraph, regardless of its original case. This value is different from `uppercase`, which capitalizes all of the characters in a paragraph. The `capitalize` value might seem a little strange at first, but keep in mind that you could use it to capitalize a list of names automatically, for example. Here are a few examples of how to use the `text-transform` property:

```
<p style="text-transform:none">This text is completely normal.</p>
<p style="text-transform:lowercase">This text is all lowercase.</p>
<p style="text-transform:uppercase">This text is all uppercase.</p>
<p style="text-transform:capitalize">This text is all capitalized.</p>
```

These examples demonstrate how to use each of the `text-transform` property values to alter the case of paragraphs.

The last property is without a doubt the trickiest in this section. The `cursor` property is used to change the appearance of the mouse pointer when it is dragged over a paragraph of text. When using the `cursor` property, set the mouse pointer to any of these standard cursor values:

default	text	hand	crosshair
wait	help	move	n-resize
ne-resize	e-resize	se-resize	s-resize
sw-resize	w-resize	nw-resize	

Each of the cursor values identifies a different cursor icon. For example, in Microsoft Windows, the `wait` cursor corresponds to the hourglass that you often see when a program is busy. Here is an example of setting the `wait` cursor for a paragraph:

```
<p style="cursor:wait">This text changes the mouse pointer to
an hourglass when you drag the mouse pointer over it.</p>
```

Lingo   The terms *mouse cursor* and *mouse pointer* refer to the same thing.

In this example, the `wait` cursor value is used to specify the hourglass mouse pointer for the paragraph. The end result is that the mouse pointer will change to the hourglass when you drag it over the paragraph. As fun as it may be to alter the appearance of the mouse pointer, I encourage you to resist the temptation to change the `cursor` style property except in situations in which it would make the Web page more meaningful or effective.

I'm cautioning you about the use of the `cursor` property because most standard cursors are used to convey information to the user. For example, the presence of the hourglass mouse pointer should mean only that a program is busy, so the user is accustomed to waiting for it to change. If you don't use the `cursor` property carefully, you could confuse the user by displaying a familiar cursor out of context. On the other hand, if your goal is to trick visitors to enter your Web site with a practical joke, feel free to use the `cursor` property at will!

This section covered several trick style properties. To get a better feel for how these properties function within a complete Web page, check out the following code:

```
<html>
<head>
  <title>Trick Styles Example Page</title>
</head>
```

```
<body style="background-color:white">
  <h1>Trick Styles Example Page</h1>
  <p style="text-decoration:underline">This text is underlined.</p>
  <p style="text-decoration:overline">This text is overlined.</p>
  <p style="text-decoration:line-through">This text is struck out.</p>
  <p style="text-transform:none">This text is completely normal.</p>
  <p style="text-transform:lowercase">This text is all lowercase.</p>
  <p style="text-transform:uppercase">This text is all uppercase.</p>
  <p style="text-transform:capitalize">This text is all capitalized.</p>
  <p style="cursor:wait">This text changes the mouse pointer to
  an hourglass when you drag the mouse pointer over it.</p>
</body>
</html>
```

The Trick Styles Web page pulls together all the code you've seen throughout this section. Figure 13-5 shows the Trick Styles Web page example as viewed in Internet Explorer.

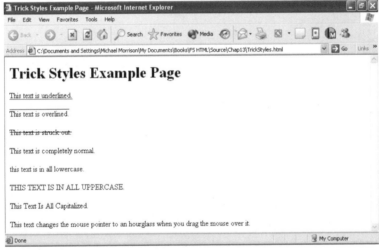

Figure 13-5 The Trick Styles Web page example demonstrates how to apply a few interesting formatting styles to text.

Key Points

- Several style properties are available for altering the size, appearance, color, and spacing of text, among other things.

- The font property is convenient for describing different aspects of a font using a single property.

- The color property sets the foreground color of text and accepts a standard color name, such as red or blue, as its value.

■   There are several background properties that allow you to set the
    background of HTML content to a solid color or even an image.

■   The `letter-spacing` and `text-indent` style properties allow you to
    alter the character spacing and indentation of text.

■   There are several margin properties that you can use to carefully con-
    trol the margins of your Web pages.

■   If you need to underline text or alter the mouse cursor when it passes
    over a paragraph, you'll find that there are styles to make these tasks
    possible.

Using Styles for Web Page Positioning

The previous chapter showed you how to use style sheets to format Web content. You may also be interested to learn that you can use style sheets to carefully control the layout and positioning of content on a Web page. For example, you can use a style sheet to specify exactly how many pixels an image should be from the edge of the page. This chapter describes several style properties that are used to control the positioning and layout of Web content. By the time you finish this chapter, you will have rounded out your knowledge of style sheets and should be prepared to tackle virtually any Web page style issue.

The Basics of Positioning with Style

As you learned in the previous chapter, cascading style sheets (CSS) support a wide range of styles used to format text in a variety of ways. In addition to these formatting styles, several other styles affect the way that Web content is positioned on a page. These positioning styles are important because you can use them to organize the layout of Web content.

One critical concept before we launch into positioning style properties: To apply positioning style properties, you have to think of each element on a Web page as if it had an invisible box around it. These boxes serve as boundaries for each image and paragraph of text on a page and identify how much space an element occupies and the position of the element relative to other elements.

When an element is used within another element—a paragraph of text within the <body> tag, for example—the element's boundary is contained within the boundary of the parent element. Figure 14-1 shows a Web page you've already seen several times. I drew the boundaries of the major elements so that you can see exactly how each element is positioned on the page.

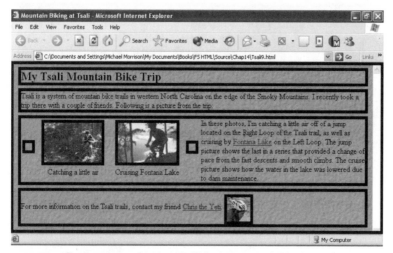

Figure 14-1 The boundaries of each major Web element are clearly shown in this modified version of the Tsali mountain bike Web page.

The positioning style properties manipulate the boundaries for elements on a page, which is useful when you produce a page according to a specified layout. Prior to style sheets, most Web designers relied on tables to organize their Web pages. The two fundamental approaches to positioning Web content using the now-popular CSS are *relative positioning* and *absolute positioning*. Relative positioning specifies the position of an element, text, or image based on its normal position. Absolute positioning, on the other hand, specifies the position of an element with respect to the parent element.

To better understand the difference between relative and absolute positioning, consider an image that appears in the body of a Web page, just after a paragraph of text. With relative positioning, changing the position of the image will position it with respect to its original location after the paragraph. With absolute positioning, however, the image will be positioned with respect to the body of the page because the <body> tag is the parent element of the image.

Note   Relative positioning is the default positioning approach used by HTML.

Figure 14-2 shows an example of a simple Web page that describes a backyard pond and includes a couple of images. This is a good Web page to use as an example of how relative and absolute positioning differ.

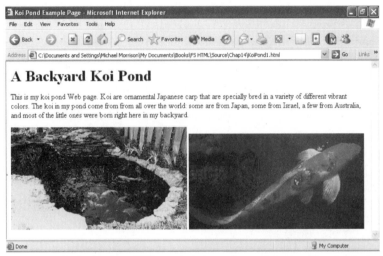

Figure 14-2 The backyard pond Web page includes two images that are positioned normally after a paragraph of text.

In this figure, two images are positioned normally following a paragraph of text (if the screen is wide enough), because they appear after the paragraph of text in HTML. This is the standard HTML approach to laying out elements on a page. Figure 14-3 shows how the page changes when you specify that the top of the second image, the big fish, is to be placed 100 pixels lower than its normal position.

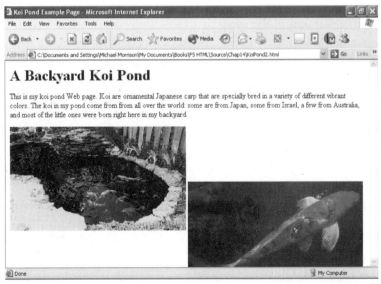

Figure 14-3 The big fish image in the backyard pond Web page is positioned 100 pixels lower than its original position by using relative positioning.

Things get more interesting when you change the pond image so that it's placed using absolute positioning. More specifically, the image is positioned so that it appears 25 pixels to the right of the left edge and 0 pixels below the top edge of the page. When using absolute positioning, you position an element with respect to its parent—in this case, the body of the Web page. Therefore, the image is positioned with respect to the entire page. Figure 14-4 shows the result of shifting the pond image 25 pixels to the right and 0 pixels below the edges of the page.

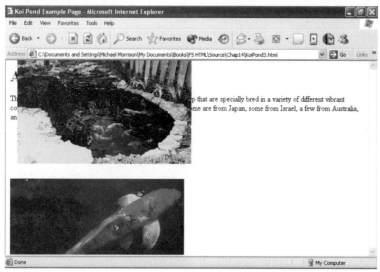

Figure 14-4   The pond image in the backyard pond Web page is positioned 25 pixels to the right and 0 pixels below the edges of the entire Web page by using absolute positioning.

As you can see in the figure, the image is positioned with respect to the upper-left corner of the Web page. The interesting aspect about the resulting page is that the image appears on top of the paragraph of text. This reveals the power of the positioning style properties; you must be careful when using them.

Notice that because the first image is now positioned using absolute positioning, it no longer factors into the relative positioning of the second image, and the second image slides over as if no other image preceded it. This again points out that the positioning styles properties are quite flexible, but that they must be used with care. Let's move on and learn how they work.

Using Relative and Absolute Positioning

You might be surprised to find out that you use only one main style property to carry out both relative and absolute positioning in CSS. However, a few support properties are required to specify the position of an element using either of these approaches. Here are the style properties involved in relative and absolute positioning:

- ■   `position`—Declares the type of positioning used for an element (`relative` or `absolute`).

- ■   `top`—Specifies the top offset of an element's position.

- ■   `right`—Specifies the right offset of an element's position.

- ■   `bottom`—Specifies the bottom offset of an element's position.

- ■   `left`—Specifies the left offset of an element's position.

The `position` style property is used to specify whether an element uses relative or absolute positioning and can be set to one of the following values: `relative` or `absolute`. When using the `position` property, you must also specify the placement of the element by using one or more of the `top`, `right`, `bottom`, and `left` properties. These properties specify the position of the element based on whether the positioning is relative or absolute. The values for these four properties can be specified in points (`pt`), inches (`in`), centimeters (`cm`), or pixels (`px`). Here is an example of setting the relative position of an image:

```
<img style="position:relative; left:0px; top:100px" src="Fish2.jpg">
```

Although it isn't obvious from the code, this is the example you saw in Figure 14-3, where the fish image was moved down 100 pixels by using relative positioning.

Figure 14-4 showed how absolute positioning affects images on a page. Here is the code for that example, which positioned an image 25 pixels over and 0 pixels down from the upper-left corner of the page:

```
<img style="position:absolute; left:25px; top:0px" src="Pond1.jpg">
```

Understand that when you use absolute positioning, an element no longer affects the layout of other items on the same page. Think of an absolutely positioned element as floating independently over the other elements on a page, as opposed to being placed next to them. In the next section, you will learn how to set the layering of elements so that you control how they appear when they overlap.

Note   You can position elements so that text flows around them, but only by using relative positioning. With absolute positioning, the positioned element essentially floats over the rest of the page independent from the other elements, including paragraphs.

Managing Overlapping Elements

You don't need to tinker much with the positioning style properties to figure out that you can move elements around so that they overlap each other. This creates an interesting opportunity for laying out pages with overlapping content. Any time an element overlaps another element, it's important to specify which one appears on top. The *z-index property*, which sets the z-index of an element, is the style property designed to do just that.

Lingo   The *z-index* of an element determines how the element is displayed with respect to any elements that it overlaps.

The layering of elements is effectively a third dimension (Z) added to the two dimensions (X and Y) that are displayed on the screen. Pretend that each element on your page is a sticky note that you stuck on your computer screen. If a red sticky note overlaps a yellow note, the red note has a higher z-index than the yellow one. If you stick a blue note on top of the red one, the blue note will have a z-index greater than both of the other notes. In HTML, the z-index determines which element appears on top of other elements.

When you set the z-index of an element, you specify it as a number. This number has meaning only with respect to other elements that you've set. In other words, setting the z-index for a single element doesn't have any effect. But if you set it for several elements, the elements with the higher numbers will appear on top of those with lower z-index values.

Tip   The z-index of an element is always specified relative to the parent of the element. This results in the element always appearing on a layer above its parent, regardless of how high you set the parent's z-index.

Here is an example of how differing z-index values for two overlapping images are set so that one of the images is displayed on top of the other:

```
<img style="position:relative; left:50px; top:-50px; z-index=1"
src="Pond1.jpg">
<img style="position:relative; left:-200px; top:0px; z-index=2"
src="Fish2.jpg">
```

The results of this code are shown in Figure 14-5. As you can see in the figure, by setting the left property to a negative value, the fish image is forced to overlap the pond image. But the fish image is displayed on top of the pond image because it has a higher z-index.

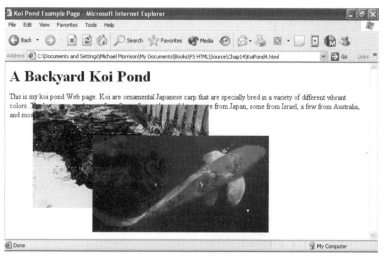

Figure 14-5 By assigning it a higher z-index value, the fish image overlaps the pond image.

Keep in mind that it's also possible to set the z-index of text to make a paragraph appear on top of an image. Here is a line of code for the paragraph of text in the example that sets the z-index of the paragraph higher than that of the images:

```
<p style="z-index=3">
```

Just to show how easy it is to change the z-index of elements to get different results, check out the following code for the images:

```
<img style="position:relative; left:50px; top:-50px; z-index=2"
src="Pond1.jpg">
<img style="position:relative; left:-200px; top:0px; z-index=1"
src="Fish2.jpg">
```

This code reverses the z-index values for the images, which should cause the pond image to appear on top of the fish image. But the paragraph still has a higher z-index than both images, so it should appear as the highest element. Figure 14-6 shows the resulting Web page.

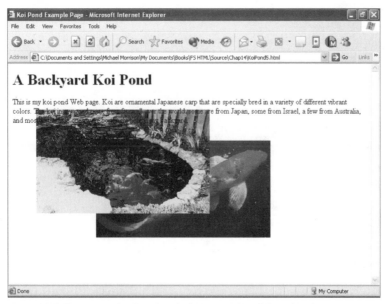

Figure 14-6 The paragraph of text has the highest z-index, followed by the pond image, and then the fish image.

If you look closely at this figure you can see that the text of the paragraph is visible over the top of the pond image. Also, notice that the pond image is now shown on top of the fish image, which is consistent with the modified z-indexes.

Tweaking the Appearance of Elements

Several positioning style properties control how an element is displayed. More specifically, you can use these properties to alter the size, visibility, and border of elements. Here are these style properties:

- width—Sets the width of an element.
- height—Sets the height of an element.
- display—Shows or hides an element.
- border-width—Sets the border width of an element.
- border-style—Sets the border style of an element.
- border-color—Sets the border color of an element.
- border—Sets the border styles of an element as a single property.

The next few sections introduce you to these style properties and describe how you can use them to control the size, visibility, and border of an element.

Changing the Size of Elements

You can set the width and height of an element with the `width` and `height` style properties. They accept familiar units, such as values: points, inches, centimeters, or pixels. When you change the width or height of a paragraph of text, you can hide part of the text if you size the paragraph smaller. When you resize an image, the browser will do its best to scale it to fit the new dimensions. Here is an example of reducing the size of an image:

```
<img style="width:200px; position:relative; top:-0.75in;
left:-0.5in" src="Fish2.jpg">
```

The results of this code are shown in Figure 14-7.

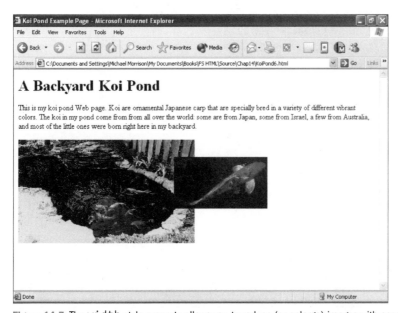

Figure 14-7 The `width` style property allows you to reduce (or enlarge) images with ease.

Tip It's usually better to reduce the size of an image using an image-editing tool so that the size of the image file is decreased. This is important because it results in the image file being transferred faster when the page is being downloaded, which results in better Web page performance. Most image-editing tools are better than Web browsers at scaling images and maintaining their quality.

In addition to images, you can also change the width and height of paragraphs, which then wrap their contents according to paragraph size. Here is an example of how to alter the width of a paragraph using the `width` style property:

```
<p style="width:375px">
```

If you apply this code to the main paragraph in the backyard pond Web page, you'll see the page shown in Figure 14-8.

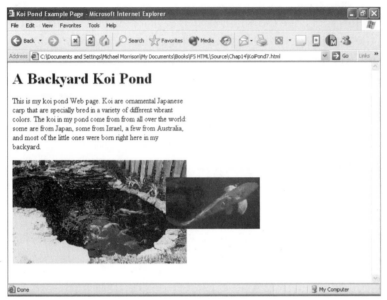

Figure 14-8 The `width` style property is valuable for setting the size of paragraphs.

Notice in this figure that the `width` property overrides the default width of the paragraph, effectively matching the paragraph width with the width of the pond image. The ability of the `width` and `height` properties to control paragraph size can be quite handy.

Tip   In addition to the units mentioned previously, the `width` and `height` properties can also be specified as percentages for elements that are placed with absolute positioning.

Showing and Hiding Elements

If I showed you a blank Web page and told you that several images were positioned on the page, would you have faith that the images were there even though you couldn't see them? The truth is that you wouldn't know for certain whether my blank page contains images unless you looked at the code because it is possible to hide an element in a Web page. Hiding an element makes it completely invisible when the page is displayed in a Web browser.

The `display` style property controls the visibility of elements and can be set to any of the following values:

- `none`—Hides an element.
- `block`—Displays an element as a block-level element.
- `inline`—Displays an element as an inline element.
- `list-item`—Displays an element as a list item.

As you might have guessed, the `display` style has a default value of either `block` or `inline`, depending on whether the element in question is a block-level or inline element. To hide an element, set the `display` style to `none`, as the following code demonstrates:

```
<img style="display:none" src="Fish2.jpg">
```

The results of this code are shown in Figure 14-9.

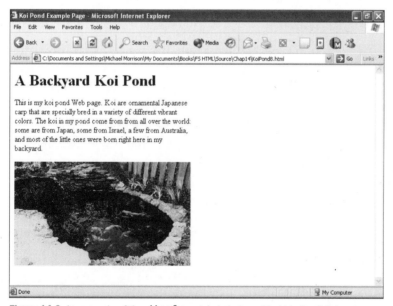

Figure 14-9 An example of the `display` style being used to hide the fish image.

You're probably curious as to why you'd ever want to hide an element so that it's never displayed. For traditional Web pages, there is no reason. However, there are situations—such as when creating dynamic Web pages with scripts—in which it's helpful to have hidden information. For a refresher on creating dynamic Web pages with scripts, feel free to flip back to Chapter 11, "Dynamic HTML."

Giving Your Elements a Border

Earlier in the chapter, I mentioned that thinking of HTML elements as having invisible boxes around them is helpful when you want to visualize the positioning and layout of elements on a page. There will be times, however, when you want to make the boundaries of some elements visible by creating a *border*—basically an outline along the boundary of the elements. But be careful; borders can be a visual annoyance if you overdo it and put them around everything.

Lingo   A *border* is a visible rectangular outline around the outside of an element in a Web page.

Here are the style properties for borders:

- `border-width`—Sets the width of the border for an element.
- `border-style`—Sets the style of the border for an element.
- `border-color`—Sets the color of the border for an element.
- `border`—Sets the border properties for an element as a single property.

The `border-width` property specifies the width of a border as one of the following standard values: `thin`, `medium`, or `thick`. You can also define the width of a border as a numeric value in units of pixels, points, centimeters, or inches.

The `border-style` property sets the style of the border to one of the following values: `none`, `solid`, `double`, `dashed`, `dotted`, `groove`, `ridge`, `inset`, or `outset`. Each of these border styles applies a different effect to the border, with the simplest styles being the `solid` and `double` styles. The default value of the `border-style` property is `none`, for no border at all.

The `border-color` style specifies the color of the border and is set to one of the standard colors that you learned in the previous chapter. You can also set the color to a custom color. To learn more about custom colors and how they are specified, refer to Appendix C, "Using Custom Colors."

The last of the border style properties is `border`, which combines the three border properties into a single property. It's a "convenience property," which means that it serves only to combine several other properties, but it's useful in making the code for a border style more concise. Here is an example of how to create a border around the paragraph of text in the backyard pond Web page:

```
<p style="width:375px; border:medium solid navy">
```

Borders can also be drawn around images. Look at this code showing how different borders are specified for the two images in the backyard pond Web page:

```
<img style="border:thick double navy" src="Pond1.jpg">
<img style="width:200px; position:relative; top:-0.75in;
left:-0.5in; border:medium dashed green" src="Fish2.jpg">
```

Figure 14-10 shows the backyard pond Web page with its three new borders.

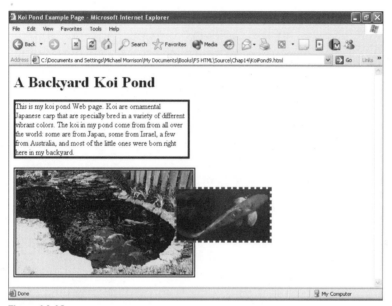

Figure 14-10 The border style is used to add borders to the elements in the backyard pond page.

As the figure shows, borders are a powerful means of clearly identifying elements on a page. When used properly, borders can serve an important visual and organizational role on Web pages.

Controlling Space on a Page

When you think about it, positioning elements is really just a matter of controlling space on a Web page. Not surprisingly, most positioning style properties directly impact or alter the space around elements. Some give you more control over the spacing of elements than others. Here are the style properties used to fine-tune the spacing of elements on a page:

- margin—Sets the margins of an element.
- padding—Sets the padding of an element.
- vertical-align—Aligns an element vertically with other elements.

The margin property should sound familiar because you ran across it in the previous chapter. If you recall, margins are used to constrain the area where text can appear in a paragraph. Margins don't apply to just paragraphs, however. Set the margin property for any element, and it serves to add space next to the element. In addition to the margin property, you can set individual margins for each side of an element using the margin-left, margin-right, margin-top, and margin-bottom properties.

Padding works like a margin, but it adds space to the inside of an element, as opposed to the outside. The inside and outside of an element refer to the invisible element boundary mentioned earlier in the chapter. A margin adds space around the outside of the boundary, which means that margin is displayed according to the parent element's style. Padding appears inside the boundary of an element, and therefore appears in the same style as the element.

Lingo   *Padding* refers to extra space added to the inside of an element, which is different from a margin that is applied to the outside of an element.

As an example, an element with a red background that's displayed in a <body> tag with a white background results in red padding for the element and a margin for the element with a white background. Likewise, if you specify a border for the element, the padding will appear inside the border and the margin will appear outside.

The padding property style is specified using a numeric measurement expressed in one of the now-familiar units. Here is an example of setting the padding for the paragraph in the backyard pond Web page:

```
<p style="width:375px; border:medium solid navy; padding:25px">
```

The results of this code are shown in Figure 14-11. As the figure reveals, the padding for the paragraph results in extra space appearing within the boundary of the paragraph element.

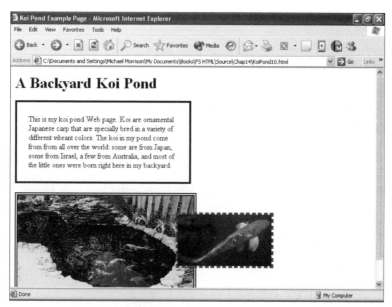

Figure 14-11 The `padding` style is used to add space around the text in a paragraph, but within the boundary of the paragraph element.

The `vertical-align` property aligns elements with each other vertically. It's often useful for aligning images of different sizes that wouldn't be aligned vertically without help. When you specify a value for the `vertical-align` property, you're specifying how an element is aligned with its parent or, in some cases, the current line of elements on the page.

Tip To align several images, place them within the same parent element and set their vertical alignments to the same value.

Here are the values that can be used with the `vertical-align` property:

- `top`—Aligns the top of an element with the current line.
- `middle`—Aligns the middle of an element with the middle of the parent.
- `bottom`—Aligns the bottom of an element with the current line.
- `text-top`—Aligns the top of an element with the top of the parent.

- `baseline`—Aligns the baseline of an element with the baseline of the parent.

- `text-bottom`—Aligns the bottom of an element with the bottom of the parent.

- `sub`—Aligns an element as a subscript of the parent.

- `super`—Aligns an element as a superscript of the parent.

Most of these property values make sense based on their descriptions, but a few require additional explanation. The `top` and `bottom` property values align elements according to the *current line* of a page, which is the location on the page where the elements naturally appear. To understand the concept of the current line, you have to consider that elements on a page are naturally arranged from left to right and then top to bottom. If you place a number of images on a page, they will appear from left to right across the page. When there isn't enough room, the next images are displayed on a new line below the previous images. The `top` and `bottom` property values align elements according to this invisible line.

The `baseline` value aligns an element with respect to its baseline and its parent's baseline. For images, the *baseline* is the same as the bottom of the image. The baseline of an element has significant meaning only when you're dealing with text. The *baseline* is the bottom of a line of text, excluding any letters that reach down below the others, such as *g* or *y*.

Here is an example of how to use the `vertical-align` property to align the tops of the two images in the backyard pond Web page:

```
<img src="Pond1.jpg">
<img style="width:200px; vertical-align:top" src="Fish2.jpg">
```

In this example, the results of this code are shown in Figure 14-12. This figure reveals that you can align images vertically with surprisingly little code.

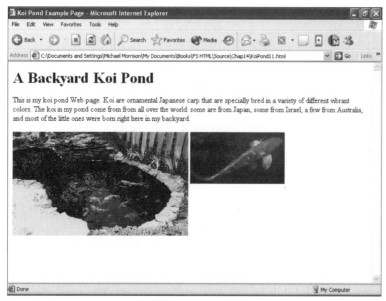

Figure 14-12 The `vertical-align` style is used to align the two images along their top edges.

Controlling the Flow of Text

In the previous section, I discussed the concept of the *current line*, which is an invisible line used to place elements on a page. It deals with the flow of elements on a page and comes into play as elements are arranged next to one another across and down the page. Part of the flow of elements is the flow of text on a page. When you mix text with other elements, such as images, it's important to control how the text flows around the other elements. Here are a few style properties that provide you with control over text flow:

- `float`—Determines how text flows around an element.

- `clear`—Stops the flow of text around an element.

- `overflow`—Controls the overflow of text when an element is too small to contain all of the text.

    The next few sections explore these style properties in more detail.

Flowing Text Around Other Elements

To control how text flows around an element, set the `float` style property of the element. It can be set to either `left` or `right`. These values determine where to position an element with respect to flowing text. So setting the `float` property to `left` results in an element positioned to the left of flowing text. Here is an example of how the `float` property is used to flow text between the two images in the backyard pond Web page:

```
<p>
<img style="float:left" src="Pond1.jpg">
<img style="width:200px; vertical-align:top; float:right" src="Fish2.jpg">
This is my koi pond Web page. Koi are ornamental Japanese carp
that are specially bred in a variety of different vibrant
colors. The koi in my pond come from all over the world;
some are from Japan, some from Israel, a few from Australia,
and most of the little ones were born right here in my
backyard.
</p>
```

The results of this code are shown in Figure 14-13. As you can see in the figure, the pond image is positioned to the left of the flowing text with the fish image to the right. You don't need to set the `float` property for the paragraph of text.

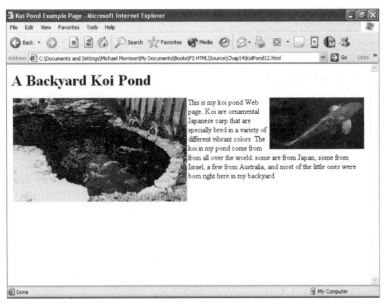

Figure 14-13 The `float` style is used to set the way text flows around the two images in the backyard pond Web page.

Stopping the Flow of Text

Just as the `float` property controls the flow of text around elements, you can prevent text from flowing next to an element by using the `clear` property. The `clear` property can be set to `none`, `left`, `right`, or `both`. The default value for the `clear` property is `none`, indicating that text is to continue flowing normally. The `left` value denotes that text is to stop flowing around an element until the left side of the page is clear. Likewise, the `right` value means that text is to stop flowing around an element until the right side is clear. The `both` value indicates that text is to stop flowing until both sides of the page are clear of elements.

Dealing with Overflow Text

Earlier in the chapter, you learned that you can change the size of an element using the `width` and `height` properties, but keep in mind that making it too small might prevent you from seeing all of it. The text that doesn't fit within the paragraph is known as *overflow text*, and it can be dealt with in several ways.

The `overflow` property style handles overflow text and can be set to `visible`, `hidden`, or `scroll`. `Visible` automatically enlarges the element so the overflow text will fit in it; this is the default setting for the `overflow` property. The `hidden` value leaves the element the same size, allowing the overflow text to remain hidden from view. Perhaps the most interesting is `scroll`, which adds scroll bars to the element so you can move around and see the text in the element.

A Complete Positional Style Example

You've seen most of the property styles discussed in this chapter in isolation, which can sometimes make them tough to grasp from a practical perspective. The point of the examples you've seen wasn't to demonstrate good layout strategies, but to show you how the different positioning property styles work. Now it's time to pull together what you've learned and create a final version of the backyard pond Web page that has a nice visual layout. Study this code for the complete page; it includes some new content:

```
<html>
<head>
  <title>Koi Pond Example Page</title>

  <style>
    img.left { float:left }
    img.right { float:right }
    p { padding:20px; width:625px; border:medium double navy }
  </style>
</head>
```

```
<body bgcolor="white">
  <h1>A Backyard Koi Pond</h1>
  <p>
  <img class="left" src="Pond1.jpg">
  This is my koi pond Web page. Koi are ornamental Japanese
  carp that are specially bred in a variety of different
  vibrant colors. The koi in my pond come from all
  over the world; some are from Japan, some from
  Israel, a few from Australia, and most of the little
  ones were born right here in my backyard.
  </p>
  <p>
  <img class="right" src="Pond2.jpg">
  This is another view of the pond that shows how the
  fish like to congregate in one end while eating. As
  with people, they like to socialize at mealtime. Of
  course, they are more aggressive eaters than most
  people I know.
  </p>
  <p>
  <img class="left" src="Fish1.jpg">
  This picture shows a feeding frenzy of koi of all
  sizes and colors. Notice the orange fish in the
  pictureÑhis name is Big Ern. I've had him for several
  years, and he's one of the friendlier fish in the
  pond. He likes to splash about while eatingÑI suppose
  you could call him a rowdy eater.
  </p>
  <p>
  <img class="right" src="Fish2.jpg">
  Here's a close-up of Big Ern, the rowdy eater.
  </p>
  </body>
</html>
```

I'll admit that this is one of the longer pages that you've seen in this book,
but the extra code demonstrates how the positional style properties affect the
layout of the page. You'll notice in the code that the positional style properties
are specified in a style sheet rather than as local styles. This dramatically simplifies the code for the page and also makes it easier to maintain. Figure 14-14
shows the final backyard pond Web page as viewed in Internet Explorer.

Figure 14-14 The completed backyard pond Web page uses several positional style properties in its layout.

Although you can't see all of the content for this page in the figure, it gives you an idea of how the positional style properties are used to control the position of elements on the page. Granted, by most standards this is a simple layout, yet you should be able to use the general layout of this page as a starting point for applying the positional style properties to your own Web pages.

Tip   The code for this example, as well as all of the examples throughout the book, is available for download from my Web site at the following URL: *http://www.michaelmorrison.com /cbook_fshtml.html.*

Try This!   If you think the borders are a little too heavy in the pond example page, try changing the border thickness to thin.

Key Points

■ Positional style properties can be used either locally or in style sheets and give you a surprising amount of control over how elements are positioned on a Web page.

■ The two fundamental approaches to positioning Web content using style sheets are *relative positioning* and *absolute positioning*.

■   Relative positioning specifies the position of an element based on its normal position, while absolute positioning specifies the position of an element with respect to the parent element.

■   The `position` style property is used to specify whether an element uses relative or absolute positioning and can be set to either `relative` or `absolute`.

■   The z-index of an element determines how the element is displayed with respect to any elements that it overlaps and is set using the `z-index` style property.

■   The `display` style property controls the visibility of elements and allows you to show and hide elements on a page.

■   The `border` style property allows you to establish a border for an element, which is a visible rectangular outline around the outside of the element.

■   *Margins* and *padding* allow you to add extra space around the outside and inside of an element, respectively.

■   The *current line* is an invisible line used to place elements on a page, and it comes in quite handy when you need to carefully control how elements are arranged next to one another across and down the page.

Integrating Multimedia with Your Web Pages

In HTML, multimedia refers to the mixing of audio, video, and Web pages. Standard HTML allows you to work with text, images, and even animated images. But I've held off mentioning sound and traditional video until now. This chapter explores the possibilities of adding sound and video to your Web pages by using HTML. So pull that microphone and video camera out of the closet and brush up on your directing skills. Action!

Understanding Plug-ins and Helper Applications

If you've ever seen a Glade air freshener in a bathroom, you know what I'm talking about when I refer to a *plug-in*. Web browsers have their own version of plug-in—without the refreshing scent. Browser plug-in programs display Web content that the browser can't, such as video clips. A lot of multimedia content falls outside the realm of standard browser support, which is why plug-ins enter the picture. You may not even realize that your browser is using a plug-in because the plug-in typically appears directly in the browser window. In other words, you won't see another program launch when a plug-in is activated.

Note   If you've spent any time on the Web, you've probably run across an Adobe Acrobat file, also known as a PDF file, which requires the Adobe Acrobat Reader plug-in to be read. If you don't have the appropriate plug-in, your browser usually tells you where you can obtain it on the Web.

A Web browser examines the extension of the multimedia file to figure out how to handle its content. This extension is sufficient for the browser to determine what kind of file it is and whether it's necessary to use a plug-in. As an example, when a browser encounters files with a .jpg or .gif file name extension, it recognizes the files as standard browser images and has no problem displaying them. But if a browser encounters a file with a .pict or .tif extension—nonstandard in browser terms—the browser will search for the plug-in that you need to view the image.

Note   PICT and TIFF are image formats not commonly used in Web pages. This is primarily because these image formats don't compress image sizes as efficiently as JPEG or GIF, so they are more appropriate for desktop publishing where image size isn't such a critical issue.

If a plug-in for a certain file type isn't available, the browser will look for a *helper application*. A helper application differs from a plug-in; it's a separate program launched independently of the browser. Just as you might use Windows Media Player to play a video or *MP3* music file, a helper application is launched outside of the browser to display an image or video, or to play a piece of audio.

Lingo   MP3 is a music format that allows you to store and play digital music on your computer. MP3 music is now supported on several portable digital music players, and was widely covered by the media because of the legal battle between the music recording industry and the popular Napster music file-sharing service.

Because it's less distracting to see a media file displayed directly within a Web browser, the browser attempts to find a plug-in first and then looks for a helper application if the search fails. If the browser finds neither one, it typically prompts you to save the file to your local hard disk.

A browser generally recognizes files from a standard media type known as *Multipurpose Internet Mail Extensions (MIME)*. This collection of file types was used originally to encode different types of files so that they could be sent easily as e-mail messages. Today, MIME types are also used as the basis for identifying files for browsing purposes. Table 15-1 contains the different MIME types that you will likely encounter as you work with multimedia files.

Table 15-1   Common MIME Types

Extension(s)	MIME Type	Media Type
.gif	image/gif	Image
.jpg, .jpeg, .jpe	image/jpeg	Image
.tif, .tiff	image/tiff	Image
.pic, .pict	image/pict	Image
.xbm	image/x-xbitmap	Image
.wav	audio/x-wave	Audio
.au, .snd	audio/basic	Audio
.aiff,, .aif	audio/aiff	Audio
.mpg, .mpeg, .mpe	video/mpeg	Video
.qt, .mov	video/quicktime	Video
.avi	video/x-msvideo	Video

MIME types are used to identify different multimedia files that often appear on the Web. The MIME type names listed in Table 15-1 are somewhat cryptic, but fortunately it's not important for you to remember them. Just understand that each type of multimedia format has an associated media type that a browser uses to determine what to do with the file. You can see in the last column that each of the MIME types boils down to one of three fundamental types of media: an image, an audio clip, or a video clip. A few MIME types are directly supported in your browser, but others require a plug-in to view or listen to them. Some types require a helper application if no plug-in is installed. It ultimately depends on the browser you are using and what plug-ins you have installed.

Note   Not all file types have MIME types associated with them. If a Web browser encounters a file type that doesn't have a MIME type, it uses the operating system's file associations to search for a helper application.

Working with Sound

A computer is a digital machine. All information on a computer is stored as a series of 0s and 1s. This means that sound on a computer is also digital. However, sound in the real world isn't digital, and it must be converted to be stored and played on a computer. *Sampling* made its mark on the music industry in the eighties when rap artists sampled rhythm and blues melodies and drum beats and used them in their own songs. After lengthy litigation, sampling is now permitted, provided that one has permission from the original artist.

Lingo   The process of converting a real-world sound to a digital computer sound is known as *sampling*.

Sampling is important because sounds must be sampled to be playable within a Web page. The manner in which a sound is sampled determines both its quality and the size of its file. There is a significant trade-off in determining the ideal sampling approach to achieve maximum sound quality without requiring a huge sound file. It's tough to get CD quality sound out of small sound files. On the other hand, large sound files result in long download times. This is not a good thing!

The duration of a sound affects its size proportionately. And some sounds are too long to trim down to a reasonable size. Some sounds are, theoretically, infinite in length. For example, an Internet radio station broadcasts digitally over the Internet in real time. Because the broadcast is continuous, there is no way to limit the size of the sound file. In fact, it's hard for the user to tell if there is a sound file because there isn't really a start or an end to the audio clip. This brings us to the distinction between two types of sound on the Web: *static sounds* and *streaming sounds*.

Lingo   *Static sounds* are those that have a defined end and typically must be downloaded completely before you can start listening to them. They are good for storing short sound clips. *Streaming sounds* usually don't have a defined end, and can be played while they are being downloaded. Their primary benefit is that they can be quite long, and they can be played without waiting until the entire sound has been downloaded.

The general rule is that you should use static sounds for shorter sound clips and rely on streaming sounds for sounds with longer download times. Live audio broadcasts on the Web are treated as streaming sounds. Although streaming sounds are ideal in many ways, there are a few drawbacks: They often require a special audio server, and they are more difficult to prepare.

Don't forget that you can't use copyrighted sounds without the copyright owner's written permission. So be careful when sampling sounds from copyrighted sources.

Note   Some sound collections that you might assume are in the public domain are actually copyrighted. Most collections come in the form of an audio CD containing a variety of sound effects. Read the fine print and be sure you can legally use the sounds, or get written permission from the publisher.

Creating Your Own Sounds

Because the majority of the sounds out there are copyrighted, you may want to create your own sounds for your Web pages. You can record with a microphone or use sampled sounds from a stereo cassette deck or VCR. The microphone is the easiest route; most computers these days come equipped with one. If you have some sounds in mind from a prerecorded cassette or home movie, you will need to connect an external sound source to your computer. To sample a sound, you use a special program called a sound editor. If your computer came with a microphone and a sound card, it probably has a sound editor already installed. In fact, all computers with Windows come with a simple sound editor called Sound Recorder.

Note If you have a Creative Labs sound card, your computer probably also has Wave Studio already installed. It is a full-featured sound editor with interesting effects to spice up sounds.

There is basically one way to clean up a sampled sound for use on the Web, regardless of the sound's source. Sample the sound and play it back to make sure that it's okay. It's likely that the sound will be either too loud or too soft. You can judge the volume by looking at the sound's *waveform* in a sound editor.

Lingo The *waveform* of a sound is its graphical appearance plotted over time.

If the sound waveform goes beyond the top or bottom of the waveform display, you know it's too loud. If you can barely hear it, it's too soft. You can either adjust the input level for the sound device and resample the sound or use amplification effects provided by the sound editor. Amplification effects allow you to make a sound louder or softer.

The best way to fix the volume problem is to adjust the input level of the sound device and resample the sound. For example, in Windows you can easily adjust the microphone or line input level using the Volume Control application shown in Figure 15-1. To launch the Volume Control application, just follow these steps:

1 Click the Start button in Windows.

2 Select All Programs, followed by Accessories, and then Entertainment.

3 Select Volume Control to launch the application.

Note that the content of the Volume Control window is determined by the audio hardware and software on your computer and may look a bit different than the figure.

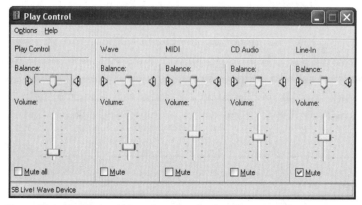

Figure 15-1   The Windows Volume Control application allows you to alter the level of the microphone and line input.

Once you get the volume of the sound at a level you like, you'll want to clip the sound to remove unwanted portions. *Clipping* a sound means zooming in on the waveform in a sound editor and cutting out unwanted silence or other sounds. This is important because it removes unneeded parts of a sound, such as silence at the beginning and end. The shortened sound plays more quickly and takes up less file space.

Try This!   Windows includes several built-in sounds that are used throughout the system to indicate certain events. To find out what sounds are already on your system, just perform a search on files with the .wav file extension. To get started, click the Start button and then Search.

Once you have a sound clipped, it should be ready to roll, but first check out the effects that are available with your sound utility. Simple effects range from reverb to echo; advanced effects include fading and phase shifts. It's up to your imagination and discerning ear.

Finding Sounds

If you don't have the vocal skills of Michael Winslow—the self-proclaimed master of 10,000 sound effects in the *Police Academy* movies of the eighties and nineties—don't despair. You can seek an outside sound source. The best source for prerecorded sounds is sound archives on the Web, and there are many available with an array of sounds. Keep in mind that you need to be careful about the copyrights of these sounds, too. In general, sounds in an archive are safe to use, but always double-check.

I've found the Microsoft Design Gallery Live useful for finding sounds. It's also great for clip art and other Web site images. It has numerous sounds, and is unique because you can search the sounds by keyword. Figure 15-2 shows the Design Gallery Live Web site, located at *http://dgl.microsoft.com/*.

Figure 15-2 Microsoft's Design Gallery Live provides an archive of sounds that you can search using keywords.

Another good place to find sounds is the World Wide Web Virtual Library, which maintains an audio page with links to sound archives. It is located at *http://www.comlab.ox.ac.uk/archive/audio.html*. Yet another good sound source is the Yahoo! audio archive, located at *http://dir.yahoo.com/Computers_and_Internet/Multimedia/Audio/Archives/*. Examples of what you'll find on these archive sites are animal sounds, military sounds, spoken phrases, and sound effects of all kinds, from bubbling liquids to screeching tires.

Archived sounds may be stored in different formats. Currently, the most common is the WAV format, Microsoft's standard Windows sound format. Sounds stored in the WAV format are also known as *wave files*, or simply *waves*. All WAV sounds are static sounds. RealAudio and RealMedia are two other sound formats widely used on the Web. RealAudio is used for static sounds, and Real-Media for streaming sounds. If you plan to place short sound clips in your Web pages, your best bet will be to find sounds in WAV or RealAudio formats, although RealAudio sounds require a special browser plug-in.

Note   Another sound format you might run across in your search is the *Musical Instrument Digital Interface (MIDI)* format, which is used to store music in very small files. MIDI files usually have
the .mid extension. They can be used in most browsers to provide simple music without taking up
much space.

Adding Sounds to Your Web Pages

Finally, we get into the fun stuff! Let's use HTML code to add sound to a Web
page. Note that there are three approaches to using sound, and that they differ
with respect to how a sound is played when the browser encounters it in a Web
page. Here are the ways you can use a sound in a Web page:

- Link to the sound, in which case an external helper application will
  play it.

- Embed the sound, in which case the browser or a plug-in will play it.

- Set the sound as the background sound, in which case the browser or
  a plug-in will play it as soon as the page is opened.

Many users find it annoying when a Web page starts playing sounds immediately upon being opened in a browser. You should strongly consider giving
the user the option of playing a sound. This is primarily an issue when it comes
to background sounds, which we will get to soon.

Linking to Sounds

Linking to a sound from a Web page is the cleanest, simplest way to use sounds
on the Web. Playing the sound is optional for the user, and the browser relies on
a helper application to play that sound. To link to a sound from a page, use the
familiar <a> anchor tag. You may recall that the href attribute of this tag is used
to identify the target of the link, in this case the URL of the sound file. Here is an
example of how you link to a sound using the <a> tag:

```
<p>
Click <a href="Funny.wav">here</a> to listen to a funny sound clip!
</p>
```

This code reveals how easy it is to link to sounds in your Web pages. You
may find it more interesting to link sounds to an image, such as an ear or a

speaker. Here is example code from a Web page that uses small images as links to sounds of animals that live in a pond:

```
<html>
<head>
  <title>Pond Friends</title>
</head>

<body>
<h2>Pond Friends</h2>
<table cellspacing="20">
<tr>
  <td>
  <img src="Pond.jpg">
  </td>

  <td>
  <p>
  This is a picture of my backyard pond. Several different
  types of animals live in the pond, and they all make
  distinctive sounds. Here are a few of the animals that
  inhabit the pond:
  </p>
   <bl>
  <li>Frogs <a href="Frog.wav"><img src="Speaker.gif"
  border="0"></a></li>
  <li>Mosquitos <a href="Mosquito.wav"><img src="Speaker.gif"
  border="0"></a></li>
  <li>Ducks <a href="Duck.wav"><img src="Speaker.gif"
  border="0"></a></li>
  </bl>
  </td>
</tr>
</table>
</body>
</html>
```

Tip   The code for this example, as well as all of the examples throughout the book, is available for download from my Web site at the following URL: *http://www.michaelmorrison.com/ cbook_fshtml.html.*

Figure 15-3 shows how this Web page uses a small image of a speaker to serve as the link to sound clips.

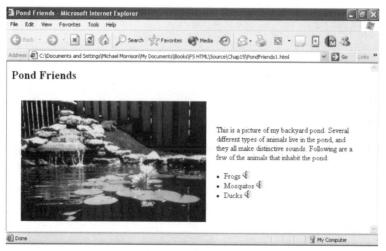

Figure 15-3 The Pond Friends Web page uses a small speaker image to serve as a link to animal sounds.

Okay, I exaggerated a little on the Pond Friends Web page—my pond doesn't have ducks. (However, it does have some hefty *koi*, those colorful Japanese fish, which to me are more appealing than ducks.) Getting back to the sound aspects of the Pond Friends Web page, click one of the speaker images, as shown in Figure 15-4, and a helper application launches to play the sound.

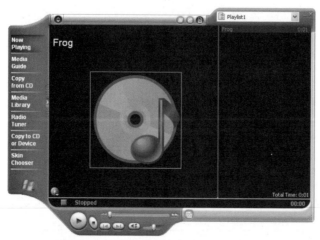

Figure 15-4 Click one of the speaker links in the Pond Friends Web page, and a helper application launches to play the appropriate sound.

If you don't like the idea of using a helper application to play sounds, you may want to consider embedding sounds in your pages.

Embedding Sounds

A browser can play a sound embedded in a Web page without a helper application. In some ways, this is more appealing for the user because it doesn't involve another window popping up. On the other hand, browsers are more limited in the types of sound files that they can play as embedded sounds. Stick with the WAV format and you'll probably be just fine. To embed a sound in a Web page, use the `<embed>` tag. The URL of the sound file is specified in the `<embed>` tag by using the `src` attribute. Here is an example of how to embed a sound using the `<embed>` tag and the `src` attribute:

```
<embed src="Frog.wav">
```

Although this code works fine, it results in the sound being played automatically when the page is first opened in the browser. It also results in the display of a large multimedia console with play, pause, and stop buttons, along with a volume control. These are nifty features, but the multimedia console takes up a lot of space on the screen, and you usually want an embedded sound to take up minimal space.

These problems are solved with additional attributes of the `<embed>` tag: `width`, `height`, `hidden`, and `autostart`. The `width` and `height` attributes allow you to set the size of the multimedia console; a minimum size of 25 × 25 pixels leaves enough room for a play button—ideal for most embedded sounds. The `hidden` attribute, if set to `true`, will hide the multimedia console entirely. The `autostart` attribute allows you to set whether the sound plays automatically when the page opens. Here is an example of how the previous embedded sound example might be modified using these attributes:

```
<embed src="Frog.wav" width="25" height="25" autostart="false">
```

> **Tip** The `<embed>` tag also supports the `align` attribute, which serves the same purpose as it does with the `<image>` tag. It aligns the multimedia console for the sound with respect to any surrounding content.

Here is the code for the Pond Friends Web page that you saw previously, modified to use embedded sounds instead of linked sounds:

```
<html>
<head>
  <title>Pond Friends</title>
</head>

<body>
<h2>Pond Friends</h2>
```

```
<table cellspacing="20">
<tr>
  <td>
  <img src="Pond.jpg">
  </td>

  <td>
  <p>
  This is a picture of my backyard pond. Several different
  types of animals live in the pond, and they all make
  distinctive sounds. Following are a few of the animals that
  inhabit the pond:
  </p>
  <bl>
  <li>Frogs <embed src="Frog.wav" width="25" height="25"
  autostart="false"></li>
  <li>Mosquitos <embed src="Mosquito.wav" width="25"
  height="25" autostart="false"></li>
  <li>Ducks <embed src="Duck.wav" width="25" height="25"
  autostart="false"></li>
  </bl>
  </td>
</tr>
</table>
</body>
</html>
```

As you can see, this code no longer includes the anchor tags, but uses
<embed> tags to embed the sounds on the page. Figure 15-5 shows that the
resulting page displays small play buttons for each sound, as opposed to the
speaker image link.

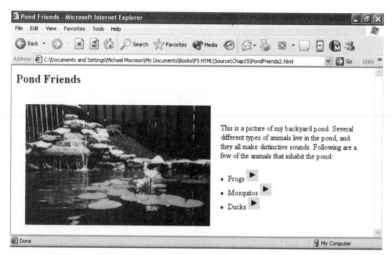

Figure 15-5 The embedded sounds on the Pond Friends Web page are identified by small play buttons that play a sound when clicked.

When you click any of the play buttons, the appropriate animal sound plays directly in the browser. This is more convenient for the user than linked sounds, provided the browser supports the embedded sound format.

Caution   Although you will need version 7 or later of Windows Media Player for any of these examples, I've noticed that some of the earlier releases of version 7 do not support this use of the `width` and `height` attributes to access the Media Player's control bar. In Windows Media Player, open the Help menu and select About Windows Media Player. Ensure the version number is 7.00.00.1956 or later. If it is not, then log onto the Internet, open the Help menu, and select Check For Player Upgrades; your version of Media Player will be updated and these examples should play accurately.

Try This! Jazz up the Pond Friends Web page by adding a few new creatures, along with their respective sounds. Feel free to use any of the sound resources mentioned throughout the chapter, including your own voice if you think you can belt out a decent sound effect!

One last `<embed>` attribute to know is `loop`, which allows you to loop a sound multiple times. Specify a number of repetitions in the `loop` attribute. Or set it to `true`, and the sound will continue to loop until the user clicks the stop button on the multimedia console. This assumes you've made the stop button accessible by using a higher value for the `width` attribute. Otherwise, the user won't be able to stop the sound without leaving the page. If your intent with the `loop` attribute is to establish a background sound, such as music that plays continuously, consider setting it as the background sound for the page.

Using Background Sounds

I don't like recommending solutions that are applicable only to a specific browser, but I must point out that Internet Explorer supports a tag for background sounds: `<bgsound>`. A background sound is one that is played when the user first opens a Web page, similar to an embedded sound with its `autostart` attribute set to `true`. However, background sounds don't have a visual presence on the page, so you don't have to worry about sizing the multimedia console. Like embedded sounds, the `<bgsound>` tag has a loop attribute that can be set so that a sound plays a certain number of times. Or set the `loop` attribute to `infinite`, in which case the sound will play until the user leaves the page. Here is an example of how you might set a background sound for a page:

```
<bgsound src="Music.wav" loop="infinite">
```

It's important to use a relatively subtle sound. Otherwise, you run the risk of driving people away from your site. Some people, myself included, are genuinely annoyed by most background sounds. Also, consider that many people work in office environments in which unexpected sounds can be a problem. They may enjoy listening to music while surfing the Web but dislike hearing someone else's background sounds at the same time.

Working with Video

Virtually anyone can buy a digital video camera for under U.S.$1,000 and create videos and movies. Inexpensive video-editing software makes it relatively painless to edit video, add professional wipes and fades between scenes, and overlay music and sound effects. Video has entered the digital age and opened up the possibility for the next Steven Spielberg to emerge from any home studio. Knowing how many aspiring Spielbergs are out there, I'm not surprised that video has made its way onto the Web in a big way.

Like sounds, videos can be either static or streaming. The majority are streaming because video files are much larger than sound files. Waiting for a video file to download can be a real drag; I have a cable modem, fast by most standards, and some videos still take several minutes to download.

Creating Your Own Videos

As I said, it's easier than ever to create your own videos if you have access to either a traditional video camera or one of the newer digital models. You'll need a special video card in your computer, with a connector for hooking the camera to the computer and transferring the video, or a separate device that allows you to connect a camera to your computer via a USB or FireWire port. Many newer computers come standard with video inputs for pulling video from a camera, along with video-editing software. If you have a PC without a graphics card, you can install one or use an external video input device. One is the Dazzle Digital Video Creator, which plugs into your computer's universal serial bus (USB) port and captures videos from a video camera, allowing you to edit them on your PC.

Note   PCs these days include *USB ports*, which allow you to connect different kinds of devices to your computer. For example, many digital cameras communicate with computers using a USB port. *FireWire* is another kind of port that is ideally suited for video because it is incredibly fast.

Regardless of the hardware and software used to create videos, the result is basically the same. You end up with a video file that can be played back using a video player. Popular formats for static video files include Moving Picture Experts

Group (MPEG); Audio-Video Interleaved (AVI), which is promoted by Microsoft; and QuickTime, which is promoted by Apple. MPEG videos have a file name extension of .mpe, .mpg, or .mpeg. AVI videos use .avi, and QuickTime movies use a file name extension of .mov or .qt. All three formats can be used on the Web, although each requires a plug-in that is determined by the browser you're using.

Finding Videos

If you don't aspire to be the next Martin Scorsese, you might consider using existing videos for your Web pages. Streaming video is used on the Web more often than static video, so there aren't as many video archives. There are a few sources, however; you just have to hunt for them. Keep in mind that most video archives are specific to a certain topic, such as movies or sports.

Some of the best sources for video archives are movie-related Web sites. For example, the Web site Jurassic Punk, at *http://www.jurassicpunk.com/* includes videos of the latest movie trailers. This is a great way to find out about new movies. Another movie-related site with loads of videos is Jim Carrey Online—mostly his movie clips. Carrey fans will be in Carrey heaven at *http://www.jimcarreyonline.com/videoclips/*.

If you're looking for something more educational, check out Volcano World, which has several video clips of erupting volcanoes. The video section of Volcano World is located at *http://volcano.und.nodak.edu/vwdocs/movies/ movie.html*. Also take a look at the National Oceanic and Atmospheric Administration (NOAA) Web site located at *http://www.pmel.noaa.gov/vents/geology/ video.html*. The New Millennium Observatory off the coast of Oregon filmed intriguing videos of underwater volcanoes.

Adding Videos to Your Web Pages

You'll be glad to learn that adding videos to your Web pages is virtually identical to adding sounds. The next two sections explore the details of adding videos to Web pages, revealing the similarities of coding sound and video in HTML.

Linking to Videos

The <a> anchor tag allows you to link from your Web pages to videos; you used it earlier in the chapter to link sounds. Not surprisingly, the href attribute of this tag is used to identify the URL of the video file. Here is an example of how to link to a video using the <a> tag:

```
<p>
Fortunately, Junior's first home run was immortalized on
<a href="HomeRun.avi">video</a>.
</p>
```

In this code, the word *video* serves as the text link to the video file HomeRun.avi. When you click the word video to activate the link, the HomeRun.avi video is displayed by a helper application, such as Windows Media Player.

Similar to the technique for sounds used earlier in the chapter, it is also possible to link to a video with an image. Here is an example of code from a Web page that uses a small image of a piece of film as the link to an ice hockey video:

```
<html>
<head>
  <title>Hockey Skills</title>
</head>

<body>
<h2>Hockey Skills</h2>
<p>
Hockey is a game of considerable skill. One of the toughest
skills to develop is that of a quick, powerful, yet accurate
shot. Some shots go so far beyond the realm of normal skill
that they are just about unbelievable. This video clip
demonstrates what I'm talking about. <a href="HockeyShot.avi">
<img src="Film.gif" border="0"></a>
</p>
</body>
</html>
```

Figure 15-6 shows how this Web page looks when viewed in Internet Explorer.

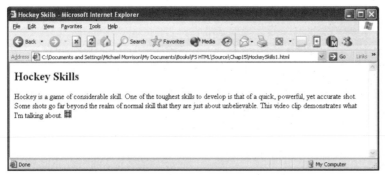

Figure 15-6 The Hockey Skills Web page uses a small film image to serve as a link to an incredible hockey video.

When you click on the little film image on this page, a helper application plays the video, as shown in Figure 15-7.

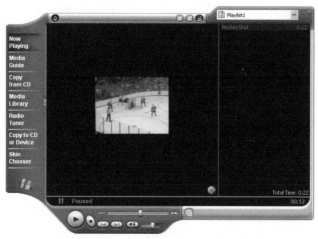

Figure 15-7 When you click the film link in the Hockey Skills Web page, a helper application launches to play the video.

As with playing sounds, you may prefer to embed videos directly in a page so that they are played directly within the browser, as opposed to being played in a separate helper application. If so, you'll be interested in the next section. Keep in mind that video formats vary considerably, which means that browsers are more likely to delegate the specifics of supporting different video formats to helper applications. On the other hand, some plug-ins allow you to play embedded video.

Embedding Videos

To embed a video in a Web page, you use the <embed> tag, which is the same tag you used earlier in the chapter to embed sounds. The URL of the video file is specified in the <embed> tag by the src attribute. Here is an example of how to embed a video using the <embed> tag and the src attribute:

```
<embed src="HomeRun.avi">
```

Embedded videos have the same issues as embedded sounds in terms of how they are presented to the user. The same attributes of the <embed> tag alter the presentation and control of the videos: width, height, autostart, and loop. The autostart attribute allows you to set whether the video is played automatically when the page opens, and the loop attribute determines how many times the video plays. Unlike the width and height attributes for embedded sounds, these attributes are critically important for embedded videos because they determine the viewing area of the video.

Here is the Web page titled Hockey Skills from the previous section, modified to use an embedded video:

```
<html>
<head>
  <title>Hockey Skills</title>
</head>

<body>
<h2>Hockey Skills</h2>
<p>
Hockey is a game of considerable skill. One of the toughest
skills to develop is that of a quick, powerful, yet accurate
shot. Some shots go so far beyond the realm of normal skill
that they are just about unbelievable. This video clip
demonstrates what IÕm talking about.<br>
<embed src="HockeyShot.avi" width="200" height="200"
autostart="false"></a>
</p>
</body>
</html>
```

This code no longer includes the anchor, but instead uses the `<embed>` tag to embed the video on the page. Figure 15-8 shows how the video is displayed on the page when viewed in a Web browser.

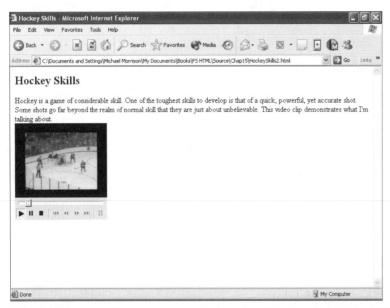

Figure 15-8 The embedded video is shown directly on the Web page called Hockey Skills.

Along with playing the video on the Web page, you can also control the video using the multimedia console buttons along the bottom of the video image.

Dealing with Other Types of Multimedia

In addition to the multimedia file types mentioned in this chapter, there are other types that you might run across on the Web. Here are some of these types of multimedia:

■ Java applets and animations

■ Flash movies and animations

■ Virtual 3-D worlds

Although all of these media types are interesting in their own right, it would be too ambitious to cover all of them in this chapter. There are tons of Java books out there for learning to use Java applets and animations. You can also check out the official Web site for Java at *http://java.sun.com/*. Flash is another widely used technology for creating animations as well as full-blown cartoons and games. To learn more about Flash and how to use it in your Web pages, visit the Macromedia Web site at *http://www.macromedia.com/*.

And finally, there are several technologies for creating and adding virtual 3-D worlds to your Web pages. One such technology comes in the form of a browser plug-in called Rover and a special XML-based language—3DML—used to describe 3-D worlds. Rover and 3DML are products of Flatland Online and are very cool technologies. Check them out at the Flatland Web site at *http://www.flatland.com/*.

Key Points

■ The only thing stopping multimedia from becoming the central focus of the Web is the limited connection speeds imposed by current modems and networks; multimedia content takes up a lot of space and takes a considerable amount of time to download.

■ High-speed connections, such as those offered by cable and DSL modems, are opening the door for more multimedia-rich Web sites.

■ Browser plug-in programs display Web content that browsers can't, such as video clips.

■ A helper application differs from a plug-in; it's a separate program launched independently of the browser.

■   The MIME (Multipurpose Internet Mail Extensions) collection of file
      types is used to identify different multimedia files that often appear on
      the Web.

■   The familiar <a> anchor tag is used to link to a sound or video clip
      from a Web page.

■   The <embed> tag is used to embed a sound or video clip in a Web page.

■   In Internet Explorer, you can use the <bgsound> tag to play a back-
      ground sound for a Web page.

Part IV

Beyond HTML with XML

Part IV leads you a few steps beyond HTML and introduces you to XML, which is one of the key technologies shaping the future of the Web. You will learn how to organize data using XML, as well as how to use a special type of style sheet to process and transform XML documents for display within a Web browser. This part concludes by examining the merger of HTML and XML, which is the new *extensible* hypertext markup language known as XHTML.

Chapter 16

Organizing Data with XML

As I'm sure you know, there's a great deal of information floating around out there on the Internet. Not surprisingly, little of this information is structured in a meaningful way, other than being formatted for easy viewing, which sometimes makes it difficult to find what you're looking for. Granted, search engines do a good job of dealing with the chaos of the Web's colossal information overload but, for most of us, an added degree of organization and structure would be welcome. Fortunately, the industry is rapidly adopting a technology that aims to provide this.

I'm referring to *XML*, which you learned in Chapter 1, "An Introduction to HTML, DHTML, and XML," stands for *Extensible Markup Language*. Like HTML, XML allows you to use tags to create Web pages and other documents. In addition, XML is designed to be completely open-ended; you can create your own tags to give pages unique meaning. This isn't possible with HTML. You will learn in this chapter that XML introduces a whole new way of thinking about the Web and electronic information in general. It is sure to challenge and broaden your perspective about Web pages.

Getting to Know XML

Because Chapter 1 dealt with XML at a conceptual level, I want to dive in with the XML language and show you how it works. If you recall, XML is a generic language used to describe other markup languages such as HTML. Knowing this, you'll find XML to be extremely general and open-ended. It's not until you begin working with specific *XML vocabularies* that the true power of XML comes into full view. So as you learn about XML, try to think about how it might affect the HTML markup you've used so far.

Lingo   An *XML vocabulary* is a markup language designed using XML that applies to a specific type of content. For example, MathML (Mathematical Markup Language) is an XML vocabulary that allows you to create mathematical equations using markup code.

The first thing to understand about XML is that it makes a clear distinction between *markup* and *content*.

Lingo   *Markup* consists of the tags and attributes used to describe information in an XML document; *content* is the information itself.

In the following example of HTML code, can you guess which parts are markup and which are content?

```
<p>Let's sing a lament, the world isn't round it's <i>twisted
and bent</i>.</p>
```

In this HTML code, the `<p>`, `<i>`, `</i>`, and `</p>` tags are all markup; the remaining sentence text is content. Here, the markup is used to describe the appearance of the content, which is typical of HTML code. XML markup is often more descriptive and doesn't necessarily have anything to do with the appearance of content. Here is an example of a hypothetical XML document:

```
<question answer="true">The world's termites outweigh the
world's humans ten to one. True or False?</question>
```

In this code, a hypothetical question-and-answer XML vocabulary is used to mark up content for a True/False question. Notice that the question is marked up using the `<question>` tag; the answer is specified by the `answer` attribute. None of this markup has anything to do with the content's appearance; instead, it focuses on its meaning. However, the markup is instantly familiar because it's formatted in a manner similar to HTML.

Although I've talked in terms of tags when describing the creation of XML documents, the actual structure is determined by *elements*.

Lingo   An *element* is a discrete piece of information within an XML document, typically corresponding to a tag or a set of tags.

For example, in the question markup you just saw, there is an element named `question` that is marked in the document by using the `<question>` and

</question> tags. It's helpful to think in terms of elements when you're analyzing an XML vocabulary instead of thinking in terms of tags. Another way to explain elements is to say that they describe the structure of XML documents.

An element can have both start and end tags, as in the question element, or a single empty tag. An HTML example of an element with both start and end tags is the p paragraph element, which has both the <p> and </p> tags. An HTML element with a single empty tag is the img image element, which has only the <img/> tag. Notice that I closed the empty <img/> tag with a forward slash (/) before the closing angle bracket (>). This is important in XML; all empty tags must have a closing slash. This is the first of several picky XML coding conventions that you need to get used to.

XML elements are capable of containing content, child elements, or both. Content in XML is often referred to as *character data*, to indicate that it consists of characters of text. When an element contains child elements, it means that they're nested within the element. Although this may sound tricky, you are already experienced with nested elements. In fact, you just saw an example of HTML code that included both nested child elements and character data. Here is the sentence I just showed you:

```
<p>Let's sing a lament, the world isn't round it's <i>twisted
and bent</i>.</p>
```

In this code, the p element contains the i element as a child element, along with the character data for part of the sentence. The i element also contains the character data twisted and bent. When you look at examples such as this, it becomes apparent that XML is not as complicated as it sounds.

Note XML is a very formal language, so it helps to get used to terms like *character data*. I've made an effort to dress down XML as much as possible, but some of the formality is necessary to explain things accurately.

The XML language consists of several components that describe the makeup of different parts of a document. Here are the major XML components:

- Element tags
- Entity references
- Comments
- Processing instructions
- Document type declarations

Don't worry if these components sound technical because you're about to
see that they're actually easy to understand. Their significance is that they
describe the fundamental structure of the XML language, dictating the makeup
of all XML documents. With a solid understanding of these components, you'll
be able to read and understand the overall structure of any XML document, not
to mention gain a new perspective on HTML.

Because I'm the kind of guy who loves to get in over my head when I learn
new things, I'm going to use a similar approach here by explaining the XML
components in the context of a real XML document. Don't worry if the document
doesn't make sense immediately, because it will soon enough. The document
I'm talking about uses a special XML vocabulary to mark up an audio collection.
You could use a document like this to catalog all of your CDs and tapes. Here
is the audio collection XML document:

```
<?xml version="1.0"?>
<!DOCTYPE audiocollection SYSTEM "AudioCollection.dtd">

<audiocollection>
  <!-- This is the Rock section of the collection. -->
  <audio type="rock" review="5" year="1990">
    <title>Cake</title>
    <artist>The Trash Can Sinatras</artist>
    <track>Obscurity Knocks</track>
    <track>Maybe I Should Drive</track>
    <track>Thrupenny Tears</track>
    <track>Even the Odd</track>
    <track>The Best Man's Fall</track>
    <track>Circling the Circumference</track>
    <track>Funny</track>
    <track>Only Tongue Can Tell</track>
    <track>You Made Me Feel</track>
    <track>January's Little Joke</track>
    <comments>Brilliant first release from the most underrated
    band in existence.</comments>
  </audio>

  <!-- This is the Jazz section of the collection. -->
  <audio type="jazz" review="5" year="1993">
    <title>Criss-Cross</title>
    <artist>Thelonious Monk</artist>
    <track>Hackensack</track>
    <track>Tea for Two</track>
    <track>Criss-Cross</track>
    <track>Eronel</track>
    <track>Rhythm-A-Ning</track>
    <track>Don't Blame Me</track>
    <track>Think of One</track>
```

```
    <track>Crepuscule with Nellie</track>
    <track>Pannonica</track>
    <comments>Excellent collection of Monk across five
    different sessions.</comments>
  </audio>
</audiocollection>
```

Even though I haven't formally introduced you to the details of the XML language, you can probably study this document for a few moments and make out most of its meaning. This is because XML tags tend to be pretty descriptive. By the way, Internet Explorer allows you to view XML documents and interact with them to some degree.

Try This! Use the audio collection XML document as a basis for entering your own audio collection in XML. Just change the relevant audio entries in the document so that they refer to your own collection. Also, keep in mind that you can add additional entries to the document via the `<audio>` tag.

XML documents don't necessarily include any information about how they are to be displayed, and Internet Explorer doesn't try to interpret the meaning of the audio collection document. Instead, it focuses on highlighting the different structural parts. If you look carefully, you'll see a hyphen (-) to the left of some of the elements. Clicking this hyphen allows you to close the element, thereby hiding the information contained within it. This could be helpful in large XML documents. When you close an element, the hyphen turns into a plus sign (+), which can be used to reopen the element. Figure 16-1 shows the audio collection document with both of the audio elements closed.

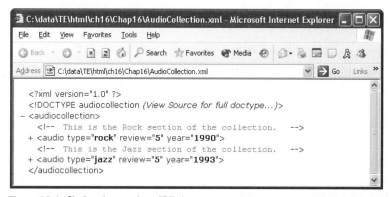

Figure 16-1 Closing elements in an XML document can help you to see the higher level of the document's structure.

Now that you've seen the audio collection document from different angles, let's use it to learn about the primary XML components.

Understanding Elements and Tags

As you may have guessed, tags form the basis of all XML documents and are used to mark up elements. This is evident in the example of the audio collection by the `artist` element. It's marked up using the `<artist>` and `</artist>` tags. The distinction between elements and tags is admittedly subtle; think of elements as logical pieces of markup, and tags as specific text strings used to represent elements in XML documents.

Earlier in the chapter, I mentioned that elements can have both start and end tags, in which case they contain character data. Or they can be empty. Empty elements must be closed with a forward slash (/). A good example of an empty element in HTML is the `br` element, which is used to create a line break on a page. The `br` element doesn't contain any character data and according to XML standards must be coded as `<br/>`. Many HTML developers code empty elements without the closing slash, but the future of HTML is slanted toward XML, so you should get in the habit of closing empty elements properly.

Note   Web browsers are flexible and don't care about the XML empty-element forward-slash rule, but this may change as the Web becomes more structured. Even if browsers don't tighten up regarding Web page structure, you may find it important to validate your HTML documents in the future. You will learn more about document validation later in the chapter.

Note that the forward slash used in empty tags is a carryover of the forward slash used with end tags. For example, consider that all end tags begin with a forward slash: `</html>`, `</body>`, `</p>`, and so on. Using a forward slash at the end of an empty tag is like combining a pair of start and end tags into a single tag. As evidence that this is the motivation behind the forward slash, I must point out that it's possible in XML to code an empty tag as a pair of tags, like this:

```
<br></br>
```

In this example, a line break is coded as a pair of tags, instead of the empty `<br/>` tag. Although the two-tag variation is valid XML, the empty tag approach is preferable because it's more concise.

Referencing Entities

Because of the rigid structure of XML, there are some pieces of information that must be specially encoded in order to include them as content. For example, the apostrophe character (') serves a special purpose in XML and must be specially coded if you intend to use an apostrophe as part of document content. To understand, consider the following XML content:

```
Last summer we visited Pike's Peak.
```

Because XML interprets apostrophes as markup, you must use a special technique to identify the apostrophe in Pike's Peak as content.

Lingo   An *entity reference* is a way of referring to a piece of data by using a special name.

An entity reference is basically a unique name that identifies a piece of XML data. You use an entity reference by enclosing the reference between an ampersand (&) and a semicolon (;). The standard entity reference for an apostrophe character is ', which means the previous XML content would be coded like this:

```
Last summer we visited Pike&apos;s Peak.
```

I realize this code isn't easy to read, but the ' entity reference clarifies that the apostrophe is XML content, not markup. You must also use an entity reference for the ampersand character because the ampersand character is used to identify entity references. You must use the entity reference & for an ampersand that is content.

Entity references are usually unique to the specific document in which they appear. However, there are several built-in entity references. Table 16-1 shows the built-in entity references that are available for use in all XML documents:

Table 16-1   **Built-In Entity References in XML**

Entity Reference	Description
&amp;	Ampersand character (&)
&quot;	Double-quote character (")
&apos;	Apostrophe character (')
&lt;	Less-than character (<)
&gt;	Greater-than character (>)

Using Comments

Like HTML, XML allows you to create comments that aren't interpreted as document markup or content. Comments are useful for adding notes that explain a certain part of a document, or maybe to mention an aspect of the document that you intend to improve upon later. Document markup and content is designed for interpretation by your computer; it's either processed or displayed, but comments are there solely for your benefit as the XML author. Put another way, comments are ignored when an XML document is processed and/or displayed.

You can place comments in a document anywhere content appears, which makes it possible to add comments throughout a document if you so desire. Comments are unique because they are enclosed by special symbols. More specifically, you start a comment with <!- and end it with -->. Here is an example of a simple comment:

```
<!-- Copyright (c) 2003 Tailspin Toys -->
```

This code shows how you could add a copyright notice to your XML documents with a comment. Comments are used a few times in the audio collection document, as the following code reveals:

```
<!-- This is the Rock section of the collection. -->
<!-- This is the Jazz section of the collection. -->
```

> **Caution**   The only significant limitation on comments is that you can't use double-hyphens (--) in the text of a comment.

Using Processing Instructions

Contrary to what I've led you to believe, XML documents don't consist of markup, content, and comments only. In fact, a couple of other pieces of information commonly show up in XML documents. One is *processing instructions*, special commands passed along to the programs that process or view the XML document. Processing instructions are easily distinguished from other XML components because they always start with <? and end with ?>. For example, here is a processing instruction that you will see in virtually every XML document:

```
<?xml version="1.0"?>
```

Notice that in this code the processing instruction begins with <? and ends with ?>. Inside the instruction, you may notice that the structure is similar to tags. This is because processing instructions typically include a name followed by an attribute/value pair. The previous processing instruction example is used to identify an XML document as adhering to version 1 of the XML standard. This processing instruction was used at the beginning of the audio collection document and is an important part of all XML documents.

> **Note**   The latest version of XML as of this writing is 1, the only version so far.

Declaring the Document Type

The last XML component you need to understand is *document type declarations*, which are extremely important because they describe the structure of an XML document.

Lingo   A *document type declaration* appears near the top of an XML document just below the xml processing instruction and identifies the document's root element and document type definition. The *document type definition (DTD)* is responsible for describing the tags and attributes capable of being used in the document, along with the relationships between them.

The document type declaration takes care of the following three primary tasks:

- Specifies the document's root element (for example, html is the root element of HTML documents)

- Defines elements, attributes, and entities specific to the document

- Identifies an external DTD for the document

This document type declaration stuff is confusing, so let me clarify its purpose. One of the principle features of XML is the ability to validate documents based on whether they adhere to the strict XML rules. In addition to making sure that a document follows the fundamental language rules of XML, it's also important to see that it adheres to the specific language rules of the markup language it is based on. For example, it's possible for a Web page to completely adhere to XML language rules yet completely violate HTML rules. A simple example of how this is possible is if you use the <joke> tag I mentioned previously on a Web page. You can code the <joke> tag so that it's perfectly legal in XML, but HTML has no <joke> tag, so the tag violates HTML.

The point is that XML documents have two different levels of *correctness*. The first is determined by whether a document meets the strict language requirements of XML. If it does follow these rules, it's considered a *well-formed document*. The second level of correctness is determined by whether a document adheres to a DTD for a particular markup language such as HTML. If the document passes this test as well, then it's referred to as a *valid document*. It's considered an accolade of the highest order for an XML document to be valid. Ideally, all XML documents—and ultimately all Web pages—would be valid documents. It goes without saying that a valid document is also a well-formed document, but the reverse is not always true.

Let's now circle back to the document type declaration for a document, whose main purpose is to identify the root element of the document as well as the DTD, which is usually contained in an external file. The DTD is essential for creating valid documents, and the audio collection document includes its document type declaration on a single line of code:

```
<!DOCTYPE audiocollection SYSTEM "AudioCollection.dtd">
```

In this code, the root element of the document is identified as `audiocollection`, with the external DTD being in the external file AudioCollection.dtd. This DTD can be used to validate the document, which you will learn about in Chapter 18, "XHTML: XML Meets HTML." The main point to understand now is the structure of the document type declaration and how it identifies the root element and external DTD.

In case it isn't obvious, the root element of a document is the element that contains all other elements. In HTML documents, the root element is `html`. In the audio collection document, it's `audiocollection`.

Modeling XML Data

By now you're probably thoroughly confused by document type declarations and how they are used to describe XML documents. This section will help clarify the role of both document type declarations and DTDs so you can fully understand why they are an important part of XML.

In case it's not abundantly clear yet, XML is all about structuring information. Almost every facet of XML is directly aimed at accomplishing this so that people can better understand information. To structure information, it's necessary to establish a model for the data. An XML *document model* serves as a template that determines what kind of information can appear in the document, as well as how it's structured.

XML document models are also sometimes referred to as *schemas*, and are used to describe a class of data. For example, the information contained within the audio collection document you saw earlier in the chapter could be considered a class of data: audio data. Once you've established a class of data by using a schema, you can create highly structured documents that can be tested for validity. The benefit of having valid documents is that they can be accurately processed with automated programs such as search engines.

An XML schema describes the arrangement of markup and content within a valid XML document; the document must strictly adhere to a schema to be considered valid. Knowing this, you can think of a schema as an agreement between an XML document (perhaps a Web page) and the XML vocabulary (HTML) in which it's written.

Consider a simplified, real world analogy. If you meet someone and he gives you his phone number, you expect the number to be in a certain format. If he gives you an 8-digit number, you immediately know something is wrong. Domestic phone numbers adhere to a 10-digit format. This format is the schema that you use to determine that the 8-digit number is invalid. Although this example is simplified, it nonetheless shows how we employ schemas in many areas of our lives other than Web development.

Note   It's perfectly legitimate to create XML documents without schemas, in which case the documents can be well-formed, but not valid.

The specific role of a schema is to describe an XML vocabulary, naming every tag and attribute, as well as their relationships with each other. Of course, a document without a schema can use any custom tag or attribute. This is fine, but it precludes the document from being considered valid. And as you now know, validity is the ultimate goal of all XML documents. If documents without schemas can use any tags or attributes, then it's fair to say that schemas impose constraints on how documents of a certain type can be structured. More specifically, schemas constrain the structure of documents in two ways:

1   They define the data model, which determines the specific order and nesting of elements.

2   They establish the data types of document data.

The first function is the most important because it determines which elements can be used in a document and how they relate to one another. DTDs rely primarily on this approach for describing document structure, and are weak in establishing data types for document data. DTDs represent the standard approach for describing XML document structure, but are at risk of being replaced by an alternative called XML Schema.

XML Schema is a newer approach that Microsoft promotes that includes rich support for describing document data. DTDs do a great job detailing which tags and attributes can be used in a document, as well as how they can be nested. But XML Schema goes a step farther—you can nail down the data types of document content. The next two sections introduce you to both DTDs and XML Schema and show you how to use each to establish the structure of the audio collection document.

Working with DTDs

DTDs serve as the standard schema approach for describing the structure of XML documents. Although DTDs represent the original schema approach for XML, they aren't without flaws. One complaint is that they use a specialized language for describing the structure of XML vocabularies. Although this language is simple, it's cryptic and seemingly unnecessary when you consider that XML could be used to describe document structure. The only upside to the special language used in DTDs is that it's compact, making most DTDs relatively small. The DTD language describes the structure of documents using individual characters such as question marks, asterisks, and plus signs; hence, its cryptic look.

Even so, DTDs are easy to follow once you understand what the different characters mean, and they benefit from being concise. For proof, take a look at the following DTD, which describes the structure of the audio collection XML document:

```
<!ELEMENT audiocollection (audio)+>

<!ELEMENT audio (title, artist+, track+, comments?)>
<!ATTLIST audio
  type (rock | pop | jazz | classical | country | soul |
  hiphop | comedy | other) "rock"
  review (1 | 2 | 3 | 4 | 5) "3"
  year CDATA #IMPLIED>

<!ELEMENT title (#PCDATA)>

<!ELEMENT artist (#PCDATA)>

<!ELEMENT track (#PCDATA)>

<!ELEMENT comments (#PCDATA)>
```

As you can see, there isn't a lot to this DTD. The main part to understand is the relationship between the elements. Notice that the root audiocollection element is listed first. The word audio in parentheses next to the audiocollection element indicates that the audiocollection element contains the audio element as a child element. The plus sign (+) next to audio indicates that the audio element can appear multiple times within the audiocollection element.

You'll also see that the audio element contains several child elements of its own: title, artist, track, and comments. The plus signs next to artist and track indicate that there can be multiple elements of each. The question mark (?) next to comments indicates that the comments element is optional but can be used only once. This is the cryptic mumbo-jumbo DTD language I mentioned previously. It's fairly easy to understand but not necessarily intuitive.

Back to the audio element. It has three attributes, as noted by the ATTLIST notation in the DTD: type, review, and year. The type and review attributes are interesting because they specify a list of possible values along with a default value for each ("rock" for type and "3" for review). This is an important part of the DTD because you must adhere to the attribute lists for the type and review attributes when you create audio collection documents. In other words, the values for these attributes must be one of the values appearing in the lists. The year attribute is a text attribute that can contain any kind of text data; the CDATA notation indicates that the attribute can contain *Character DATA*.

Try This! Modify the `type` attribute so it includes additional audio types, such as `metal` and `ambient`. This demonstrates how a DTD can grow to accommodate additional kinds of information.

You may notice that the remaining elements in the DTD contain #PCDATA, or *Parsed Character DATA*. This is a fancy way of saying that the elements contain text content.

There are certainly more subtleties to DTD design than I've mentioned in this brief explanation of the audio collection DTD, but I think I've given you an idea of how a DTD lays the ground rules for XML vocabularies. More important, DTDs provide the guidelines to which XML documents can be compared to determine validity.

Working with XML Schema

I mentioned previously that Microsoft offers a more powerful alternative to DTDs. This approach uses XML as the language describing document structure and also allows you to use specific data types. The Microsoft alternative to DTDs is known as XML Schema, and it's quite interesting because it uses a custom XML vocabulary to describe XML documents. This might seem strange at first, but all it means is that you create an XML Schema as an XML document using tags and attributes, much like you create an HTML document. The only thing necessary for you to do differently is learn how to use the XML Schema tags and attributes.

Rather than spending time sifting through the details of the XML Schema vocabulary, let's look at an example. Here's the code for a schema developed using XML Schema that describes the structure of the audio collection document:

```
<?xml version="1.0"?>

<Schema name="AudioCollectionSchema"
  xmlns="urn:schemas-microsoft-com:xml-data"
  xmlns:dt="urn:schemas-microsoft-com:datatypes">
  <ElementType name="title" content="textOnly"/>

  <ElementType name="artist" content="textOnly"/>

  <ElementType name="track" content="textOnly"/>

  <ElementType name="comments" content="textOnly"/>

  <AttributeType name="type" dt:type="enumeration"
    dt:values="rock pop jazz classical country soul hiphop
    comedy other" default="rock"/>
```

```
<AttributeType name="review" dt:type="enumeration"
  dt:values="1 2 3 4 5" default="3"/>

<AttributeType name="year" dt:type="int"/>

<ElementType name="audio" content="eltOnly">
  <element type="title" minOccurs="1" maxOccurs="1"/>
  <element type="artist" minOccurs="1" maxOccurs="*"/>
  <element type="track" minOccurs="1" maxOccurs="*"/>
  <element type="comments" minOccurs="0" maxOccurs="1"/>
  <attribute type="type"/>
  <attribute type="review"/>
  <attribute type="year"/>
</ElementType>

<ElementType name="audiocollection" content="eltOnly">
  <element type="audio" minOccurs="1" maxOccurs="*"/>
</ElementType>
</Schema>
```

Tip   The code for this example, as well as all of the examples throughout the book, is available for download from my Web site at the following URL: *http://www.michaelmorrison.com/ cbook_fshtml.html.*

Although it isn't nearly as compact (or as cryptic), this schema is roughly the equivalent of the DTD for the audio collection document that you saw in the previous section. The schema is a little easier to understand than the DTD because it uses XML tags and attributes. For example, the `minOccurs` and `maxOccurs` attributes of the `<element>` tag are used to determine how many times an element may appear as a child, as opposed to the strange character codes used to carry out the same chore in the DTD.

In addition, the content of each element is specified clearly in the `content` attribute, set to `eltOnly` (elements only), `textOnly` (text only), `mixed` (elements and text), or `empty`. Perhaps the most significant improvement of XML Schema over DTDs is that it uses specific data types. For example, the `year` attribute is specified as type `int`, which means that it's an integer number.

Knowing how XML Schema improves on its DTD equivalent, you might think that all XML vocabularies use XML Schema to describe their structure. However, this isn't the case currently. The reality is that DTDs existed before XML and are widely used in large information management programs. This means that they aren't going anywhere in a hurry. The other compelling reason not to throw away DTDs is that they work. XML Schema might work better, but such changes take time to catch on. For now, you may find yourself creating both a DTD and a schema for any XML vocabularies that you dream up.

The Practical Side of XML

So far, this chapter has spent a great deal of time delving into the theory of XML and how it works as an organizational technology for information. What I haven't spent much time doing is assessing the role of XML in your life as a Web page creator. Sure, your new XML knowledge can be put to great use impressing your geeky friends the next time document structure becomes the hot topic at a lunch meeting. But how exactly does XML benefit you in terms of your Web pages?

The relevance of XML to Web pages is twofold. First and foremost, the Web is evolving toward a more structured information repository, and is a topic you may want to explore at another time. For now, just take my word that XML is dictating the future of HTML. The second aspect of XML that relates heavily to Web pages is the use of specialized XML vocabularies to mark up special types of information. Custom XML vocabularies will allow you to create documents containing information that can be tied into your Web pages.

The discussion of DTDs and XML Schema in this chapter assumed to some degree that you're interested in creating your own XML vocabulary. For example, the audio collection document uses a custom XML vocabulary with its own set of tags and attributes. Although this is a powerful use of XML—and quite liberating—you probably won't be creating your own XML vocabularies often, if ever. But you will use vocabularies that others created. A wide variety of XML vocabularies exist for marking up all kinds of interesting data in XML documents. Here are some examples, along with the types of data they model:

- **MathML**   mathematical equations
- **3DML**   three-dimensional virtual worlds
- **VoxML**   interactive speech
- **SMIL**   multimedia integration
- **RELML**   real estate listings
- **HRMML**   human resource management
- **XMLNews**   news articles
- **P3P**   personal privacy

As you can see, XML vocabularies vary greatly in the kinds of data they model. If you include any of these kinds of data in your Web pages, consider using an XML vocabulary to mark up the data.

Key Points

■   Extensible Markup Language (XML) is a generic markup language used to describe other markup languages, such as HTML.

■   An XML vocabulary is a markup language designed using XML that applies to a specific type of content.

■   An element is a discrete piece of information within an XML document, typically corresponding to a tag or set of tags; elements are capable of containing content, child elements, or both.

■   In XML, empty elements must be closed with a forward slash (/).

■   Comments are useful for adding notes that explain a certain part of a document and are created by starting the comment with `<!--` and ending it with `-->`.

■   A document type *declaration*—not to be confused with a document type definition (DTD)—appears near the top of an XML document just below the `xml` processing instruction, and identifies the document's root element and DTD.

■   The DTD is responsible for describing the tags and attributes capable of being used in the document, along with the relationships between them.

■   DTDs serve as the standard schema approach for describing the structure of XML documents.

■   XML Schema is a newer approach to XML data modeling (promoted by Microsoft) that improves upon DTDs by allowing you to describe document data precisely.

Chapter 17

Styling XML with XSL

As I'm sure you know, most television ads attempt to make their products look stylish to convince us that we'll be hip if we own them or use them. Although we all understand and appreciate style to different degrees, I think it's safe to say that we are style-conscious creatures. Knowing this, it stands to reason that we might as well consider style when dealing with Extensible Markup Language (XML).

It's fair to say that XML by itself is pretty much devoid of style. XML is a calculated, supremely logical markup language that doesn't leave any room for style—and that's a good thing. XML is about rigidly structuring information so that it can be processed consistently and understood without question. However, there comes a time when even the most uptight, unstylish person has to dress up for a special occasion. And the same thing applies to XML. Fortunately, there are several technologies that make it possible to stylize XML documents so they can be displayed attractively. If you are a style junkie, then you can think of styling an XML document as the XML equivalent of a personal makeover.

Style Sheets and XML

Styling an XML document refers to the process of describing how you want the information in the document to appear visually. Because the information typically doesn't include special cues for how it should appear, it's entirely up to you to establish a set of styles that control its appearance.

Lingo   A *style sheet* is a special document containing a list of styles that apply to the information when using an XML document.

Style sheets are used to determine how to display the XML information in a program such as a Web browser. Style sheets are needed because many, if not most, XML documents aren't designed to be viewed directly. This separation of content from formatting is one of the design goals of XML; it encourages the distinction between pure information and the manner in which it is to appear.

As an example, consider the weather report on local television. On the screen, you see a colorful map with neat graphics showing rain, wind, sun, and other weather elements as they sweep across the country. However, the information driving that map is really just a bunch of numbers that indicate the temperature, wind speed, relative humidity, and barometric pressure at given points on the map. Weather software takes the data and uses it to generate the colorful map. Or to put it another way, the weather software stylizes the data so that it's easier to view and understand. For all you know, the weather data could be stored in an XML document. If that were the case, then a style sheet would dictate the weather map's appearance.

More specifically, a style sheet converts the information in an XML document into a form suitable for presentation. With a Web browser, a style sheet converts an XML document into a suitable HTML document that can be viewed in the browser.

Hey! Hold on there—how did HTML suddenly enter the picture? As you know, HTML is used primarily to display information on a Web page, viewable in a Web browser. One way to obtain a graphical/stylized version of an XML document is to selectively convert it to an HTML document. I use the word "selectively" because you may not want every piece of information in an XML document to be displayed.

In Chapter 12, "Style Sheet Basics," you learned how to use cascading style sheets (CSS) to add style to HTML documents. CSS can certainly be used with XML documents, but it isn't as powerful as another style sheet technology known as Extensible Style Language (XSL). XSL is a powerful XML vocabulary used to stylize XML documents.

Understanding XSL

XSL is a style sheet technology used to convert, or *transform*, XML documents into other formats. The idea is that by transforming a document, you can reformat it to be suitable for viewing in an existing program, such as a Web browser.

Keep in mind, however, that XSL is not targeted simply at transforming XML documents into HTML documents. XSL is very general and can be used to transform XML documents into virtually any other markup language.

This is significant because Web browsers aren't necessarily the only applications to which XML is relevant. What if your favorite fast-food restaurant wanted to code their menu in XML? A computer inside the restaurant would need to transform this XML code into a form that could be displayed on a screen at the drive-through window, and possibly even be read aloud to the customer. This might seem like a bit of a stretch, but XML and XSL are that broad in their goals.

Moving away from fried foods, let's clarify exactly what it is that XSL brings to the XML table:

- XSL transforms XML documents into other document formats.

- XSL adds styles to XML documents by using special formatting rules.

These two facets of XSL are carried out by two different parts of the XSL technology: *XSL Transformation* (XSLT) and XSL Formatting Objects.

Lingo   *XSL Transformation* allows you to transform XML documents into other document formats, such as HTML. *XSL Formatting Objects* is a newer XSL technology that provides many of the same styling features as CSS, plus many new ones.

Both XSLT and XSL Formatting Objects are XML vocabularies; you use them by creating XML documents with elements and attributes that describe how to carry out the transformation or styling process.

Note   Unfortunately, XSL Formatting Objects is so new that it isn't yet supported in any Web browsers. However, XSLT is supported in Internet Explorer, so you can use it now. Because XSLT is the only part of XSL that is currently supported in Web browsers, the remainder of the chapter focuses solely on it. You'll be learning how to use XSLT to transform XML documents for viewing in Web browsers.

Applying XSL to XML Documents

Like an HTML document, an XSL style sheet must be processed to be useful. Although they can be processed in any type of XML program, they will be processed primarily by Web browsers, at least in the immediate future. It's important to understand the connection between the style sheet and XML documents—and how those documents are transformed by applying the style sheet.

Envision an XML document as an upside-down, tree-like structure of elements —like the directory tree for your hard disk—with a single *root element* at the top that represents the trunk of the tree. Any elements appearing beneath the root element are considered *branches* of the tree. This XML tree continues to grow as additional elements are nested within each other. As examples, the `html` element is the root element of HTML documents; the `audiocollection` element is the root element of the audio collection document you saw in the previous chapter. The root element is significant because it represents the starting point for an *XSL processor.*

Lingo   An *XSL processor* is an application that processes an XSL style sheet and uses that style sheet to transform XML data in an HTML document. In most cases, you will rely on an XSL processor that is built into a Web browser, such as Internet Explorer.

When an XSL processor processes a style sheet, it looks for templates that describe special patterns in an XML document.

Lingo   A *template* in an XSL style sheet simply describes *how* the XML information is to be transformed whenever it is encountered.

The XSL processor determines which XML information to transform by searching for information that matches a certain *pattern*. A pattern could be something as simple as an element name. Whenever the XSL processor encounters an element named `artist`, for example, it applies a certain template to transform the data. The pattern-matching process begins with the root element of the document and continues throughout the entire document.

When the XSL processor finishes working through an entire XML document, matching patterns and applying templates, you have a complete transformation of the original XML document. If you transform an XML document into an HTML document, it can be displayed in a Web browser. So if you open an XML document in Internet Explorer, its style sheet will automatically be processed and applied to the document to generate an HTML document that can be displayed in the browser window. Someone viewing the resulting Web page would never know what was going on behind the scenes to give the XML data its appearance.

Peeking Inside a Style Sheet

So far I've done my best to bore you with abstract theory surrounding XSL style sheets and how useful they are. Now it's time to move beyond theory and dig into the guts of XSL style sheets and how they are structured. As you begin to learn the coding specifics of XSL style sheets, understand that this is only an introduction. XSL is a broad, often complex technology, so I've distilled the basics and will give you enough fundamental knowledge to start using XSL style sheets.

The basic structure of XSL style sheets is surprisingly straightforward. As we've discussed, XSL style sheets basically consist of two types of information: patterns and templates. The next two sections explore how patterns and templates are used to transform XML documents for display purposes.

But first, let's look at the overall structure of XSL style sheets, specifically the `stylesheet` element, required as the root element of all XSL style sheets. This element, along with several other XSL elements and attributes, is part of the XSLT vocabulary. To use elements and attributes in this vocabulary, you first declare the *namespace* where they're contained.

Lingo   A *namespace* is an identifier for XML documents, and in this case serves to identify the XSL vocabulary.

Here is an example of how to use the `stylesheet` element to declare the XSL namespace:

```
<xsl:stylesheet xmlns:xsl="http://www.w3.org/TR/xsl/">
```

This code makes all the elements and attributes in the XSL namespace available and assigns them the prefix `xsl`. This is standard practice in all XSL style sheets. The implication of this code is that you must precede all XSL element and attribute names with the prefix `xsl`. This will make much more sense in the next two sections as you begin to see how patterns and templates are coded in XSL.

Drilling for Data with Patterns

You learned earlier in the chapter that when an XSL style sheet is processed, patterns are used as the basis for finding XML data to transform. More specifically, a pattern identifies an element or attribute, in an XML document, that corresponds to a branch of the XML "tree."

Although this may sound abstract, patterns are identified in a familiar manner. Patterns look much like paths in a file system such as your hard drive, except that patterns specify elements and attributes, while paths specify folders and files. As an example, consider the `head` element that appears within the `html` element of an HTML document. To identify the `head` element using a pattern, you simply refer to it as `html/head`.

Don't forget that the significance of patterns is to identify a portion of an XML document for transformation. When the XSL processor matches up a chunk of XML data by using a pattern, it shuttles the data to a template to be transformed. (More on templates in the next section.) If you want to process an entire XML document using a single pattern, specify the pattern as a single forward slash (/); this identifies the root element of the document. When specifying other patterns, the pattern for the root element is assumed; this pattern for the root element is known as the *root pattern*. That's why the html/head pattern you just learned didn't begin with a forward slash. Patterns are referenced with respect to the root pattern (/).

Transforming Information with Templates

Templates are used in XSL to carry out the transformation of XML data. When an XSL processor matches a pattern in a style sheet, the XML data associated with the pattern is routed through a template and transformed. An XSL style sheet can contain as many templates as necessary to carry out a transformation, or as few as one. When multiple templates are used in a style sheet, each corresponds to a different section of an XML document. Think of templates as little workers that take on the task of transforming different sections of an XML document.

Keep in mind that XSL is an XML vocabulary, so XSL style sheets are coded using XML. The element used to define a template in a style sheet is xsl:template. A pattern is associated with a template by the match attribute of the xsl:template element. As an example, the following code shows how to start a template matched to the root element of a document:

```
<xsl:template match="/">
```

The template in this code will transform the document beginning with the root element, which means the entire document will be processed by the template. You will typically create templates that match elements beneath the root element. Here's another example of a more complete template that matches the artist element of the audio collection document:

```
<xsl:template match="audiocollection/audio/artist">
</xsl:template>
```

As you can see, the artist element is specified by listing its parent elements. Notice the closing </xsl:template> tag, which is necessary for all templates. To carry out a transformation on data within the artist element, you must use the <xsl:value-of/> tag inside the template, as the following code demonstrates:

```
<xsl:template match="audiocollection/audio/artist">
  <b>Artist: </b><xsl:value-of/>
</xsl:template>
```

This code shows that the data stored in the artist element can be formatted for display purposes by placing the bold text "Artist:" in front of it. If you recall, the <b> tag is used in HTML to apply a bold font to text. In this code the xsl:value-of element serves as a placeholder for the content in the artist element. The xsl:value-of element is one of several elements used to create templates that transform XML documents. Here are the most commonly used of these elements, all of which are included in the standard XSL namespace you learned about previously in this chapter:

- xsl:value-of—inserts the value (content) of an XML element or attribute.

- xsl:if—performs a conditional match for a template.

- xsl:for-each—loops through the elements in an XML document.

- xsl:apply-templates—applies a template to an XML document.

These elements are explained in more detail in the next few sections. Later in the chapter, you'll create a style sheet that formats and displays the audio collection document.

The value-of Element

The xsl:value-of element is used to insert the value of an element or attribute into a transformed document. You have the ability to place HTML code around the xsl:value-of element, which affects how the value is displayed in the resulting Web page. This allows you to include HTML code in a style sheet, with placeholders for XML data inserted via the xsl:value-of element. Here is an example of a template that uses the xsl:value-of element to display the title element of the audio collection as a large heading:

```
<xsl:template match="title">
  <h1><xsl:value-of/></h1>
</xsl:template>
```

Note the absence of the parent elements (audiocollection/audio) from the match attribute in this code. This is because you will use the xsl:for-each element to cycle through the elements in an XML document, alleviating the need to specify the full pattern for the title element. This will make more sense in the section in which you learn about the xsl:for-each element.

The if Element

Like an if statement in a programming language such as Java or BASIC, the xsl:if element is used to conditionally match an element or attribute in a template. To establish the condition that's matched, the xsl:if element uses the same `match` attribute that you learned about earlier with the `xsl:template` element. The most common use of the `match` attribute is to check for a specific value in an element or attribute. Here is an example of how you might use the `xsl:if` element to match only jazz entries in the audio collection:

```
<xsl:if match="@type=jazz">
  <xsl:apply-templates select="audio"/>
</xsl:if>
```

In this example, the `type` attribute of the `audio` element is used as the basis for the conditional match. More specifically, the value of the `type` attribute must be `jazz` for the match to occur. If it does, the template for the `audio` element is applied and the audio data is transformed. The net effect of this code is that the audio collection data is filtered so that only jazz entries are transformed and displayed. It's important to note that the `@` symbol in the code is used to signify that `type` is an attribute, not an element.

The `for-each` Element

Perhaps the most powerful of the XSL template elements is the `xsl:for-each` element. It's used to create a loop that steps through all the elements in an XML document to match patterns and apply templates. The `select` attribute of the `xsl:for-each` element determines which elements of the document are included in the looping process. It's also possible to alter the order of the looping by setting the `order-by` attribute of the `xsl:for-each` element. The best way to understand how the `xsl:for-each` element works is to look at a quick example:

```
<table>
<xsl:for-each order-by="+ review"
  select="audiocollection/audio">
  <tr>
    <td><xsl:value-of select="artist"/></td>
    <td><xsl:value-of select="title"/></td>
    <td><xsl:value-of select="@review"/></td>
  </tr>
</xsl:for-each>
</table>
```

This example begins to show the power of XSL. The `xsl:for-each` element is used in this code to step through all the `audio` elements in the audio collection document. The order in which the elements are processed is determined by the `order-by` attribute, which states that the elements should be ordered according to their review, and in increasing order (`"+ review"`). Within the `xsl:for-each` element the artist, title, and review values for each `audio` element are formatted together as a row of table data. This code takes the audio collection document and formats it as an HTML table so that it can be viewed in a Web page.

The `apply-templates` Element

The `xsl:apply-templates` element is used to apply a template to a portion of an XML document. Templates improve the organization of style sheets by isolating the transformation code associated with each part of an XML document. Before applying a template with the `xsl:apply-templates` element, you must first use the `match` attribute of the `xsl:template` element to specify the element or attribute that's transformed by the template. Here is an example of how the `match` attribute is used with the `xsl:template` element to identify the `comments` element of the audio collection document:

```
<xsl:template match="comments">
  <b>Comments:</b><br/><xsl:value-of/><br/><br/>
</xsl:template>
```

Notice that the `match` attribute is set to `"comments"`, which means that the template applies to only `comments` elements within the document. The code within the template then uses the `<xsl:value-of/>` tag to insert the value of the `comments` element and transform it for display purposes with the help of some HTML code.

Once you've defined a template with the `match` attribute of the `xsl:template` element, you can then use the `xsl:apply-templates` element to apply the template to the style sheet. Here is an example of how to use the `xsl:apply-templates` element to apply the "comments" template:

```
<xsl:apply-templates select="audiocollection/audio/comments"/>
```

This code causes the style sheet to associate `comments` elements with the "comments" template. The result is that `comments` elements appearing in an XML document are transformed according to the "comments" template of the style sheet.

Constructing Your Own XSL Style Sheet

Admittedly, XSL style sheets aren't the easiest things in the world to comprehend, so it's natural if you're feeling a bit overwhelmed at this point. XSL style sheets go several steps beyond HTML and even XML, and can almost be considered a type of programming. In fact, you were somewhat equipped for this chapter thanks to what you learned back in Chapter 11, "Dynamic HTML." In many ways, you can think of XSL as a type of scripting language even though it's completely focused on processing XML documents.

Now that you've had a breather and are ready to proceed, I have good news: The remainder of this chapter focuses on creating an XSL style sheet that will transform the previous chapter's audio collection document into an HTML document that's viewable in a Web browser. Not only is this a good example of an XSL style sheet, but it opens up the possibility for you to create your own collection documents in XML and then integrate them into your Web site by using an XSL style sheet.

Before getting into the details of the style sheet, it's worth revisiting the audio collection XML document to make sure you remember how it's structured. Here's the code:

```xml
<?xml version="1.0"?>
<?xml-stylesheet href="AudioCollection.xsl" type="text/xsl"?>
<!DOCTYPE audiocollection SYSTEM "AudioCollection.dtd">

<audiocollection>
  <!-- This is the Rock section of the collection. -->
  <audio type="rock" review="5" year="1990">
    <title>Cake</title>
    <artist>The Trash Can Sinatras</artist>
    <track>Obscurity Knocks</track>
    <track>Maybe I Should Drive</track>
    <track>Thrupenny Tears</track>
    <track>Even the Odd</track>
    <track>The Best Man's Fall</track>
    <track>Circling the Circumference</track>
    <track>Funny</track>
    <track>Only Tongue Can Tell</track>
    <track>You Made Me Feel</track>
    <track>January's Little Joke</track>
    <comments>Brilliant first release from the most underrated
    band in existence.</comments>
  </audio>

  <!-- This is the Jazz section of the collection. -->
  <audio type="jazz" review="5" year="1993">
    <title>Criss-Cross</title>
    <artist>Thelonious Monk</artist>
    <track>Hackensack</track>
    <track>Tea for Two</track>
    <track>Criss-Cross</track>
    <track>Eronel</track>
    <track>Rhythm-A-Ning</track>
    <track>Don't Blame Me</track>
    <track>Think of One</track>
    <track>Crepuscule with Nellie</track>
    <track>Pannonica</track>
    <comments>Excellent collection of Monk across five
    different sessions.</comments>
  </audio>
</audiocollection>
```

Tip   The code for this example, as well as all of the examples throughout the book, is available for download from my Web site at the following URL: *http://www.michaelmorrison.com/cbook_fshtml.html.*

As you can see, the audio collection document starts with an `audiocollection` element as its root element. Beneath this root element are a couple of `audio` elements that are used to mark up individual entries in the audio collection. Each `audio` element then contains several other child elements (`title`, `artist`, `track`, `comments`), along with a few attributes (`type`, `review`, `year`). With this document structure in mind, it makes sense that an XSL style sheet for the document would need to step through the individual `audio` elements and format each one for display. If you recall, the `xsl:for-each` element allows you to step through elements in an XML document. Here is the beginning of the `xsl:for-each` element that makes this possible for the audio collection document:

```
<xsl:for-each select="audiocollection/audio">
```

As each `audio` element is processed within this loop, you will want to apply templates to transform different parts of the document. Here is the complete `xsl:for-each` element, which applies templates for the most important parts of the audio collection document:

```
<xsl:for-each select="audiocollection/audio">
  <xsl:apply-templates select="title"/>
  <xsl:apply-templates select="@year"/>
  <xsl:apply-templates select="artist"/>
  <xsl:apply-templates select="track"/>
  <xsl:apply-templates select="comments"/>
</xsl:for-each>
```

A loop is established that steps through each `audio` element in the XML document and applies templates for the `title` element, `year` attribute, `artist` element, `track` element, and `comments` element. In case you're wondering, the @ symbol in the code is used to signify that `year` is an attribute, not an element. Now it's time to put these templates together to transform each of the elements and attributes. Here are the templates for this style sheet:

```
<xsl:template match="title">
  <b>Title: </b><i><xsl:value-of/></i>
</xsl:template>

<xsl:template match="@year">
  (<xsl:value-of/>)<br/>
</xsl:template>
```

```
<xsl:template match="artist">
  <b>Artist: </b><xsl:value-of/><br/>
  <b>Tracks:</b><br/>
</xsl:template>

<xsl:template match="track">
  <xsl:value-of/><br/>
</xsl:template>

<xsl:template match="comments">
  <b>Comments:</b><br/><xsl:value-of/><br/><br/>
</xsl:template>
```

Although this template code looks somewhat messy on the surface, if you look closely at how each element and attribute is transformed, you'll realize that it's quite simple. For example, look closely at the template for the `title` element. All it does is display the text "Title:" in bold, followed by the value of the `title` element in italics. The template for the `year` attribute continues by placing the `year` value in parentheses, followed by a line break. We'll look at the results of this code in just a moment. But first, it's important to examine the entire audio collection style sheet (AudioCollection.xsl), which follows:

```
<?xml version="1.0"?>
<xsl:stylesheet xmlns:xsl="http://www.w3.org/TR/WD-xsl">
  <xsl:template match="/">
    <html><head><title>Audio Collection XML Example</title></head>
      <body bgcolor="#FFFFFF">
        <h2>My Audio Collection</h2>
        <xsl:for-each select="audiocollection/audio">
          <xsl:apply-templates select="title"/>
          <xsl:apply-templates select="@year"/>
          <xsl:apply-templates select="artist"/>
          <xsl:apply-templates select="track"/>
          <xsl:apply-templates select="comments"/>
        </xsl:for-each>
      </body>
    </html>
  </xsl:template>

  <xsl:template match="title">
    <b>Title: </b><i><xsl:value-of/></i>
  </xsl:template>
```

```
<xsl:template match="@year">
  (<xsl:value-of/>)<br/>
</xsl:template>

<xsl:template match="artist">
  <b>Artist: </b><xsl:value-of/><br/>
  <b>Tracks:</b><br/>
</xsl:template>

<xsl:template match="track">
  <xsl:value-of/><br/>
</xsl:template>

<xsl:template match="comments">
  <b>Comments:</b><br/><xsl:value-of/><br/><br/>
</xsl:template>

</xsl:stylesheet>
```

The most interesting aspect of this style sheet is that it includes a consider-able amount of familiar HTML code. That's because the document created by the transformation of the audio collection is an HTML document; it must conform to the structure of a complete HTML document. That's why you see the <html>, <head>, and <body> tags in the code. Also important is how the main section of the style sheet is the template for the root element (/), which contains the loop that steps through the audio elements and applies the remaining templates in the style sheet.

Try This! To get a different visual appearance out of the audio collection style sheet, simply change the manner in which each element is formatted in the XSL code. For example, use standard HTML physical formatting tags within the XSL code to change the manner in which they are displayed.

The code for the audio collection style sheet is interesting in terms of its organization, but it wouldn't mean much if you couldn't use it. Fortunately, you can use it to transform the audio collection document and view the results in Internet Explorer.

If you noticed that the actual document opened in Internet Explorer is the AudioCollection.xml document, you may be curious about how Internet Explorer knows that there's a style sheet for the document. You must use a special processing instruction (`xml-stylesheet`) in the XML document to indicate that it has an XSL style sheet. The following code shows how this processing instruction appears in the audio collection XML document:

```
<?xml-stylesheet href="AudioCollection.xsl" type="text/xsl"?>
```

Notice in this code that the file name of the XSL style sheet is specified in the `href` attribute. This makes it possible to create different style sheets that provide different ways of viewing an XML document. To use a different style sheet, just change the value of the `href` attribute in the processing instruction.

Key Points

- Styling an XML document refers to the process of describing how you want the information in the document to appear when viewed in a Web browser.

- A style sheet is a special document that contains a list of styles that apply to the information when using an XML document.

- XSL is a style sheet technology used to transform XML documents into other formats, such as HTML.

- It's helpful to think of an XML document as being organized as an upside-down, tree-like structure of elements with a single root element at the top of the tree.

- XSL style sheets consist of two main types of information, patterns and templates, which are used to match and transform XML content.

- The XSL `value-of` element serves as a placeholder for the content in an element.

- The `xsl:apply-templates` element is used to apply an XSL template to a portion of an XML document.

Chapter 18

XHTML: XML Meets HTML

XHTML, or Extensible HTML, is a technology developed to add structure to HTML code and establish ground rules for a better, more powerful Web. XHTML is the application of XML to HTML; in other words, the rigid rules of XML are applied to familiar HTML elements and attributes. This additional structure takes HTML to a new level of consistency and compatibility. Browsers and other Web-based programs will eventually have the ability to perform advanced processing of HTML documents.

This chapter explores XHTML and how it came to be. You'll examine the differences between XHTML and HTML and learn why XHTML offers the possibility for a brighter future with a more structured Web. Along with learning XHTML background and theory, you'll find out how to create and validate XHTML documents—as well as convert HTML documents to XHTML.

The Significance of XHTML

It would be easy for me to say that because XML is an interesting technology, people should go ahead and blend it with HTML. This might be true, but busy Web developers need a much better reason to tinker with anything beyond HTML. You might not realize that much of what's on the Web looks good because Web browsers do an impressive job of displaying pages built from butchered HTML code that violates fundamental rules of the HTML language. It's a good thing browsers don't pop up error messages every time a Web page is coded improperly.

The Problem with HTML

If you ask your average Web surfers, they would say that the Web works just fine. But if you ask an experienced Web page designer about the difficulties with HTML structure, you would likely hear something I can't print. It's not that it's a flawed technology; it's that HTML has been forced to solve a problem it was never intended to solve. HTML was originally designed to share technical notes among scientific researchers, which required little in the way of formatting for display.

However, the HTML language changed dramatically when the first Web browser appeared. HTML was the most convenient approach at hand for creating Web pages. New features that were quickly added to HTML only twisted the language into performing unsupported actions, such as laying out graphical information. To make matters worse, browser vendors scrambled to add new features that worked on only their browsers.

Of course, the leniency of browsers shielded users from Web developers' coding inconsistencies, but at what cost? The cost is complicated HTML processors in Web browsers, not to mention Web pages that don't work reliably across different browsers.

The XHTML Solution

So how does XML solve the problems of HTML? As you know, XML can give structure to virtually any kind of information; XHTML is a specific XML vocabulary you use to create highly structured Web pages. XHTML enforces the structure of XML within the HTML language, which is quite beneficial for Web designers and users alike. One huge benefit is that XHTML documents can be validated, which means they can be analyzed for correctness. Don't worry; I'm not talking about political correctness. In this case, *correctness* means that an XHTML document meets all of the coding requirements of the XML language, as well as adhering to the rules of an XHTML schema or document type definition (DTD).

Note   To refresh your memory, schemas are used to describe the structure of an XML document. DTDs represent the default schema technique used with XML documents.

Validated XHTML code is extremely important because it alleviates the need for browsers to perform complex analysis of documents to determine how they should be displayed. It also puts an end to the coding tricks that some Web designers use to make Web browsers do things they weren't intended to do. For example, there have been some known discrepancies between the manner in which different browsers process certain HTML tags. By taking advantage of such discrepancies, Web designers have sometimes been able to get interesting effects on one browser at the expense of other browsers.

One solution to the HTML formatting problem is the now-popular style sheet. But style sheets don't address the fundamental structural problem of HTML. Only by enforcing the rules of XML can you tie up the loose ends of HTML. This is where XHTML comes in.

Unfortunately, XHTML won't have an impact on the Web overnight, which means unstructured HTML will likely be around for a long time. One of the reasons is because XHTML and style sheets involve a steeper learning curve, so Web developers will likely take their time switching over. XHTML also requires planning, which isn't something all Web designers take the time to do. So browsers will continue supporting unstructured Web pages, but developers will phase in structured XHTML code as its benefits become more visible. Visual Web design tools will likely play an important role in this goal because many Web designers already use them. They automatically generate code for Web pages, which is an ideal way to transition to XHTML.

The Leap from HTML to XHTML

At this point, you're probably thinking that XHTML is a complicated technology that requires you to learn a completely new approach to creating Web pages. As much as I love practical jokes, I wouldn't spring that on you in the last chapter of a book primarily about HTML. The truth is that XHTML isn't all that different than HTML. The latest version of HTML, 4, has solved many of the problems in earlier versions. It's a short leap from HTML 4 to XHTML. Throughout the remainder of this chapter, we'll assume that sample HTML documents are based upon HTML 4.

> **Note**   HTML isn't installed like new versions of software programs. You can't upgrade from HTML 3 to HTML 4 because HTML is built into Web browsers. You upgrade to a new version of HTML by upgrading your Web browser.

The process of converting an HTML document to XHTML primarily involves making subtle coding changes. Although this can be tedious, you don't need to make sweeping changes to the overall design and layout of an HTML document. It's helpful to run through a checklist that highlights the primary differences between the two markup languages. Here are the main requirements of XHTML documents that should be taken into account when you consider bringing HTML documents up to XHTML standards:

- Place a document type declaration at the top of the page.
- Declare an XHTML DTD in the document declaration.
- Declare an XHTML namespace in the html element.
- Ensure that the head and body elements are present.

- Make the `title` element the first element in the `head` element.

- Make element and attribute names lowercase.

- Ensure that non-empty elements have end tags.

- Ensure that empty elements consist of an empty tag or a start-tag and end-tag pair.

- Assign values to attributes.

- Enclose attribute values in quotation marks.

> **Note**　Because valid XML documents must be well formed, you must ensure that an HTML document is well formed when you convert it to XHTML. You may recall that a well-formed XML document is one that meets the rigid language requirements of XML.

You'll notice that most of these requirements highlight the greater degree of structure inherent in XHTML. Fortunately, you can modify most HTML documents according to these requirements without too much pain and suffering. Later in the chapter, you will work through the steps for converting an HTML document to XHTML.

XHTML and Its Need for Acceptance

At various times during our formative years, most of us yearn for acceptance. If you agree that the need for human acceptance reaches a peak during the teen-age years, then it's safe to say that XHTML is an adolescent technology. XHTML documents need approval, which means that they are deemed accurate and correct in the eyes of others. *Others* in this case are software programs such as Web browsers. Add to that the Web-based programs that process XHTML code. These might be e-commerce programs that handle orders for an online store or they might be search engines.

The Three XHTML DTDs

The standard XHTML DTDs target certain kinds of XHTML documents. Specifically, three XHTML DTDs provide varying levels of detail for XHTML, resulting in three different classifications of XHTML documents.

> **Note**　The XHTML DTDs were created by the World Wide Web Consortium, or W3C, which oversees most Web-related technologies. You can learn a great deal about HTML and XHTML by visiting the W3C Web site at *http://www.w3.org/*.

The three XHTML DTDs provide flexibility in using different XHTML features. They are divided according to the number of XHTML features they
include. So if you create an XHTML Web page that doesn't require advanced features such as frames, you can use a minimal DTD. Smaller DTDs result in faster
validation, which is a significant benefit to using an XHTML DTD that includes
only the support you need. This matters, because at some point in the future,
XHTML documents will be verified as they are being displayed. Obviously, the
faster the validation process, the better.

Here are the three XHTML DTDs listed in order of increasing XHTML
features:

- Strict: No HTML presentation elements are available, such as `font`,
  `table`, etc.

- Transitional: Adds HTML presentation elements to the strict DTD.

- Frameset: Adds support for frames to the transitional DTD.

The strict DTD is the most streamlined of the three and provides a minimal
XHTML language for creating documents without any presentation elements.
This might sound limiting when you consider that XHTML documents are typically designed for viewing in Web browsers. The idea is that you format such
documents for display using style sheets instead of presentation elements. Not
surprisingly, the strict DTD is the most efficient and enables the fastest validation
of XHTML documents.

The transitional DTD picks up where the strict DTD leaves off, adding support for presentation elements. You already know that one of the main purposes
of XML is to separate presentation code from content, which the transitional
DTD violates. Although this may be true, most Web designers won't be giving
up presentation elements for style sheets anytime soon, so you can think of the
transitional DTD as a concession for stubborn Web designers. The transitional
DTD is useful when converting HTML documents to XHTML because it includes
most of the HTML features found in Web pages. But it doesn't include support
for frames, which display multiple Web pages in a single browser window.

The most full-featured XHTML DTD is the frameset DTD, which takes the
transitional DTD a step farther by adding support for frames. Frames are coded
using presentation elements, so the same rules governing the separation of content and formatting apply to the frameset DTD. It's the most complex of the
three DTDs and the slowest to validate documents.

Document Validation Requirements

The validation of an XHTML document requires one of the three XHTML DTDs and fulfillment of the following rules:

- A document type declaration (DOCTYPE) must appear in the document prior to the root element.
- The root element of the document must be html.
- The root element of the document (html) must designate an XHTML namespace using the xmlns attribute.

The first requirement shouldn't come as a surprise given that XHTML DTDs are required to validate XHTML documents. But the last two requirements are unrelated to the DTD. The root element of all XHTML documents must be html, which indicates that the document is in fact an HTML document. This is an interesting requirement, indicating that XHTML is simply a structured version of HTML—not a new language. In other words, XHTML doesn't change the root element to xhtml; the idea is to require minimal changes to HTML documents to be able to validate them as XHTML documents.

The last validation requirement for XHTML documents enforces the use of the XHTML namespace. The xmlns attribute of the root element used to stipulate this namespace is a standard XHTML namespace, as specified by the W3C. The next section describes the code required to specify the DTD and namespace for a valid XHTML document.

Declaring an XHTML DTD and Namespace

Declaring an XHTML DTD and namespace within an XHTML document is straightforward and requires entering only a few standard lines of code. The DTD is declared at the top of a document before the html root element. The following code shows how the strict DTD is declared:

```
<!DOCTYPE html PUBLIC "-//W3C//DTD XHTML 1.0 Strict//EN"
  "DTD/xhtml1-strict.dtd">
```

This document type declaration identifies the strict DTD as a public resource hosted by the W3C. Don't worry about the specifics, because this code is always entered exactly as you see it here. It appears in any XHTML document based on the strict DTD. Transitional and frameset DTDs also have standard document type declarations. Next is the document type declaration for the transitional DTD:

```
<!DOCTYPE html PUBLIC "-//W3C//DTD XHTML 1.0 Transitional//EN"
  "DTD/xhtml1-transitional.dtd">
```

The document type declaration for the frameset DTD is similar:

```
<!DOCTYPE html PUBLIC "-//W3C//DTD XHTML 1.0 Frameset//EN"
  "DTD/xhtml1-frameset.dtd">
```

It's important to include one of these document type declarations in every XHTML document because a valid XHTML document must specify a DTD. Just be sure to use the appropriate DTD for the required level of XHTML support.

To ensure that a document is valid, you must also declare an XHTML namespace in the root `html` element. This namespace is a standard XML namespace that must appear in every XHTML document. Here is the code used to declare the XHTML namespace in the root `html` element:

```
<html xmlns="http://www.w3.org/1999/xhtml">
</html>
```

As the code shows, the `xmlns` attribute of the `html` tag is used to specify the standard XHTML namespace. Like the declaration of the DTD in the document type declaration, the declaration of the XHTML namespace in the `html` element is required for all valid XHTML documents. Also like DTDs, this code is standard code that will be the same in all of your XHTML documents.

Validating an XHTML Document

XHTML documents require a special software tool that carries out the validation process. It can be a stand-alone tool or one that's incorporated into a Web program such as a Web browser. Either way, the tool's job is to validate an XHTML document to make sure that it adheres to one of the three XHTML DTDs.

Document validation is extremely valuable for XHTML Web page design because it detects errors in XHTML code, helping to ensure that documents are properly displayed in Web browsers. You'll likely want to get in the habit of validating all XHTML documents that you create. Ideally, Web browsers would support XHTML validation so you could test XHTML Web pages. Until then, you'll have to validate XHTML documents some other way.

The W3C has a tool called the W3C Validator that is quite useful in validating XHTML documents. The interesting part about the W3C Validator is that it's an online tool; you don't have to download or install anything to use it. It validates both HTML and XHTML documents and is available on the Web at *http://validator.w3.org/*.

To validate a document using the W3C Validator, enter the document's URL into the Address box and click Validate This Page. Figure 18-1 shows the results of validating an HTML document using the W3C Validator. The document wasn't coded according to the rigid rules of XHTML for a transitional DTD, and several errors were found.

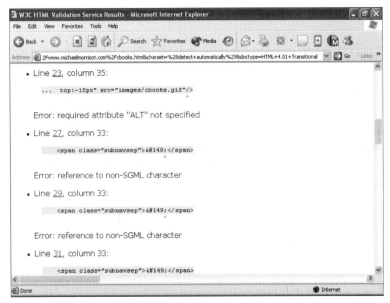

Figure 18-1 Not surprisingly, the W3C Validator finds a lot of errors when attempting to validate a conventional HTML document.

With the W3C supporting XHTML as the future of the Web, we can expect browsers to support XHTML validation in the near future.

Creating an XHTML Document

This is the last chapter in the book, and I hope you're comfortable creating HTML documents by now. Creating XHTML documents is similar to creating HTML documents. The important thing to remember is to observe the rigid rules of the XML language and XHTML vocabulary. It's also important to include the standard XHTML DTD and namespace declarations. Here is code for a basic XHTML document that includes a heading and a paragraph, along with a link to a Web page:

```
<!DOCTYPE html PUBLIC "-//W3C//DTD XHTML 1.0 Transitional//EN"
  "DTD/xhtml1-transitional.dtd">
<html xmlns="http://www.w3.org/1999/xhtml">
<head>
  <title>Microsoft Link</title>
</head>

<body>
<h1>Microsoft
</h1>
<p>
```

```
Click <a href = "http://www.microsoft.com/">here</a> to go to the Microsoft
Web site.
</p>
</body>
</html>
```

This simple XHTML Web page reveals the basic structure of a valid XHTML document. It includes the all-important document type declaration with the transitional XHTML DTD specified. The XHTML namespace is also declared with the xmlns attribute of the <html> tag. The remainder of the document follows the familiar structure of an HTML Web page, containing both head and body sections. Notice the small coding differences, such as all attributes are enclosed in quotation marks and all start tags are accompanied by end tags. You might find this document useful as a template for creating XHTML documents of your own. Figure 18-2 shows the document as viewed in Internet Explorer.

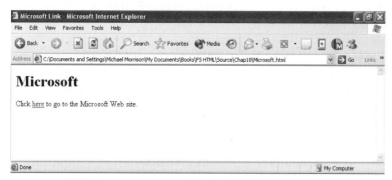

Figure 18-2 HTML documents are opened easily and viewed in Internet Explorer.

Creating more complex XHTML documents is no different than creating this simple document, except that you include a wider range of tags. Keep in mind that I used a simple text editor, Windows Notepad, to enter the code for this XHTML document. Unfortunately, as of this writing no visual Web design tools that I am aware of generate XHTML code, so you have to code XHTML by hand for the time being.

Try This! Try your hand at creating your own XHTML document from scratch. Just make sure to follow the stricter rules of XHTML, and include important standard pieces of information such as the XHTML DTD and namespace declarations.

Another option is to first create an HTML document in a Web design tool such as Microsoft FrontPage and then convert it to XHTML. This saves time if you find it easier to build Web pages visually.

Converting to XHTML

The future belongs to XHTML, but today the Web is built on conventional HTML code that violates most XHTML rules. You can use XHTML for new documents, but it's likely that you will convert existing HTML documents to XHTML at some point. If you create Web pages with a visual Web design tool, then you'll need to convert generated code to XHTML.

XHTML Conversion Guidelines

The good news is that you can follow simple guidelines to convert HTML to XHTML code. These guidelines flow directly from the differences between HTML and XHTML that you've learned about. These differences are primarily picky language details and therefore don't involve significant changes to HTML documents when you convert them.

Use this checklist of syntax differences between HTML and XHTML to make changes in the HTML code:

1   Add a document type declaration that indicates the appropriate standard XHTML DTD. Note that the transitional DTD usually works best for most HTML documents.

2   Declare the XHTML namespace in the html element.

3   Ensure that all elements and attributes are defined in the XHTML DTD.

4   Convert all element and attribute names to lowercase.

5   Match every start-tag with an end-tag.

6   At the end of all empty tags, replace > with />.

7   Enclose attribute values in quotation marks ("").

8   Assign values to attributes even if they are empty quotation marks.

9   Set the values of required attributes.

You will have a valid XHTML document if you carefully apply this list. Although it might be tedious, it's relatively painless once you're in the habit of eliminating the offending HTML syntax.

Converting an HTML Document to XHTML

Take a look at the following HTML code for a Top Ten Movies Web page to see
how simple it is to convert to XHTML:

```
<html>
<body bgcolor=silver text=navy>
<h1>Sparky's Top Ten Movies Page</h1>
Hello, this is the Top Ten Movies page for me, Sparky
the Clown.
The following list of movies are my all-time favorites,
and hopefully you'll like some of them too. If you have
any questions or movie recommendations, please feel free to
<a href=mailto:sparky@sillyclowns.com>send me e-mail</a>.

<p>

<table>
<tr>
  <td>
    <img src=Movie.gif align=left>
  </td>

  <td valign=top>
    Here are the movies:
    <ol>
    <li>Quick Change</li>
    <li>Shakes the Clown</li>
    <li>Killer Klowns from Outer Space</li>
    <li>Funny Bones</li>
    <li>Dumbo</li>
    <li>Big Top Pee-Wee</li>
    <li>The Greatest Show on Earth</li>
    <li>He Who Gets Slapped</li>
    <li>Freaks</li>
    <li>It</li>
    </ol>
  </td>
</tr>
</table>
</body>
</html>
```

This HTML document contains a Web page that might be included on the
Web site for Sparky the Clown, whose personal Web page you first created back
in Chapter 2, "Your First HTML Web Page." Even though this code contains several coding inconsistencies, it can be viewed with no problems in a Web
browser. Figure 18-3 shows the Sparky's Top Ten Movies Web page as viewed in
Internet Explorer.

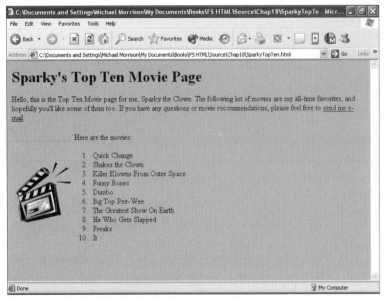

Figure 18-3 The Sparky's Top Ten Movies Web page displays well in a Web browser even though it contains some problematic HTML code.

If you carefully applied the conversion checklist to the Top Ten Movies Web page, you would find several problems that need to be addressed. To get an informed opinion of the *validity* of this document, I suggest running it through the W3C Validator at *http://validator.w3.org/*. To do so, follow these steps:

1 Point your browser to the W3C Validator Web site at *http://validator.w3.org/*.

2 Click the Upload Files link.

3 Browse your hard disk to locate the file to be validated.

Figure 18-4 shows the result of this attempt to validate the Top Ten Movies HTML document.

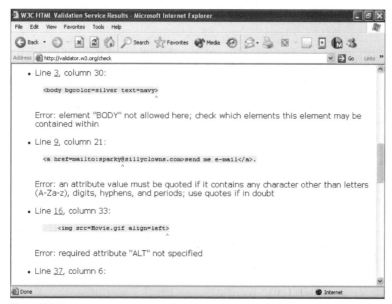

Figure 18-4 The W3C Validator reveals the problems with the Sparky's Top Ten Movies Web page that prevent it from being considered a valid XHTML document.

In addition to validating documents, W3C Validator tracks down problematic code. By working through the code's problems, you'll gain a better understanding of how to convert HTML documents to XHTML. So let's work on this Web page and bring it up to XHTML standards.

The first step in converting the Top Ten Movies document from HTML is to add the standard document type declaration and namespace declaration for the document. The following code shows how:

```
<!DOCTYPE html PUBLIC "-//W3C//DTD XHTML 1.0 Transitional//EN"
  "DTD/xhtml1-transitional.dtd">
<html xmlns="http://www.w3.org/1999/xhtml">
```

These three lines of code should appear at the beginning of the document; note that the third line of code replaces the existing <html> tag.

A quick look at the previous HTML code for the Web page reveals that there is no head section. A headless XHTML document is not only gruesome, but also just not allowed. The following code adds a suitable head to the document:

```
<head>
  <title>Sparky's Top Ten Movies Page</title>
</head>
```

Now, let's move on to the other problems with this Web page, keeping the conversion checklist in mind. A start-tag and end-tag problem occurs with the `<p>` tag, which is missing a matching `</p>` end tag. This is a common error in Web pages because many Web designers think of the `<p>` tag as a divider between paragraphs. As you know, the `<p>` and `</p>` tags enclose paragraphs, not divide them.

The empty tag problem applies to the `<img>` tag, which should end with `/>`. This coding detail was introduced by XML, so it doesn't appear on many Web pages. You'll need it for any empty elements in the Web pages that you convert to XHTML. Also, little HTML code uses quotation marks for attribute values unless a multiple-word value is necessary. So you'll need to add quotation marks around attribute values when you convert to XHTML.

Setting the values of any required attributes is the last problem on the Top Ten Movies Web page. It requires a subtle fix, but it's necessary for XHTML document validation. Although you probably didn't realize it, `alt` is a required attribute of the `<img>` tag. You must give it a value, even if it's just a pair of empty quotation marks (`""`). However, you might as well give the attribute a meaningful value if you're going to the trouble of setting it.

Applying these simple conversion rules is sufficient to convert the Top Ten Movies document to XHTML. This is the successfully converted code for the new XHTML version of the Web page:

```
<!DOCTYPE html PUBLIC "-//W3C//DTD XHTML 1.0 Transitional//EN"
  "DTD/xhtml1-transitional.dtd">
<html xmlns="http://www.w3.org/1999/xhtml">
<head>
  <title>Sparky's Top Ten Movie Pages</title>
</head>

<body bgcolor="silver" text="navy">
<h1>Sparky's Top Ten Movies Page</h1>
<p>
Hello, this is the Top Ten Movies page for me, Sparky the
Clown.The following movies are my all-time favorites, and
hopefully you'll like some of them too. If you have any
questions or movie recommendations, please feel free to
<a href="mailto:sparky@sillyclowns.com">send me e-mail</a>.
</p>

<table>
<tr>
  <td>
    <img src="Movie.gif" alt="Movie icon" align="left"/>
  </td>
```

```
   <td valign="top">
     Here are the movies:
     <ol>
     <li>Quick Change</li>
     <li>Shakes the Clown</li>
     <li>Killer Klowns from Outer Space</li>
     <li>Funny Bones</li>
     <li>Dumbo</li>
     <li>Big Top Pee-Wee</li>
     <li>The Greatest Show on Earth</li>
     <li>He Who Gets Slapped</li>
     <li>Freaks</li>
     <li>It</li>
     </ol>
   </td>
</tr>
</table>
</body>
</html>
```

Tip   The code for this example, as well as all of the examples throughout the book, is available for download from my Web site at the following URL: *http://www.michaelmorrison.com/cbook_fshtml.html*.

You might want to run the XHTML document through the W3C Validator at *http://validator.w3.org/* to double-check this conversion. Figure 18-5 shows the results of validating the newly converted XHTML document using the W3C Validator.

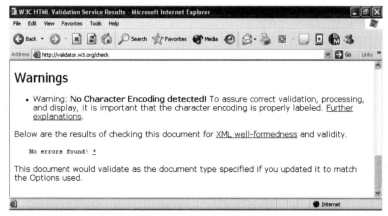

Figure 18-5 The newly converted Sparky's Top Ten Movies Web page passes the W3C Validator with flying colors.

Although it initially looks as if the W3C Validator is reporting errors, a closer inspection reveals that the newly converted Top Ten Web page passed the validation with no errors.

Try This! By now you've probably created a few HTML Web pages on your own. If so, run one of them through the W3C Validator, and then use the XHTML knowledge you've learned in this chapter to convert the document to XHTML. Just make sure the document validates properly under the W3C Validator when you're finished.

Key Points

- The fact that the future of the Web is being described in terms of XHTML is encouragement enough for all Web designers to get up to speed.

- XHTML presents a solution to several problems inherent in HTML.

- A *correct* XHTML document is one that meets all the coding requirements of the XML language as well as adhering to the rules of an XHTML schema or DTD.

- There are three standard XHTML DTDs that provide varying levels of detail for XHTML, resulting in three different classifications of XHTML documents.

- The DTD for an XHTML document is declared at the top of the document before the html root element.

- Document validation is extremely important to XHTML Web page design because it allows you to detect errors in XHTML code.

- The W3C Validator is an online tool that is quite useful in validating XHTML documents.

HTML Quick Reference

This appendix serves as a quick reference for the most commonly used tags in HTML. This reference doesn't go into painstaking detail about each tag; it focuses on the start and end tags and their meanings.

Structural Tags

Structural tags are used in HTML to describe the overall structure of a Web page, such as the head and body. Table A-1 lists the HTML structural tags you'll see most often.

Table A-1   The Most Commonly Used HTML Structural Tags

Start Tag	End Tag	Meaning
`<html>`	`</html>`	Encloses HTML codes
`<head>`	`</head>`	The head of the page
`<title>`	`</title>`	The title of the page
`<body>`	`</body>`	The body of the page
`<!--`	`-->`	A comment that won't be displayed

Text Tags

Text tags are used a great deal in Web pages to organize and format text content. Table A-2 lists the most commonly used HTML text tags.

Table A-2   The Most Commonly Used HTML Text Tags

Start Tag	End Tag	Meaning
`<p>`	`</p>`	A paragraph of text
`<div>`	`</div>`	A block of content
`<span>`	`</span>`	Inline content
` `	n/a	A line break, which initiates a new line
`<hr/>`	n/a	A horizontal line, often called a rule
`<font>`	`</font>`	The font used for text
`<b>`	`</b>`	Bold text
`<i>`	`</i>`	Italic text
`<h1>...<h6>`	`</h1>...</h6>`	Headings
`<tt>`	`</tt>`	Typewriter text

List Tags

List tags make it possible to organize Web content into unordered lists, ordered lists, and even definition lists. Table A-3 shows the most commonly used HTML list tags.

Table A-3   The Most Commonly Used HTML List Tags

Start Tag	End Tag	Meaning
`<ul>`	`</ul>`	An unordered (bulleted) list
`<ol>`	`</ol>`	An ordered (numbered) list
`<li>`	`</li>`	An item in a list
`<dl>`	`</dl>`	A definition list
`<dt>`	`</dt>`	A term in a definition list
`<dd>`	`</dd>`	A definition in a definition list

Table Tags

Table tags make it possible to create tables that can organize tabular data or control the layout of a Web page. Table A-4 lists the most commonly used HTML table tags.

Table A-4   The Most Commonly Used HTML Table Tags

Start Tag	End Tag	Meaning
`<table>`	`</table>`	A table
`<tr>`	`</tr>`	A row in a table
`<td>`	`</td>`	A cell of data within a table row
`<th>`	`</th>`	A table heading
`<caption>`	`</caption>`	A table caption

Form Tags

Form tags allow you to create data entry forms that you can use to obtain information from visitors to your Web pages. Table A-5 shows the most commonly used HTML form tags.

Table A-5   The Most Commonly Used HTML Form Tags

Start Tag	End Tag	Meaning
`<form>`	`</form>`	A form
`<input>`	`</input>`	An input field in a form
`<select>`	`</select>`	A selection list in a form
`<option>`	`</option>`	An option in a form
`<textarea>`	`</textarea>`	A scrolling multi-line text field in a form

Miscellaneous Tags

In addition to the tags shown in Tables A-1 through A-5, there are some popular HTML tags that don't fit the standard categories. These miscellaneous tags are listed in Table A-6.

Table A-6   The Other Most Commonly Used HTML Tags

Start Tag	End Tag	Meaning
`<img/>`	n/a	An image
`<a>`	`</a>`	An anchor hyperlink
`<map>`	`</map>`	An image map
`<area>`	`</area>`	An area within an image map
`<meta>`	`</meta>`	Additional information for a Web page
`<style>`	`</style>`	A style sheet
`<link/>`	n/a	A link to an external file

Appendix B

HTML Resources on the Web

I hope this book serves your every HTML need, but that probably isn't very realistic thinking. You'll need additional information about HTML at some point, and I'd like to be able to help you expand your HTML knowledge base. Numerous online resources offer more information or even a second opinion and can fill you in on the complexities of HTML and other Web technologies. This appendix highlights some of the Web sites I've found most useful as a Web designer.

By the way, if you're interesting in getting the HTML code and support files for the examples shown throughout the book, they are available from my Web site via the following link: *http://www.michaelmorrison.com/cbook_fshtml.html*. Enjoy!

■ **Microsoft Developer Network** (*http://msdn.microsoft.com/*)
The Microsoft Developer Network is a massive software development resource that covers an unbelievable range of technologies related to Microsoft products and services. More importantly to HTML, the site contains a dizzying amount of information on every facet of Web design. Sections of the site are devoted to HTML, CSS, and DHTML, and there are related sections on security and streaming media, to name but a few of the topics. I encourage you to visit this site and have a look around.

■ **Webmonkey**   (*http://www.webmonkey.com/*)
Webmonkey is an excellent resource for learning about the practical
side of Web design. One of the strong appeals of the Webmonkey site
is its numerous short tutorials on virtually all aspects of HTML and Web
page design. There are even how-to articles on topics such as using a
scanner to scan and edit photographs for your Web pages. Good stuff!

■ **HTML Goodies**   (*http://www.htmlgoodies.com/*)
Like Webmonkey, HTML Goodies is rich in tutorials. It's organized into
the primary areas of Web design and includes articles and discussions
related to almost any facet of HTML that you can imagine.

■ **HTML Help**   (*http://www.htmlhelp.com/*)
HTML Help promotes the creation of Web pages that function
smoothly across all Web browsers. Emphasis is on developing HTML
code that's highly browser-independent. Even if you're okay with supporting a single browser, this is still a good resource to learn about
how browser inconsistencies affect HTML code.

■ **The HTML Writer's Guild**   (*http://www.hwg.org/*)
If you're one of those people who have always dreamed of being part
of a guild, here's your chance. The HTML Writer's Guild is an organization of Web designers consisting of approximately 150,000 members.
The HTML Writer's Guild Web site includes resources for designers and
is priced reasonably if you feel the need to belong. At the very least,
the HTML Writer's Guild T-shirts are pretty cool.

■ **World Wide Web Consortium**   (*http://www.w3.org/*)
If you want the absolute bottom line on an issue related to HTML,
DHTML, XML, or CSS, the World Wide Web Consortium (W3C) Web
site is the place for you. The W3C oversees HTML specifications and is
the governing body for most Web standards. Although much of the
documentation reads like a legal treatise, it's nevertheless the last word
on the structure of the Web.

■ **Electronic Frontier Foundation**   (*http://www.eff.org/*)
The Electronic Frontier Foundation (EFF) doesn't have anything to do
directly with HTML or Web page design. It relates to the entire Internet
and its continued availability to all of us. Every Web user should have
a basic knowledge of their civil rights with respect to the Internet, and
the EFF Web site is a great place to learn about them.

Appendix C

Using Custom Colors

Color plays an important role in Web pages and impacts HTML code in a variety of ways. You typically specify a color as the value of an attribute or style property. For example, the `bgcolor` attribute for the `<body>` tag allows you to specify the background color of a Web page. Likewise, the `color` style property allows you to set the color of text. Both approaches allow you to use standard colors such as `yellow`, `red`, `orange`, and so on. However, you may want a higher degree of flexibility in your use of color, in which case you should consider creating a custom color.

Each color on a Web page is described by a combination of three primary colors: red, green, and blue. A color described using this system is known as an *RGB color*: *R* for red, *G* for green, and *B* for blue. Just as you mix different colors of Play-Doh to come up with different colors, you vary the amount of the red, green, and blue color components to create custom colors in HTML.

Each of the color components range in value from 0 to 255, but you don't specify the color components as ordinary decimal numbers (base 10). Instead, you must use the hexadecimal number system (base 16) on which computers rely. The primary advantage to the hexadecimal approach is that it allows you to describe a complete color in six digits. The downside is that hexadecimal numbers are tricky to work with if you aren't a math whiz.

Note   Unlike decimal numbers, *hexadecimal numbers* are described using a strange-looking combination of letters and numbers. Instead of numbering from 0 to 10, the hexadecimal system consists of numbers from 0 to F. Think of the letters A through F as continuing on from 9, in that A is 10, B is 11, and so on. So, if you're working with two-digit hexadecimal numbers, the lowest is 00, and the highest is FF.

Following is an example of a hexadecimal number that identifies a simple color: #FF00FF. Note that six digits follow the number symbol (#). The first two digits (FF) specify the hexadecimal value of the red color component, the second two digits (00) specify the value of the green color component, and the final two digits (FF) identify the value of the blue color component. The actual color described by this number is fuchsia.

Because the hexadecimal value 00 represents the lowest value a two-digit hexadecimal number can have, and FF represents the highest value, you can learn a great deal about HTML colors by examining the RGB values of the standard HTML colors. Table C-1 shows the hexadecimal value for each of the 16 standard HTML colors.

Table C-1   RGB Values of Standard HTML Colors

Color	Value	Color	Value
white	#FFFFFF	green	#008000
black	#000000	silver	#C0C0C0
red	#FF0000	gray	#808080
lime	#00FF00	maroon	#800000
blue	#0000FF	olive	#808000
yellow	#FFFF00	navy	#000080
aqua	#00FFFF	purple	#800080
fuchsia	#FF00FF	teal	#008080

The first colors in this list are relatively easy to figure out, because you can see how the maximum and minimum hexadecimal values are used for each color component. As the list goes on, however, it gets tougher to visualize the colors. Even so, this is still a good way to learn how to create custom colors of your own. Start with a known color in the list and experiment by tweaking the hexadecimal values for each of its color components.

To specify a custom color on a Web page, use the hexadecimal value preceded by the number symbol: `<body bgcolor="#1100FF">`. Similarly, the following code shows a custom color used in a `style` property: `<p style="color:#1100FF">`. You now know how to move beyond the standard HTML colors and create custom colors for your own Web pages.

Index

Michael Morrison

is a writer, developer, toy inventor, and author of a variety of computer technology books and inter-active Web-based courses. In addition to his primary profession as a writer and technical consult-ant, Michael is the creative lead at Stalefish Labs, an entertainment company he cofounded with his wife, Masheed. The first commercial debut for Stalefish Labs is a traditional social/trivia game called *Tall Tales: The Game of Myths, Legends, and Creative One-Upmanship*.

When not glued to his computer, playing hockey, skateboarding, or watching movies with his wife, Michael enjoys hanging out by his *koi* pond. You can visit Michael on the Web at *http://www.michaelmorrison.com/*.

The manuscript for this book was prepared and submitted to Microsoft Press in electronic form. The pages were composed by nSight, Inc., using Adobe FrameMaker+SGML for Windows, with text in Garamond and display text in ITC Franklin Gothic Condensed. Composed pages were delivered to the printer as electronic pre-press files.

Cover Designer:	Tim Girvin Design
Interior Graphic Designer:	James D. Kramer
Compositor:	Mary Beth McDaniel
Project Manager:	Tempe Goodhue
Copy Editor:	Stephanie English
Technical Editor:	Christopher M. Russo
Proofreaders:	Stephanie English, Katie O'Connell
Indexer:	Jack Lewis

Microsoft *Press*

Learn how to get the job done every day—
faster, smarter, and easier!

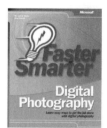   

**Faster Smarter
Digital Photography**
ISBN: 0-7356-1872-0
U.S.A. $19.99
Canada $28.99

**Faster Smarter
Microsoft® Office XP**
ISBN: 0-7356-1862-3
U.S.A. $19.99
Canada $28.99

**Faster Smarter
Microsoft Windows® XP**
ISBN: 0-7356-1857-7
U.S.A. $19.99
Canada $28.99

**Faster Smarter
Home Networking**
ISBN: 0-7356-1869-0
U.S.A. $19.99
Canada $28.99

Discover how to do exactly what you do with computers and technology—faster, smarter, and easier—with FASTER SMARTER books from Microsoft Press! They're your everyday guides for learning the practicalities of how to make technology work the way you want—fast. Their language is friendly and down-to-earth, with no jargon or silly chatter, and with accurate how-to information that's easy to absorb and apply. Use the concise explanations, easy numbered steps, and visual examples to understand exactly what you need to do to get the job done—whether you're using a PC at home or in business, capturing and sharing digital still images, getting a home network running, or finishing other tasks.

Microsoft Press has other FASTER SMARTER titles to help you get the job done every day:

Faster Smarter PCs
ISBN: 0-7356-1780-5

Faster Smarter Microsoft Windows 98
ISBN: 0-7356-1858-5

Faster Smarter Beginning Programming
ISBN: 0-7356-1780-5

Faster Smarter Digital Video
ISBN: 0-7356-1873-9

Faster Smarter Web Page Creation
ISBN: 0-7356-1860-7

Faster Smarter HTML & XML
ISBN: 0-7356-1861-5

Faster Smarter Internet
ISBN: 0-7356-1859-3

Faster Smarter Money 2003
ISBN: 0-7356-1864-X

To learn more about the full line of Microsoft Press® products, please visit us at:

microsoft.com/mspress

Get a **Free**
e-mail newsletter, updates,
special offers, links to related books,
and more when you
register on line!

Register your Microsoft Press® title on our Web site and you'll get
a FREE subscription to our e-mail newsletter, *Microsoft Press
Book Connections.* You'll find out about newly released and upcoming
books and learning tools, online events, software downloads, special
offers and coupons for Microsoft Press customers, and information
about major Microsoft® product releases. You can also read useful
additional information about all the titles we publish, such as detailed book descriptions, tables of contents and indexes, sample
chapters, links to related books and book series, author biographies,
and reviews by other customers.

Registration is easy. Just visit this Web page and fill in your information:

http://www.microsoft.com/mspress/register

Microsoft·

Proof of Purchase

Use this page as proof of purchase if participating in a promotion or rebate offer on
this title. Proof of purchase must be used in conjunction with other proof(s) of
payment such as your dated sales receipt—see offer details.

Faster Smarter HTML & XML
0-7356-1861-5

CUSTOMER NAME

Microsoft Press, PO Box 97017, Redmond, WA 98073-9830